OVER THE WIRE
AND ON TV

CBS and UPI in Campaign '80

OVER THE WIRE AND ON TV

CBS and UPI in Campaign '80

Michael J. Robinson and Margaret A. Sheehan

Russell Sage Foundation

New York

The Russell Sage Foundation

The Russell Sage Foundation, one of the oldest of America's general purpose foundations, was established in 1907 by Mrs. Margaret Olivia Sage for "the improvement of social and living conditions in the United States." The Foundation seeks to fulfill this mandate by fostering the development and dissemination of knowledge about the political, social, and economic problems of America. It conducts research in the social sciences and public policy, and publishes books and pamphlets that derive from this research.

The Foundation provides support for individual scholars and collaborates with other granting agencies and academic institutions in studies of social problems. It maintains a professional staff of social scientists who engage in their own research as well as advise on Foundation programs and projects. The Foundation also conducts a Visiting Scholar Program, under which established scholars working in areas of current interest to the Foundation join the staff for a year to consult and to continue their own research and writing. Finally, a Postdoctoral Fellowship Program enables promising young scholars to devote full time to their research while in residence for a year at the Foundation.

The Board of Trustees is responsible for the general policies and oversight of the Foundation, while the immediate administrative direction of the program and staff is vested in the President, assisted by the officers and staff. The President bears final responsibility for the decision to publish a manuscript as a Russell Sage Foundation book. In reaching a judgment on the competence, accuracy, and objectivity of each study, the President is advised by the staff and a panel of special readers.

The conclusions and interpretations in Russell Sage Foundation publications are those of the authors and not of the Foundation, its Trustees, or its staff. Publication by the Foundation, therefore, does not imply endorsement of the contents of the study. It does signify that the manuscript has been reviewed by competent scholars in the field and that the Foundation finds it worthy of public consideration.

Transcripts from CBS News used with permission, © CBS Inc. 1980. All rights reserved. Originally broadcast over the CBS Television Network in 1980.

United Press International wire material used with permission, © United Press International 1980.

Library of Congress Catalog Number: 82-50356
Standard Book Number: 0-87154-722-8

For Stanley and Edith Robinson,
and for Rourke and Anne Sheehan—
our parents.

Contents

Part III: Conclusions and Implications

Acknowledgments

LOOKING back on our research, we are less impressed by Newton's having discovered the law of gravity than by his having done so with no outside funding. We had only a vague notion as to how much it would eventually cost to watch television and read the wire during one presidential year. We thank first the Russell Sage Foundation for making possible our watching, our reading, and our writing.

Byron Shafer, program officer at Russell Sage, deserves more credit than anybody else. In mid-1979, Byron expressed interest in our doing something about news media coverage of presidential politics. And, when we thought there was not time enough left to gear up for Campaign '80, Byron did everything short of turning back his watch to persuade us that we really could be ready for the Iowa caucuses.

William C. Adams, associate professor at George Washington University, helped us set up our project at George Washington, and he also read drafts of our book as if he were copy editor. It is safe to say that without his help, there would not have been a Media Analysis Project.

Bill Adams also introduced us to Fay Schreibman, then director of the Television News Study Center, which is housed in the Gelman Library at George Washington University. The Study Center permitted us to use its audio-visual facilities and its microfilm collection. Fay Schreibman gave us special accommodations and access to the video-tape equipment, even though she knew how little we knew about what makes SONY run.

Dean Burton Sapin at George Washington's School of Public and

International Affairs agreed to meet with us at least half a dozen times before it was clear there would ever be a research proposal, let alone a Media Analysis Project—we appreciate his early support. Professor Louis Mayo and his assistant, Pamela Smith, who oversee the Program in Policy Studies for Science and Technology, helped us find office space at George Washington, and they kept us in our office even after the grant money had run out. John Logsdon, Director of the Graduate Program in Science, Technology and Public Policy, also permitted us to work on at George Washington past the end of our grant.

Philip Robbins, chairman of the Department of Journalism at George Washington, did something for us that nobody should ever have to do for anyone: he monitored the UPI teletype every weekday for a year. When it broke down, Phil not only had the machine fixed, he also managed to replace all the wire copy that we lost during the breakdowns.

Norman Ornstein, Visiting Scholar at the American Enterprise Institute, read the first draft, correcting errors in fact and logic. Norman's editorial hand and photographic memory have continuously influenced our writing.

Debbie Rundell and Anne Higgins, both at the White House, provided us with facts only the White House staff could provide.

Dean Eugene Kennedy at the Graduate School of Catholic University performed another crucial service: he gave us two years leave time from Catholic University to complete this work. We appreciate the furlough.

In a sense, we worked for all of these people; they were our supervisors and benefactors. But equal credit goes to the people who worked for us. This is a study of over six thousand news stories, in the main part from Campaign '80, but also from Campaign '60 and Campaign '40. Somebody had to read or watch those stories—and every story was read or watched at least three times. We did lots of reading ourselves, but the bulk of the quantitative work was done by a dozen friends who were also employees.

Nancy Conover was the first person we hired, and despite all her forays into the unknown, she remained with the project until the end. Laura Halbleib read wire stories for us until she moved back to New Mexico, probably because she needed a permanent rest from UPI wire copy. Sue Ann Hannigan trained for two months but never really had the chance to serve as a full-time reader.

ACKNOWLEDGMENTS

Three people also came on as "pinch" readers: Amy Miller, Michael Ruth, and Keith Eddins. We used John Sheehan as a "utility" man. Every Washington-based project should have an intern, and Carol Fletcher was ours. Eve Rogers typed from drafts of manuscripts that were illegible and incomprehensible.

We had originally intended to do our own computer work. That idea lasted a month, then we found Eric Strassler. His work saved us a half year's wasted time. Barbara Howe keypunched the fifteen thousand IBM cards that Eric had to carry around with him.

Susan Sullivan worked more months but fewer hours than any other employee. A born editor, Susan read drafts or listened to them over the phone. Nobody offered better suggestions for cutting out extraneous information. It was Sullivan who imposed the original quarantine on surplus apples and oranges in chapter 1.

Liz Noyer, Laura Newman, and Lisa Jahoda joined us at the very last and helped us meet our final deadline. Priscilla Lewis was our editor at Russell Sage. We needed her very badly.

Art Miller at Michigan, Cliff Zukin at Rutgers, and Herb Asher at Ohio State gave us access to national survey data. S. Robert Lichter at George Washington and Stanley Rothman at Smith College were able to provide us with voting patterns and personality measures for people who work at CBS News.

Jody Powell, Tom Donilon, and Gael Doar (all from the Carter campaign) granted us long and entertaining interviews. Mark Bisnouw, John Anderson's first press secretary in 1980, also donated his time to discuss Anderson's extraordinary press campaign. Lyn Nofziger, press secretary to the Reagan campaign in its later stages, agreed to give us his perspective on press in 1980, and we were delighted to have it.

Finally, we thank the campaign journalists and editors from CBS and UPI who spent dozens of hours talking with us about our findings and their reporting. Everyone we asked agreed to see us or speak with us over the phone. All permitted us to tape their remarks and quote them directly. In a few instances, despite what amounted to attributional carte blanche, we have chosen to impose anonymity on their quotations. And, despite a perception of national reporters being antiacademic, we found our respondents to be interested in our admittedly academic exercise.

Despite their interest, nobody at CBS or UPI seemed thrilled with the idea that we had been checking up on them for one full year. Nobody enjoys finding out that his work has been inspected day in and day out. But if anybody can appreciate the need for a watchdog, it ought to be the members of the national press.

Preface

TELEVISION invites hyperbole. Three weeks before the election, then Vice-President Walter Mondale told the press that "if I had to give up . . . the opportunity to get on the evening news or the veto power . . . I'd throw the veto power away!" Television news, said Mondale, "is the president's most indispensable power."

This was not Geraldo Rivera talking. This was, at the time, the man next in succession to hold the veto power. And Mondale was not alone in his assessment. John Connally presented his own memorable hyperbole concerning television in Campaign '80: "On a scale of ten the importance of media is at least an eight, everything else is two."

Talk like that produces books. Since 1976, more than half a dozen full-length books about media and presidential politics have been published. At least three more are expected before 1984. Given the surplus of books about the topic, one might think we hardly need another study of presidential television. But if nothing else our book is different from the recent rest—different in what it does and different in what it does not do.

First, we have *not* attempted another voter study. We have surveyed a nonrandom sample of press secretaries, campaign officials, editors, and national reporters; nobody in our surveys could be legitimately classified as mass public. Second, we have not done an investigation of the history, background, or behavior of the White House press corps. This is not a book about newspeople. Third, we have not tried to pinpoint the press winners and losers in Campaign '80, or to gauge the precise impact of the media on election day. Finally, we have not written about the effect of broadcast technology on campaign strategy per se.

We have spent our energy on three other topics—topics that generally receive less play in research about news. First, by using the historic standards of journalism—objectivity, fairness, seriousness, and comprehensiveness—we have tried to measure just how well network news (CBS) and the national wires (UPI) did in covering Campaign '80. Second, we have attempted to show, qualitatively and quantitatively, how traditional print and contemporary network journalism compare and contrast in covering the same campaign. Third, we have used our findings about campaign news to speculate about politics under a new system of political reporting. We have tried to sort out the broader implications of moving from newspapers to networks as our principal medium for following elections and campaigns. We conclude with a list of possible consequences drawn from the separate realities of print and electronic journalism—consequences for politicians, for press secretaries, for us all.

We have divided the book into three parts. For those who insist on a quick read—and don't much care about statistical evidence—chapter 1, combined with chapters 9 through 13, will summarize our conclusions and spell out the implications. For those who are interested in our methodology, chapter 2 describes what we did, and how and why we did it. Chapters 3, 4, 5, 6, 7, and 8 indicate how CBS and UPI did at achieving basic press values. Although most chapters deal only in campaign news coverage, chapter 8 is unique. It contains findings on press coverage of the "official" presidency, all the news about Jimmy Carter when he exercised his *formal* duties of office, not when he campaigned.

During this political generation, America has changed the periscope and lens through which it tracks political leaders on the surface of a political campaign. New lenses mean new perspective. In politics, new perspective entails new "realities." As we interpret history, network news has produced the second most important transformation in political journalism in the last 100 years. Not since the adoption of "objective journalism" near the turn of the century has anything affected the shape of campaign news quite so much as network television. Even ignoring the enormity of the audience and the credibility of the source, network journalism as a news form has influenced our political vocabulary and the relations between media, public, and government.

There are limits, however. The changes in campaign journalism from print to network are evolutionary, not revolutionary. If we were president, we would try to be more realistic than Walter Mondale: We would keep the veto power and sacrifice television news time. But having made the choice in favor of the veto, we would still want to know everything we could about the content and calculus of the nation's most popular news source. And know something about the consequences as well. In the end, content, calculus, and consequences of political news reporting are what this book and our research are all about.

PART I

Introduction

Chapter 1

Carter's Day—
"He'd Rather Not
Have Been
in Philadelphia"

There is more license in broadcasting.

—HELEN THOMAS, UPI

We didn't want their campaign to dictate our agenda.

—LESLEY STAHL, CBS NEWS

ON September 3, 1980, Jimmy Carter took his campaign to Philadelphia. As usual, the national press went along for the ride. To cover Carter, CBS sent White House correspondent Lesley Stahl and United Press International sent Helen Thomas, UPI's chief White House reporter since 1974.

These women are not cub reporters; between them Stahl and Thomas have been covering Washington politics for over thirty years. But seasoned though they are, these reporters work for their news organization, not on their own. Although both write under a byline, each represents a news source, if not a news medium.

It was Stahl and CBS together that produced the "hard copy" about

Carter's day in Philadelphia. It was Thomas, writing in the tradition and mode of UPI, who covered those same events for the late night wire. So comparing their copy tells us less about Stahl and Thomas than about journalism, less about individuals than traditional American print and contemporary network news.

Most of this book deals quantitatively in making comparisons between television news and twentieth-century "traditional print." But as a case study, Carter Day in Philadelphia points up qualitatively and vividly the fundamental similarities and differences between hard copy filed at the networks and hard copy that goes out over the wire.

We start with UPI and Thomas:

> After three days on the campaign trail, President Carter is clearly convinced that the once divided Democratic Party is now closing ranks behind his candidacy. . . .
>
> At the windup of a day of campaigning in Philadelphia Wednesday, Carter said in an interview on WPVI-TV that since the political convention last month he has seen "a remarkable coalescing of unity within the Democratic Party."
>
> In the interview and at a black Baptist Church, Carter mentioned that Sen. Edward Kennedy, D-Mass., his rival in the primaries, had telephoned him to express his hope that the Democratic Party "will be united" in November . . . .
>
> Former Kennedy supporters also have taken their cue and are falling into line. They include Philadelphia Mayor William Green, who never left Carter's side during his visit to drum up votes, particularly among ethnic groups and blacks.
>
> Also Wednesday, Carter won endorsements from three powerful unions that had endorsed other candidates in the primaries . . . .
>
> In his speech from the pulpit to an enthusiastic gathering in Zion Baptist Church in Philadelphia, Carter warned that a Democratic Party divided as it was in 1968 could lead to a Republican victory in November.
>
> During the day, he toured the Italian market, shaking every hand in sight, and had a corned beef and cabbage lunch at an Irish restaurant. . . .
>
> Carter also said he thinks the recession has bottomed out, but he didn't have any good news to report about the immediate prospects for release of the American hostages in Iran.

This is quintessential wire copy. In the finest traditions of traditional print, Thomas tells us what Carter said, when he said it, and to whom. It emphasizes the old political factors—the party and the working man.

Now for the day's events according to CBS and Stahl. Introduction and leitmotif were provided by subanchor Charles Kuralt:

KURALT: You remember that great old photograph of Calvin Coolidge wearing a war bonnet. Campaigning politicians have a need to identify themselves with every segment of the population, the old, the young and the ethnic. It's a tradition. And as Lesley Stahl reports, President Carter stayed busy today—following tradition.
STAHL: What did President Carter do today in Philadelphia? He posed, with as many different types of symbols as he could possibly find.

There was a picture at the day care center. And one during the game of bocci ball with the senior citizens. Click, another picture with a group of teenagers. And then he performed the ultimate media event—a walk through the Italian market.

The point of all this, obviously, to get on the local news broadcasts and in the morning newspapers. It appeared that the President's intention was not to say anything controversial. . . .

Simply the intention was to be seen, as he was, and it was photographed, even right before his corned beef and cabbage lunch at an Irish restaurant with the popular mayor Bill Green . . . .

There were more symbols at the Zion (black) Baptist Church. . . .

Over the past three days the President's campaign has followed a formula—travel into a must-win state, spending only a short time there but ensuring several days of media coverage. . . .

And today the President got a bonus, since the Philadelphia TV markets extend deeply into neighboring New Jersey—another must-win state.

This is *not* the kind of report the Carter campaign was hoping for. After the election, we asked Carter's press secretary, Jody Powell, about his response at the time. Powell remembered the piece but pretty much dismissed it, saying, "by that point. . . you almost expected that sort of coverage and you just sort of rolled with it. . . ."* Although he had hoped for better press than Stahl was offering here, Powell had no major reservations about the CBS coverage of the Philadelphia trip.

We, however, do have reservations about the piece. Our reservations are analytical, not professional: They involve overstating the comparison between Stahl and Thomas, hence between CBS and UPI. CBS did not file hard news stories like this every day. The color dial has been turned up slightly in the CBS case. Stahl's piece is not quite so archetypical of "Evening News" as the Thomas piece was for

*Quotations not referenced are drawn from personal interviews with the authors.

UPI. But despite that fact, these two versions of Carter Day in Phila-delphia—wire and electronic—still tell us much about national cam-paign news coverage, old-style and new-fangled.

Starting with fundamental similarities, both these campaign stories were about Jimmy Carter, as were most of them in 1980. On CBS and UPI three-quarters of the stories referring to any candidate men-tioned Carter at some point. Even excluding all "official" press stories about Carter as president, candidate Carter got far more coverage than anybody else.

Second, these two reports were essentially objective or, at the very least, "objectivistic." Objectivistic is to objective as honesty is to truth. In both conditions, somebody is at least trying to achieve a preferred goal. Objectivistic is a reasonable substitute for objective, and most press stories we saw in Campaign '80 were, at a minimum, objectivistic. And, without a doubt, Thomas's piece on Carter met all the criteria. The wire story drew almost no conclusions about Carter without attributing the inference to some legitimate source—usually Carter.

The CBS piece came much closer to crossing the line of objectivity —closer than most hard news stories on "Evening News" did. Stahl made two assertions about motive and strategy that were not at-tributed. The premise that the Italian market was the "ultimate media event" seemed to us somewhat less than objective, if not inaccurate, especially given that several thousand reporters had cov-ered the Democratic Convention three weeks before. But what keeps this piece inside the limits of objectivistic reporting is that nobody, including the Carter people, thinks Stahl was wrong in her basic analysis. Gael Doar, who handled Carter's press advance that day, told us that Stahl's piece "made me cringe, first, because it made the president look as if he had done something wrong, something nobody else does, and second, because she [Stahl] was absolutely right about all the photo opportunities." In American journalism, as in law, truth is its own defense. By that standard, Stahl's piece was, at least, objectivistic.

A third shared characteristic involves "horse racism." All national media, regardless of their prestige or financial well-being, emphasize competitiveness—the horse race. Thomas led with "horse race"— Carter's prediction that the Democrats were uniting. Half the para-graphs in her original piece dealt directly with electoral competition. Stahl's piece was all campaign strategy, which in the media is one of the higher orders of "horse racism." From start to finish, Stahl's version of Carter's day was explained as political symbolism. In the end, both reporters used winning and losing to glue together their prose.

But we also picked Carter Day in Philadelphia to symbolize the *differences* in news media. In this case, some of the differences in approach are as obvious as those between South Philly and the Main Line: UPI and CBS covered the same events but in very different ways.

Near the top of the list is the comparative need to "mediate," to interpret. UPI stories, as this case illustrates, work more on *reporting* than mediating. The Thomas story pretty much covered what Carter had said and not why he said it. Seven of thirteen paragraphs in the complete, original story were straight paraphrases or quotations from Carter's public remarks that day. CBS, in a longer piece, used Carter's words or ideas only once. As a general rule, CBS did more interpretation, while the wires did more transcription. CBS mediated; UPI reported.

CBS and UPI both employed the traditional "who, what, when, where, and why" of journalism. But "Evening News" reversed the order of priority. Thomas talked mostly about what; Stahl talked mostly about why. Sentence by sentence, CBS provided two and one-half times as much analysis in covering Carter's trip.

A much less obvious difference involves definition of candidate. Thomas linked Carter to two other traditional political institutions, the Democratic party and the American labor movement. Stahl linked Carter to the media and to symbolism. The wire related candidates to traditional political forces while networks made more of the new politics—the candidate out there by himself, or at best, out there with his pollsters.

This reflects a more important difference—network news affinity for political coverage of person and personal issues. This is *not* a question of personality journalism, journalism that deals in the psychology of the candidate. Stahl never referred to Carter's psyche, nor did anyone at "Evening News." But in Philadelphia, CBS did concentrate on the topic of campaign style. Thomas didn't bother to mention it.

Least subtle is the difference in criticism. The UPI piece neither said nor implied anything critical about Carter. If anything, the Thomas piece was upbeat, quoting Carter on restored unity in the

Democratic party, pointing to his three labor union endorsements, his warm reception at the church, and his telephone call from Ted Kennedy. None of that made the "Evening News." Instead, Stahl painted Carter as cynical poseur—a practitioner of media-based, symbolic politics. CBS presented Carter with what amounted to a classic case of bad press.

And finally, the question of format. As with most of the wire copy, Helen Thomas filed a news *item*, not a news story. Her piece had people, places, events, but it did not go anywhere much beyond that. Thomas had a "lead" but she had no particular theme. The inverted pyramid—reporting with the meat in the first paragraph—still is used in campaign wire copy, especially in hard news coverage. As is traditional with traditional print, editors could have easily taken any but the opening paragraph out of this story and it would convey pretty much the same idea.

On CBS, Lesley Stahl not only had a theme, she had a *theory*—the Carter formula for exploiting local media. And in a well-coordinated lead-in, Charles Kuralt gave the theme a fitting introduction—a brief history of the candidate's need to identify with the old, the young, and the ethnic. Kuralt and Stahl have a lesson; not just about Carter, but also about the less savory aspects of presidential campaign techniques, from Calvin Coolidge through the present.

One difference we haven't considered so far is the inherent difference between a nonstop 24-hour wire service and an all-too-frequently interrupted commercial news program. Thomas actually did several stories that day about the Carter trip. Stahl had just this piece. The wire goes on and on; "Evening News" has but 30 minutes (22 minutes, without the commercials). Can wire copy be compared with news programming in any meaningful way, or is all this an instance of comparing apples and oranges?

Actually, we have never accepted the premise that one ought not to compare apples and oranges. They compare and contrast just like boys and girls, baseball and football, the United States and the Soviet Union. One ought not to *add* apples and oranges. One can, and often does, compare apples and oranges; when, for example, deciding which to buy or which to eat.

But there is a much larger issue involved here than a frequently expressed mistake about the laws of arithmetic. In fact, apples and oranges is the very point we are trying to make. Even if we ignore the pictures and sound, and concentrate on the sentence and word, we have two different varieties of press.

Case studies should highlight important points. If Carter Day in Philadelphia were multiplied several hundred times, the result would form one of the central themes of this book: for whatever reasons, old-style print, as reflected in the wires, and contemporary television, as defined by network news, provide meaningfully different versions of the same campaign event, and, as it turns out, of the same campaign.

We found that neither fruit, evening television or day-to-day print, seemed particularly harmful, much less forbidden, in its treatment of Campaign '80. Still, the basic differences we found in Philadelphia repeated themselves throughout the year, regardless of the reporter and regardless of the candidate. Network news was more mediating, more political, more personal, more critical, more thematic than old-style print. Having sifted through several thousand campaign stories coming over the wire and on TV, we are convinced that changing the medium also tends to change the message about presidential campaigns.

If traditional print paints a different picture from the one brought to us by the networks, does the audience respond differently? We think so. As we read the last twenty years of American political history, the more modern message corresponds with the more modern response to presidential campaigns and politics. Politics have become increasingly more critical, more personal, more cynical, more analytical, more thematic. We do not know for sure that changing the message changes the outcome—whether apples and oranges have different effects on those who consume them. But if political information is a subtle form of political destiny—if we are what we eat—then we want to know as much as we can about the diet of news we have abandoned and the diet of news we have come to adopt.

Chapter 2

Press Watching in Campaign '80: Hows and Whys

The presidential bully pulpit is CBS, NBC . . . and to some extent the wires.

—JODY POWELL

Goals

WE started this study with two goals in mind. The first was to do a public service, to evaluate the performance of the national press during Campaign '80. We planned to carry out a twelve-month "press-watch," and to assess the performance of some representative segments of the press, using journalism's own criteria to measure its success or failure. Our second goal was to test what we regard as a major issue concerning national campaign press: the notion that print and electronic media differ measurably and meaningfully in the way they cover politics and campaigns.

Given these two goals, this almost had to be a study in news content, not newspeople or newsmakers. We interviewed the press secretaries for the Carter, Reagan, and Anderson campaigns and discussed our findings with more than twenty top editors and correspondents from network news and the national wires, people with special roles in covering Campaign '80. We also went back to study dozens of newspapers from Campaign "Yesteryear" (the elections of 1940 and 1960). But in the end this is a book mainly about news stories from 1980 (fifty-five hundred news stories) and what they tell us about campaign news process and performance.

We stress content, process, and performance for three reasons. The first has to do with "bias," not in the media but in contemporary press research, especially in academic research. Dennis Lowry bemoans his own finding that almost two-thirds of the scholarly research about media done in the 1970s dealt with *audience*, the overwhelming majority of it being survey research of one form or another.[1] Since 1970, the *American Political Science Review* has published only five articles that deal directly with media, less than one-half of 1 percent of the total. Every one of them has been about effects on voters or public opinion. Books about campaign media have also grown increasingly more concerned with effects on the public than with news per se or the relations between press and government.[2] The press is not the most powerful American political institution, but it is an institution in its own right, and deserves attention as such.

The second reason for studying content involves social utility. If social utility plays any part in social science, then studies which stress content have a big advantage over effects research. To us, social utility implies the possibility of reform, in this case the possibility of reforming the media. But we are convinced that news people and news organizations are responsive to research which evaluates content, not effects. We think that professional communicators (artists, novelists, entertainers, teachers, and journalists) feel greater responsibility for their product than for their byproduct. In fact, one of America's most famous journalists, Walter Cronkite, is on record saying precisely that:

> I don't think it is any of our business what the moral, political, social or economic effect of our reporting is. I say let's get on with the job of reporting the news—and let the chips fall where they may.[3]

As journalism becomes more self-conscious, information about what the news media produce—as opposed to what the news media cause—will increase the likelihood of reform, or at least the likelihood of greater self-consciousness. When, for example, Vice-President Agnew went after the networks for their actual content in 1969, he apparently improved slightly the way the networks do their job. One study found that the networks were more likely to attribute statements to identifiable sources after the Agnew assault.[4] Arnold Sawislak, senior editor at UPI, told us that academic criticism of content was one of the weightiest factors in the increasing coverage of issues during the 1980 campaign.[5] Criticize their impact, and journalists are quite likely to tell you that that's the way it is. Point out flaws in their work, and they tend to listen, defensively perhaps, but intently. Press watching, year by year, has utilitarian appeal.

There is a third reason for monitoring content. If we rely on testimony of politicians, modern audience research has not done particularly well in gauging effects. One of the most peculiar results from advanced research indicates that newspapers influence public opinion more than does national television, something we find almost impossible to believe.[6]

Much of the audience-based effects research still argues that the mass media do not much influence public opinion or political culture. Modern effects research is still arguing (though not so much as in the 1960s) the law of minimal consequences—a "law" holding that media only reinforce, rather than influence, political opinion or behavior.[7] But this "law" does not hold up very well when it is applied to recent historical observation, especially if one considers the *indirect* effects on mass politics.[8]

Knowing more about the content of media may not prove political effects, but it does give us important clues to understanding them. We have found, for example, that network news programming in the United States is twice as "presidential" in its news agenda as the national wire, and more than twice as "political"—twice as heavily focused on "campaign" news, as opposed to "official" news about political leaders. Given these differences in focus, at least two notions come immediately to mind: that replacing the wires with television has produced a more "presidential" nation, and, perhaps, a more cynical public as well. Testing these notions with survey research presents all sorts of problems, but that doesn't mean the effects aren't there.

Media are windows, and if the windows have different contours, the images of politics change, too. A more presidential window implies a more presidential politics—a more "political" lens implies a more "political" culture. But this is extremely hard to prove with audience research. Audience research is neither misguided nor unimportant. But the notion that studying news content is somehow déclassé ignores the practical, utilitarian, and theoretical advantages of that kind of work.

Blueprints

Basic methods follow from our two basic goals of evaluating press performance and distinguishing between the two worlds of American daily news. Our format combines the two göals; asking, for example, how did print perform in being objective, or fair, or comprehensive? Then, asking how did television do? We follow that model for the next six chapters, comparing the performance of print and television during the entire 1980 campaign.

DEFINITIONS

In this sort of work, definitions become blueprints. It is not enough to say we want to compare the performance of television and print in Campaign '80 until we've explained what we mean by "performance," by "television and print," and even by "Campaign '80." We use five definitions of performance: *objectivity* (chapter 3), *equity of access* (chapter 4), *fairness* (chapter 5), *seriousness* (chapter 6), and *comprehensiveness* (chapter 7). But these terms also require definition. We can cope with these terms later, one controversial definition at a time. We cannot, however, put off for later our most fundamental terminology: how we define television and print.

Television

Print and television have many faces. Even television, with far fewer faces, is local or national, public or commercial, broadcast or cable, UHF or VHF, station-centered or satellite-centered. But from the outset, we knew that network television would, for us, represent campaign television news. Network news totally dominates other forms of television in covering national campaigns. The three network programs attract almost sixty million viewers each night. No single local news program achieves even one-twentieth the audience of a network evening newscast. As for cable, even in 1980, with one out of every five families subscribing, 1 percent of the viewing population watched the Carter-Reagan debate on cable television. Each commercial network spends about 150 million dollars a year on news (three times as much as Ted Turner's Cable News Network [CNN]). In audience and in budgeting, network news *is* national television news.

Traditional Print

Deciding on network news as a representative form of television is comparatively easy, choosing a representative form of print news is not. Nothing stands for traditional print nearly so well as the networks symbolize TV news.

Newspapers, as a class, represent print, but newspapers, as a class, are distinctly nonnational. In 1980, there were seventeen hundred daily newspapers in the United States; two were national newspapers. If by national we mean coast-to-coast distribution, day-to-day, the *Wall Street Journal* and the *Christian Science Monitor* were, in Campaign '80, our only national dailies.* But neither of these comes close to being representative of traditional print. We do have two newspapers of record in the United States, the *Washington Post* and the *New York Times.*[9] But neither paper is representative of traditional ink or the print industry, which, after all, is part of the reason that they are papers of record—newspapers that scholars use to establish fact. Beyond that, neither the *Washington Post* nor the *New York Times* was, as of 1980, nationally distributed, and both remain in part local newspapers. In fact, the largest staff at the *Washington Post* works in the "Metro" (local) section.

We also considered building a composite national newspaper by using several regional papers and the newsweeklies, as Tom Patterson did in Campaign '76;[10] or "sampling" newspapers nationwide, as Art Miller did in the congressional elections of '74.[11] But these strategies are very expensive, and they present a new set of problems as well. Daily newspapers (the closest approximation of print as a national enterprise) do not actually cover national campaigns. Fewer than a dozen newspapers rely heavily on their own staff for reporting anything outside their hometown or, at best, the state. The average American daily does not provide its own news content about national

*In 1982 Gannett Company started a new national daily, *USA Today*. Given its focus, however, *USA Today* cannot yet be considered a viable example of a national paper, let alone an example of traditional print.

elections. So, comparing print with national television meant looking at the campaign news that traditional print uses, not the campaign news which traditional American print collects.

Beneath the rarified atmosphere of the prestige press, daily newspapers rely on independent news services, staff reports from the parent chain, and, above all, on the wire services for covering nonlocal news. For almost a century the wires have been the national news in the average American local daily. Since the 1840s, the major news wires have collected and disseminated the day's news for local American newspapers, and, for the last fifty years, for most local news broadcasters as well.

While there are dozens of wires, the two most conspicuous are, without question, Associated Press (AP) and United Press International (UPI). Associated Press, dating back to 1848, is older and larger and has over fourteen hundred newspaper members. UPI is much more recent and, with approximately one thousand clients, somewhat smaller. A spinoff of the old Hearst wire system, UPI was, during Campaign '80, a subsidiary of E.W. Scripps Company. As of June 1982, UPI is owned by Media News Corporation.

The most obvious difference between AP and UPI is not one of substance but of structure. The Associated Press is a news *co-op*, with each newspaper being a member of the association. UPI is a privately held organization in which newspapers are clients, buying a service from UPI. In the last twenty years, AP has grown somewhat at the expense of UPI, but both organizations have had some problem contending with the newer wire services and syndicates against which both major wires now compete.

In these last twenty years, modern news syndicates and regional news services have cut into the news monopoly that the national wires have traditionally enjoyed.[12] But, for the most part, national news in local newspapers is still wirecopy, cut and pasted to fit between the grocery ads and classifieds. Traditionally, 95 percent of the seventeen hundred American dailies subscribe to AP, UPI, or both. And these papers are not wasting their subscriptions.

As recently as 1968, the *Wall Street Journal* estimated that "the wires provide Americans with 75% of the state, national and international news they read in papers . . . ."[13] More recently, in a representative sample of 100 American newspapers, analyzed during the 1974 congressional campaign, Lutz Erbring found that 60 percent of all the national front page news came from AP.[14] Even for close-to-home issues like family planning, the wires deliver three-quarters of the copy that comes out in the local press.[15]

In April 1978 Stephen Hess studied a week's worth of print coverage of Washington news stories in twenty-two American dailies— dailies ranging from the prestigious *Los Angeles Times* down through the less-than-prestigious *Baltimore News American.* Hess found that in one paper, 88 percent of the Washington news came directly from the wires. Five papers got more than three-quarters of their Washington copy from AP, UPI, and Reuters. (Reuters is the national wire for the United Kingdom.) Overall, 57 percent of the Washington news came from the three major wires.[16]

Even in the 1980s, small local newspapers still brag about their reliance on the national wires. Strange as it may seem to those who work in or near the eastern media establishment, the banner for the local Schenectady daily proclaims: "Full AP and UPI Wire Services." Small town print not only depends on the wires, it flaunts its dependency. Wires also feed directly into broadcast journalism. Edward Epstein discovered that 70 percent of the day-to-day domestic news assignments for NBC "Nightly News" originated with AP or UPI daybooks.[17]

National campaign news, which is our principal interest, is every bit as likely to come directly over the wires. Having decided to use the wires as symbol of traditional American print, we checked back to find how much wire dependency still exists in covering presidential campaigns in what might be called the "modern era." We chose three papers; one from the East, one from the West, and one from the central states. We included one "prestige" newspaper, the *Boston Globe;* one "less-than-prestige" newspaper, the *Columbus* (Ohio) *Dispatch;* one "newspaper," the *Seattle Times.* We chose one day in each month from campaign years 1940, 1960, and 1980, and we counted the number of presidential campaign stories that came to each paper over the wire or through some other channel, such as staff, chain reports, or news syndicates.

Because editors neglect to identify the source for about 10 percent of the stories, exact percentages do not exist for any of these three campaigns. But even the now highly regarded *Boston Globe* has, across these three elections, utilized the wires in more than five cases out of ten in its hard coverage of the campaign. The *Columbus Dispatch* and the *Seattle Times* are more relevant for us; both come closer to the soul of traditional American print. Since 1940, these two dailies have, on average, taken about three-fourths of their presidential campaign coverage from the major wires. Even in 1980, in what is perhaps wrongly considered the tail-end of the wire era, Washington state's largest paper used AP and UPI copy about 80 percent of the time in hard reporting on the election.

Nothing symbolizes traditional American print completely or perfectly, but using the wires as symbolic of traditional daily print makes sense. Wires not only fill up newspapers with lots of copy, they also shape the minds of the local editors and chain reporters who decide what the local campaign news will be.[18] When it comes to monitoring campaigns, American print continues to rely on the wires. When it comes to monitoring traditional print, as authors we rely on the wires, too.

CBS and UPI as Cases

Having decided to use network television as representative of national television, and wire news as representative of traditional print, the next decision involved choosing examples of each. Rather than cut the length of our analysis (some of our most important ideas involved changes in coverage over the course of a year), we decided to limit the breadth by using only one network and one wire service.

Random selection of a network and a wire service seemed an unjustifiable scientific pretense, so we decided to use the network and the wire service which met our principal criteria for inclusion. Those criteria were *size of audience* and *professional prestige;* together they gave us a measure of importance.

Using standards of size and prestige, selecting a network was relatively simple. Among the three commercial networks, CBS News generally has maintained the largest news audience, whether considering the evening news programs, news magazines, or special events. For the last ten years, the "CBS Evening News with Walter Cronkite" (now, of course, with Dan Rather) has generally led its competitors at ABC and NBC. The 1980 Nielsen ratings showed that CBS News captured 27 percent of the viewing audience while ABC and NBC tied at 24 percent. In Campaign '80 (although it was close), CBS generally attracted the largest audience in covering the primary results, the conventions, the election night returns. Only during exceptional circumstances (for example, the ABC coverage of its own phone-in poll following the Carter-Reagan debate) did CBS lose its status as "most watched" among the networks.

In professional prestige, CBS had, as of 1980, also tended to stand a bit above the other two networks. Despite recent raids on CBS News (much of their top talent moved to NBC or to ABC during the course of this research), CBS still managed to maintain its reputation as the network of Edward Murrow. One study completed in the 1970s and conducted among more than thirteen hundred professional journalists from around the country found that CBS News ranked tenth in overall prominence as a news organization; NBC came up twelfth; ABC was fourteenth.[19] In fact, that relative ranking understates CBS's actual professional prestige. CBS News not only wound up higher in the overall ranking, it also received more "prominence points" than the other two networks combined.[20] If the *New York Times* could still justifiably be regarded as America's newspaper of record, CBS could still justifiably be considered the network of record. We, like half a dozen analysts before us, considered CBS as the one network to study when studying only one.[21]

Nor did we hesitate initially in choosing a wire—we chose Associated Press. Considering either size of audience or professional prestige, Associated Press comes out ahead of United Press International. Our own work with the *Boston Globe,* the *Columbus Dispatch* and the *Seattle Times,* shows that in 1980, AP campaign stories were twice as likely to be used in local newspapers as were stories from UPI. If there is a wire of record, it is AP.

Unfortunately, however, AP would not permit itself to become part of our record. Although it had tentatively agreed to cooperate, AP eventually decided that it would not rent us any of its daily news wire. Whatever its public position on open access to information, in this particular case, AP would not provide us open access to its wire, even if we agreed to pay normal university rates.*

Without AP, the choice became simpler. We switched to UPI. UPI

---

*Unofficially, we were told that AP management had been offended by a piece of content research that had appeared in 1979 in *Columbia Journalism Review.* Apparently, the offending article was "Inside the Wires' Banana Republics." The piece, written by Michael Massing, charged that both the AP and UPI Spanish wire were consistently supporting status quo politics in Latin America and the rest of the world.

has, of course, more clients than any wire other than AP, and does rank a very close second to AP in terms of professional excellence.[22] But UPI has, unlike AP, come upon hard financial times and is shrinking in size. So, although UPI probably does come closer to representing "old-fashioned" wire copy than AP, UPI was our admitted second choice. When we speak about the wire, we mean UPI.

Topics for Study: Objectivity, Equity of Access, Fairness, Seriousness, and Comprehensiveness

Seeking in part to compare traditional print with contemporary television, we needed grounds for comparison. Given that this was a "press watch," we decided to compare television and print in terms of their own explicit professional standards.

But unfortunately, there is no single list of standards. The original "Canons of Journalism" belong to the American Society of Newspaper Editors (ASNE), but ASNE does not speak for the profession, only for itself. Nor are the "Canons" very helpful. Published originally in 1923, the ASNE list recommends "responsibility," "freedom of the press," "independence," "truth and accuracy," "impartiality," and "fair play,"[23] a set of values roughly equivalent to a boy scout creed.

The "Canons" had, for us, one other liability: they are but one list among half a dozen. The Hutchins Commission for a Free and Responsible Journalism published its own list in 1947,[24] in part as a reaction against the "Canons." Sigma Chi Delta, the society of professional journalists, has its own set of standards. So does AP. So does UPI. John Hulteng, communications professor at Stanford, recently compiled a list of lists of press values.[25] In short, there is nothing akin to a "Ten Commandments of American journalism."

So we have distilled from several lists that do exist what we consider the five most important and testable principles: objectivity, equity of access, fairness, seriousness, and comprehensiveness. Starting in Part II, each principle is accorded its own chapter. Chapters 3 through 7 are devoted entirely to basic principles of press as practiced in Campaign '80 by CBS and UPI.

Formal Procedures

We videotaped all the weekday programs for the CBS "Evening News," starting on New Year's Day, 1980, and extending through the last day of December.* We rented backup tapes from the Television News Archives at Vanderbilt University. We also collected a copy of the UPI "A"† wire, day-by-day.

We did not use all the stories. We taped or collected only campaign or campaign-related stories. Our definition incorporated any story which: mentioned the presidential campaign, no matter how tangentially; mentioned any presidential candidate in his campaign role; mentioned any presidential candidate or his immediate family in a noncampaign, official role (almost always a story about the president); discussed to a substantial degree any campaign lower than the presidential level. We have four basic varieties of political news: full-fledged presidential campaign stories; campaign-related stories; "official" stories; and lower-level campaign stories.

Full-fledged campaign stories are easy to identify. CBS almost always used the "Campaign '80" logo to introduce these pieces; UPI generally labeled them "politics." We found just over twenty-three hundred Campaign '80 stories in 1980.

Campaign-related stories concern government officials who are running for office and who are treated as candidates only tangentially in the story at hand. These are stories that brush against the campaign, but just barely. In total, we found just under nine hundred of these campaign-related items.

"Official" stories never mention the campaign, but mention one or more of the the candidates in their official role. These pieces include a story about Jerry Brown issuing orders in Sacramento to cope with floods in Southern California, or a story about Edward Kennedy holding hearings on the effects of radiation on public health. CBS and

---

*The "Evening News" has several versions: the "Western edition"; the 6:30 P.M. edition; the 7:00 P.M. edition. For the most part we used the 7:00 P.M. edition, Eastern time. In several instances, we used the Vanderbilt Archive tapes, which employ the 6:30 news. The campaign news was usually the same, regardless of the edition.

†Each wire service really offers several news wires: an "A" wire, a "city" wire, a radio wire, etc. The "A" wire is the national, most complete wire. The "A" wire itself comes in two cycles, night and day. The "night" cycle begins at noon and goes through midnight. The "day" cycle starts at midnight and extends until noon. We used the day wire. The reason was access. We had near total access to the day wire; the night wire was less accessible.

UPI produced over two thousand of these "official" news pieces between January and December, referring to candidates as visible as Ted Kennedy and as invisible as Phil Crane. But in reality, about 90 percent of the "official" stories were about President Carter, as president. Because over one-third of all the stories were official stories, official stories merit a chapter of their own. Chapter 8, "Prime-Time Minister," compares the way wires and networks covered Carter in his official role as president in 1980.

Added to all this was a smattering of lower-level campaign stories such as stories about the vice-presidential election, the congressional campaign, state politics, even a mayor's race or two. All told there were just over fifty-five hundred stories on the day wire and CBS "Evening News" that met one of our four criteria for inclusion—22 percent of the entire newshole on CBS or UPI. Whatever else one might say, it seems near impossible to complain that the wires and networks were not interested in campaign reporting.[26]

CATEGORIES

Our two basic goals dictated much of what we finally did with each story. Obviously, given our original interest in variations in print and television, we classified every item as to news source— UPI or CBS. And, as for the "press watch," we evaluated all campaign stories for objectivity, for fairness, for seriousness, and so forth. We also collected the usual housekeeping information for every story: date, position in the newscast, length in seconds or inches, reporter, newsmaker, topic. By the end we had classified each campaign story in twenty-five different categories. Some categories were measured word by word, some sentence by sentence. But for the main, we considered the story as the most important unit of analysis.

RELIABILITY

We did not include photos or visuals or voice inflections in our work. We considered only the verbal message, and that may help explain why we were so successful, comparatively speaking, in agreeing among ourselves as to what grade or scores should be assigned to each sentence or story.

The rules and definitions we followed were not always simple. It is easy to determine the month a story appears, but much harder to arrive at agreed upon standards when classifying stories as "good press" or "bad," a measurement crucial in chapter 5, our chapter on "fairness." Poor definitions produce poor results; but there is no precise way to test the quality of one's definitions. One can only say what those definitions happen to be. But, in order to keep the research systematic and to make sure that all stories and sentences were classified the same way, "intercoder reliability" tests were performed throughout 1980.

Intercoder reliability means little more than determining how often the members of the staff, operating independently, classify ("code" is the term usually employed) the same story the same way. If reliability testing fails to meet a minimally acceptable standard—arbitrarily assigned—one has to go back and build a set of definitions that are more reliable. We have performed intercoder reliability tests among the four people (two teams) who did the classification and we have done fairly well. In total we agreed with each other more than 95 percent of the time, which is high compared with most projects like this.[27] Of course, some things are harder to agree upon, and in some measures our reliability fell as low as 75 percent.* But in general, our scoring system was reliable, that is, reproducible in its results.

SCOPE

Our approach in this book aims at being straightforward and relatively free of jargon. We have bypassed many of the more esoteric types of content analysis, most of the more complicated statistical techniques, and even some of the "heavier" issues concerning content. We have, for example, decided not to grade stories for their logical consistency or for the "grammar" of their film footage or for their linguistics.[28]

We have made these omissions for two reasons; first in order to make our findings meaningful to a general audience, and second, to maintain a sense of day-to-day reality as to what a campaign news story is. If our Washington perspective in Campaign '80 has taught us anything, it is that campaign news and campaigns lack profundity. Profound techniques sometimes overinterpret what is there and even imagine what is not. We have tried hard not to overinterpret.

*The one variable upon which we did not agree upon nearly so well—who served as principal newsmaker in each story—we have used sparingly.

And, above all, we have written for an audience that thinks about media, but doesn't often think about media research.

Presupposing Criticism

Nobody should begin this sort of work without recognizing that whatever techniques are adopted, whatever conclusions are drawn, somebody is going to be unhappy. Given what we know will follow in the next eleven chapters, we anticipate that professional media critics will think we were too easy on the press; the press will decide we were too hard; orthodox social scientists will complain our methodology is shaky; students will complain that we bothered with methodology at all. So, at the risk of providing ready-made quotations for potentially negative reviews, we have decided to admit shortcomings before we present our evidence. We confess to five weaknesses.

1. SAMPLING

We did not study all three networks. We did not study both wires. We did not study the major national dailies. And we did not study, by any stretch, all of CBS News or even the UPI wire. CBS is more than the weekday "Evening News"—much more. As of 1980, "Evening News" represented about one-third of the average weekday output, not counting documentaries. The same problem applies to the wire. UPI has two cycles, not one. There were another four thousand stories on the UPI "night" wire that we did not analyze, and the editorial staff at the Washington bureau of UPI insists that we used the "wrong" wire, the wire with less substance.*

*As they explained it to us, the editorial staff at UPI has two reasons for believing that we used the "wrong" wire: first, because more of their analytical stories appear on the night wire, particularly during the hours of 8:00 P.M. and midnight; second, because there were more issue pieces on that cycle than on the day cycle. We did a preliminary analysis of the campaign news for the first week in January and found the differences between the two cycles to be minimal. We also compared the week of October 6–10, with copy provided by UPI, and found that there was no clear evidence indicating that the day wire and night wire differed fundamentally. While we did find that the night wire had 10 percent more "issue news" than the cycle we analyzed, we also found that the night wire was 13 percent less "analytical." In other words, while the night wire did devote more of its newshole to policy issues, it also

Not surprisingly, we plead financial limitations. Given that we were convinced that we needed a study that went beyond the usual "last three months of the campaign," we were more than willing to make a trade—more days for fewer sources. Moreover, we began our research believing that the "other" two networks and the "other" wire behaved very much like their competition; that CBS, ABC, and NBC behave very much alike, and that UPI and AP were even closer together in content than the networks. We were not just guessing; a good deal of literature supports these contentions, directly and indirectly.[29] To defend ourselves, we have done a mini-comparison and find that we guessed right. For the most part, as figure 2–1 suggests, we found that differences are greater across media than within a medium.

Figure 2–1 contains six direct comparisons involving all three networks and both major wires for a sample of twelve days selected at random during 1980. These six comparisons include some of the most important elements in our research, which test, for example, the degree to which each of the five sources covered the day's campaign news descriptively, as opposed to analytically, (Frame C), or test something as crucial as the issue-orientation of all five sources (Frame E).

Looking across the six frames it becomes clear that on some dimensions all five of these national media (ABC, CBS, NBC, AP, UPI) behave much the same. On an element as fundamental as news "hardness" (the extent to which each news source dealt with concrete events during the last twenty-four hour news cycle) all five sources acted as one (Frame D).

But when the press does divide itself, the split generally separates networks and wires. Most important, in our larger study where CBS and UPI showed the greatest variation from one another, CBS wound up behaving much more like ABC and NBC, and UPI behaved more

proved to be more descriptive than the day wire, the opposite of what the UPI editorial staff told us. Finally, we found that the night wire was even more interested in campaign issues than policy issues, when compared with the day wire. In other words, it was a wash, with neither the day wire nor the night wire proving itself to be more substantive.

Because we relied completely on UPI for furnishing copy of the night wire during the second week in October, and because we found 25 percent more campaign news on the day wire, we have only minimal confidence that the day wire and night wire do behave the same way. But as it stands, we fail to share the opinion of the editors at UPI: we found the day wire and the night wire relatively similar in content.

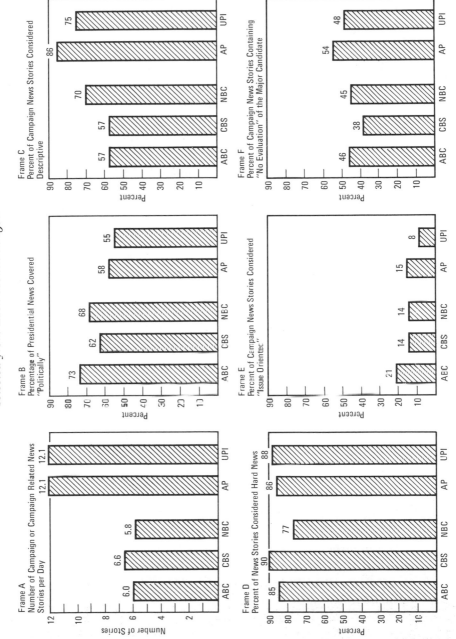

Figure 2-1

Selected Comparisons Between Networks and News Wires, One Day
Selected from Each Month in 1980

Frame A
Number of Campaign or Campaign Related News
Stories per Day

Frame B
Percentage of Presidential News Covered
"Politically"

Frame C
Percent of Campaign News Stories Considered
Descriptive

Frame D
Percent of News Stories Considered Hard News

Frame E
Percent of Campaign News Stories Considered
"Issue Oriented"

Frame F
Percent of Campaign News Stories Containing
"No Evaluation" of the Major Candidate

like AP. In other words, networks were networks and wires were wires.[30]

2. STANDARDS

This is in part a press watch; an investigation of how well CBS did and UPI did in offering news that met the standards of professional journalism. The profession itself has developed these standards not so much as rules but as norms, and most every segment of press has its own ethics manual. The profession has done almost too much in the way of defining its standards, but has never gone all the way in adopting a national code for all media. We have had to invent our own formal definitions. We have, on occasion, had to devise arbitrary standards for arbitrary standards.

Traditionally, the biggest complaint against the media, especially the networks, has been that they cover too much hoopla, not enough substance. But how much hoopla is too much? How much substance is enough? If we found, for instance, that the wire campaign news is 70 percent "issue news"—which it surely is not—we could still say that 70 percent gets a "C." But should we?

Like the journalist, we try to handle the problem by letting our descriptions speak for themselves. The fact that both UPI and CBS together devoted about four times as much to "horse race" and hoopla than to covering "the issues" does, after all, convey something, if not a grade. And so does the fact that fewer than 2 percent of the stories made any unsupported conclusions about the leadership skills of any and all of the candidates. In this press watch, we prefer first to describe, then to explain, and finally, to grade.

3. VISUALS

Marshall McLuhan became internationally famous by proclaiming that "the medium is the message." We have not so much denied McLuhan as we have tended to ignore him. Even though we are aware that among those who actually do content research the most popular and recent criticism is inattention to visuals, we have not included them.[31]

We have disregarded photographs, film, videotape, live pictures, and body language for several reasons, the first of which is practical. Assessing news visuals is difficult—more difficult than analyzing the word or the sentence. Our own early attempts to decide among ourselves what a particular gesture meant met with very limited success.

Second, it is still an open case as to whether pictures or images differ very much from the actual message. Richard Pride and Gary Wamsley analyzed network coverage of the Laos incursion and found that the visuals "said" just about what the audio "said."[32] And William Adams, who admonishes against what we have done, admits that the pictures and film are often redundant—as one might well expect them to be in a responsible news item.[33]

Third, we found on CBS "Evening News" very little meaningful visual information to consider, if by visual one means an observable nonverbal cue as to what the source was implying. Having checked and rechecked all presidential level campaign stories on the "Evening News," we found at best a handful of instances in which the journalist, per se, provided any observable body language or visual cue.

Voice inflections that "communicate" occur more often, but inflections inevitably support the verbal message. In our own opening case study of Carter in Philadelphia, Lesley Stahl, for example, did use her voice to underline her intention. But Stahl's inflection mirrored her text.

It may well be that visuals and "audials" have greater impact (some evidence supports that premise).[34] But we monitor what the media "say," not their immediate effect. And if visuals do make television messages more potent, that truth will not detract from our speculation about effects. If anything, knowing that audio-visual has greater potency will support our final conclusions.

Finally, we recognize that visuals extend well beyond the anchorman's raised eyebrow or the field reporter's grimace—wire photos (printed visuals) focus almost solely on the candidates, and quite obviously not on the reporters. But in the last analysis, we still think that not including visuals in our study is defensible, because we wanted to use common denominators in our comparisons of television and print. The common denominators are the story and the sentence; so stories and sentences become the more legitimate comparison. Not using visuals makes our comparison cleaner and simpler. If we can find differences between the two media by working in their common element of verbal expression, we will have done what we set out to do.

4. DEFINITIONS

We think a more serious problem involves definitions. Two definitions almost certain to cause complaints are: (1) our definition of "good press" and "bad press" that appears in the chapter on "fairness," chapter 5, and (2) our definition of traditional American print that we use throughout the book. Our measure of good press and bad press is "formal" but it is also problematic. A story is considered "bad press" if the ratio of negative explicit or implicit statements about a candidate runs in a story of at least three to one. A story is considered "good press" if the ratio goes the other way. In the long run, we probably err with this definition, but we err in the direction of ambiguity or neutrality. The majority of our good press stories really *are* good press. Bad press really is bad press.

We have already considered the reasoning which allows UPI to symbolize traditional print, but we offer an amendment. We really consider the wire to be a best approximation of old American print, not so much modern American print. The old print system of political campaign communication began after yellow journalism faded, around 1900, and extended on until the early 1960s. Times have changed in political communication. Wires still dominate small-time and middle-brow print. But that domination has waned somewhat during the last twenty years. So, in the last chapter of this book we shall reinterpret our findings by considering old and new print, and the prestige press as well. But for the most part, the wire represents what mass print has been for the last fifty years of campaign reporting. We know some people will reject our use of the wire as symbolic of mass print, but we believe that in print the wire still reigns, even if it tends less to rule.

5. EXTRAPOLATION

While this is a study of news content, chapters 10 through 13 speculate about the possible political implications of our findings concerning news. But there is no iron-clad proof that a particular content produces any particular political consequences. Yet it would seem highly illogical to dismiss news content as irrelevant to news consequences. In the last analysis, we try to avoid that illogic. Having found that the old print system conveys one set of messages and the new electronic system conveys a different set, we also notice that the new politics have many of the same characteristics as the new media.

The "new" media system—the television system—and the "new" political system seem to coincide. We do not know if this is merely coincidental. We imagine not, but we admit that our own work falls on only one side of the equation—the side that describes and analyzes what the news was and is, not what the news caused.

CONCLUSION

We conclude Part I of this book with a caveat about these caveats. We believe in these comparisons, and we think that tentative as the procedures may be, they get at basic truths about old news and new media, and about old politics and new politics as well. Wires once ruled the campaign news world; networks rule it today. If the message is fundamentally different in these two media, then the implications are at least important, if not profound.

PART II

Findings

Chapter 3

Objectivity: Most Objections Overruled

Our reporters do not cover stories from their point of view. They are presenting them from nobody's point of view.

—RICHARD SALANT, FORMER PRESIDENT, CBS NEWS

IN January of 1977, the Woodrow Wilson Center conducted an evening dialogue at the Smithsonian Institution in Washington. The seminar concerned "TV News and the 1976 Election." NBC sent as representative Roan Conrad, then the political editor for NBC News. Conrad, showing visible signs of frustration with the discussion papers, most of which were critical of network news decisions in Campaign '76, stunned a room full of reporters and academics by announcing that "network television news . . . is really not in the business of making assessments. We shy away from them."[1]

No assessments in network coverage of campaigns? In a way, Conrad was right—networks and much of the daily print press do shy away from assessments. Our study finds a surprising amount of reticence when it came to saying anything *explicit* about candidates or issues in Campaign '80, whether at CBS or UPI.

Obviously, all news media do make decisions and those decisions are made every operating moment. The very fact that the newshole in television and print stays about the same, day-to-day, with little respect to what is really happening, implies a bizarre sort of decision. Even in campaign news, where so much is boys-on-the-bus routine, news people make constant assessments. Editors in New York or Washington decide which candidates get a full-time reporter, or a part-time reporter or no reporter. Reporters in the field or on the bus decide what the day's lead will be for their campaign report. Producers and editors decide which story will make the program or newspaper and, if it does get used, where the story gets placed. In Campaign '80 somebody (somebodies) at each major news organization decided, for example, that Ed Clark, the Libertarian candidate, would not get full coverage in the campaign, even though Clark on election day received almost a million votes.

There are other classic examples. All media, for instance, practiced subjectivity by "state" in Campaign '80. On February 26, 1980, the state of Minnesota (population 3,800,000) held its Democratic and Republican delegate caucuses. By that date, Minnesota had managed to attract a total of three stories on CBS and UPI. New Hampshire (population 700,000) held its primary the same day; it had managed to attract ninety-four stories—and thirty-three times as much newsspace.

When applied to news focus, Conrad's remarks about news "assessments" make no sense whatever. When discussing *what* gets covered, objectivity is not really measurable. By definition, news agendas are not objective. Looking back through Campaign '80, we are forced to conclude with Lippmann that when it comes to news topics, "there are no standards, only conventions."[2]

But once media do decide what to cover—once they have made their inherently subjective choice concerning newsworthiness—they can invoke a more objective set of standards; and they do. For good or ill, the campaign stories in 1980 almost always followed the basic rules of objectivity. Perhaps a better description is *objectivistic*—in the manner of being objective. CBS and UPI proved more objectivistic than objective. But there clearly was a commitment in both media to work inside the principles and confines of what Lou Cannon somewhat disparagingly labels "Objective Reporting."*

*Lou Cannon, in his book, *Reporting: An Insider's View,* capitalizes the words in order to express his own conviction that the general rule in news is objectivity—almost to the point of fault, as Cannon sees it.

Objectivity: Most Objections Overruled

on truthfulness

Before objectivity comes truth. Truthfulness is a necessary condition for objective news; objectivity really is a first derivative of truth. All the formal standards of journalism specifically cite truthfulness as a major value.

Given that truth represents the *sine qua non* of journalistic virtue, and given that facts can be tested, one might expect here a chapter on truth. We have *not* studied the validity of CBS or UPI campaign news. We have two explanations for this, neither of which rings so true in the aftermath of the last few years.

We assumed from the outset that truth was not an "issue," at least not a major issue in press watching. In recent history, candidates have rarely worried much about the press lying or fabricating news. Candidates usually worry more about the quality than validity of coverage, in part because candidates think that media tell the truth, just not the whole truth. According to Gael Doar, one Carter press aide in the campaign, the truthfulness issue never even occurred during the campaign:

> We never even thought about the truthfulness of the stories. We were more concerned about the guy's tone—more concerned about the way the reporter perceived the public reception for the event. . . . Especially with television, we were never consciously thinking about the truthfulness of the reporting.

Even Spiro Agnew, the most outspoken critic of American media ever to be vice-president, failed to attack the press for lying, preferring instead to complain about its slant, its composition, and its power —not its facts. Only occasionally in 1980 did a major candidate attack the national press openly for dishonesty or for failure to get the facts straight. When asked about Jack Anderson's charge that he was planning a war with Iran to help himself get re-elected, Carter told a national television audience that "Jack Anderson consistently lies."[3] And Ronald Reagan, taking a much less vehement stance, criticized Bill Plante's facts in a piece Plante had done on April 3 for CBS "Evening News," a feature in which Plante made a half-dozen references to Reagan's facts being "wrong."

The history of media criticism also led us to believe that lying and inaccuracy were not much of an issue. Like politicians, even the most hostile critics of the press rarely discuss lying, fabrication, or reckless disregard for truth by the media. Edith Efron stands

35

pretty much alone among the notable media critics in arguing that the national press intentionally misleads us, and even Efron stresses bias, not falsehood.[4] Mainstream studies of national media hardly mention the problem of dishonesty.[5] No major academic study of press in the last twenty years expends any real energy on investigating factuality.*

Part of this vacuum developed because testing truth is a high-risk business, not unlike drilling for oil in a region not yet known for its reserves. For this reason even editors tend to assume that reporters are telling the truth—editors whose reputations hang on that supposition. Having had to face the fact that one of his reporters had fabricated an important story—and that, as editor, he had played a role in nominating that reporter for a Pulitzer prize—Robert Woodward, editor of the *Washington Post*, made it plain that the news business has come to *assume* honesty:

> It would be absurd for me or any other editor to review the authenticity or accuracy of stories that are nominated for prizes.[6]

Woodward, even as editor, had come to believe that when reporters file a story, it is true. Like Woodward, we took the *facts* to be a given. Certainly, we did not expect lying—at most we anticipated discrepancies.†

*Marilyn Jackson-Beeck and Robert Meadow did conduct a study fairly limited in scope—they actually bothered to learn how accurate the *New York Times* had been in merely transcribing the 1976 presidential debates. They found some important inaccuracies, though no dishonesties. For example, in the first debate, Jimmy Carter spoke about the DISC (Domestic International Sales Corporation) program. The *New York Times* referred to it as "this" and "gifts" program—an egregious error. Jackson-Beeck and Meadow, of course, attributed mistakes like this to life, and not to lying ("Ascertainment and Analysis of Debate Content," *The Presidential Debates*, ed. George F. Bishop, Robert G. Meadow, and Marilyn Jackson-Beeck [New York: Praeger, 1978], pp. 205–212).

†One organization does monitor the truthfulness of media. The National News Council, established in New York in 1973 to cope with Spiro Agnew's war with the media, investigates specific charges of distortion and lying hurled against the local and national press. Unlike most organizations dealing with the mass media, the National News Council decides matters of *fact* and, like a tribunal, decides right and wrong in those cases which have been brought to it by formal complaint.

Since its inception, case by case decisions from the Council have corroborated the general supposition about the nation's media—that facts generally prevail. In 1976, the last campaign year before 1980, the Council handled twenty-four claims against any and all levels of press (not a very large number, considering all the news sources). Exactly half of those twenty-four cases involved the networks or wires. Truth, per se, was at issue in only half of those twelve cases. Among those six instances involving major media and fact, only three concerned campaign news. And in the end, none of the final six complaints about truth at the networks or wires was upheld by the Council.[7] If the Council's findings represent reality, tracking dishonesty in press makes

The second reason for the failure to do "truth" research stems directly from the first. Having been persuaded by the earlier evidence and criticism of press, we adopted a methodology wholly inappropriate for evaluating truth. Hypothetically content analysis *can* be used to test for factuality: one can compare to see if CBS and NBC had the same "facts," or contradictory facts, concerning the same events. But that does not tell us much about which network was right, only that they differed. Without an independent observation, or a totally credible account (whatever that might be), we cannot say anything meaningful about truth, even in those instances where two or more sources covered the same event.

In the end, we found that the media do not have different facts. An analysis of twelve days of network news on all three networks produced for us not a single discrepancy as to fact. Networks not only tend to cover the same events, they tend to use the same quotes and to relate the same official statistics. The wires also used the same facts, and often the same campaign news. True or false, the facts were the facts were the facts in the media we monitored.

NEW TRUTHS ABOUT TRUTH

Although we originally decided not to concern ourselves with truthfulness, we are now more anxious about the decision. Since the beginning of 1980, at least eight instances of dishonesty at the hands of the news media have broken into public consciousness, although some of these cases began even before 1980. None of these instances involved CBS or UPI directly, although CBS has recently been involved in three situations where its accuracy, its credibility, or its practices have been brought into question.*

In chronological order those cases involve: (1) an erroneous charge by the *National Enquirer* that Carol Burnett had behaved loudly and

---

for a dull career. The Council's rulings in 1976 fail to prove that media do not lie, but those rulings do put truthfulness, as an empirical question, into perspective.

*On March 30, 1981, CBS reported that James Brady, press secretary to President Reagan, had died after having been accidentally shot in the head during the attempt on Reagan's life. Brady had not died.

Also, as Jeff Greenfield points out, at the same time that CBS maintained that Walter Cronkite's inclusion on the Board of Directors of Pan Am did not represent conflict of interest because Cronkite was no longer a regular in his news assignments, CBS News was advertising Cronkite as "our newest correspondent."

Most damning was an incident involving a 1982 CBS documentary about the Vietnam war—a documentary even CBS had to admit had misrepresented facts and quotes concerning General William Westmoreland's role in the conduct of the war.

obnoxiously at a Washington restaurant and had spilled wine on Henry Kissinger; (2) a story in the *Portland Oregonian* in which the reporter fabricated quotes that he attributed to then Governor Dixie Lee Ray during her 1980 re-election campaign in Washington state; (3) a ruse in which staff members of the ABC owned and operated station in New York, WABC, constructed fake personal letters, allegedly from viewers—letters which became the basis for a write-in talk show; (4) a televised interview with psychic Tamara Rand in which Rand and her interviewer, Dick Maurice, pretended that Rand had predicted the Reagan assassination attempt in January 1981 (the interview had been staged *after* the assassination attempt but ABC and NBC and several local stations carried tapes of the fake prediction until the ruse was uncovered and admitted); (5) the classic instance in which Janet Cooke, staff reporter for the *Washington Post*, fabricated a full-length report about a fictitious eight-year-old junkie in Washington and won a Pulitzer Prize for that feature; (6) an incident in which Michael Daly, a reporter for the *New York Daily News*, invented a British soldier stationed in Northern Ireland and then concocted an interview with that imaginary trooper, reporting it as fact; (7) a fictitious AP wire feature about drag racing in California, another instance in which the story proved to be a "composite," not fact; (8) a cover story about Cambodian life appearing in the *New York Times Magazine* that proved to be a wholly fictionalized account, concocted by feature writer Christopher Jones.*

All eight of these cases, coming so close together and involving many of the largest and most prestigious news organizations in the nation (the *Washington Post*, the *New York Times*, ABC Television, Associated Press, and the *New York Daily News*), have made assertions about truthfulness in media a lot more problematic. A *Newsweek* poll conducted just after the Janet Cooke affair indicated that one-third of the public believed that the hoax was not an isolated incident and that "reporters often make things up."[8]†

---

*A ninth case, still not resolved, involves a piece on "20/20," ABC's newsmagazine. CBS affiliate WBBM in Chicago has charged Geraldo Rivera and "20/20" of "shoddy journalism," accusing Rivera of not presenting all the facts it had concerning an arson ring in Chicago.

†We cannot know whether these several highly-publicized indiscretions, one after another, mean that the press has been growing more corrupt, or, on the other hand, that the discoveries only come back-to-back as a string of coincidences. We do, see, however, something akin to the Watergate syndrome—the Janet Cooke syndrome, perhaps. In these conditions, journalists and politicians take practically every unsavory incident, major and minor, as symbols of the inherent corruption of big press. We expect more press exposés of press between now and the next campaign. The

Nonetheless, we think that news from a major network or a major wire is less vulnerable to the kind of thing we saw in the Janet Cooke debacle or the Michael Daly affair or the Christopher Jones case, especially in presidential campaign reporting. Cooke and Daly were doing independent feature stories, based on quotations coming from highly unofficial sources. Campaign news almost always comes as "pack journalism." It would be hard to make up important facts about campaign events, where all the reporters and editors traveling on the same bus or plane have constant opportunity to compare one person's reports with everybody else's story. Campaign reporting may not always represent Truth, capital T, but given its composition, it is not likely to be dishonest. We have, however, no way of proving that in this research. We test only objectivity.

DEFINING OBJECTIVITY

Press people have almost as many definitions of objectivity as they have sources. In 1923, the ASNE defined objectivity to be news "free from opinion or bias of any kind,"[9] This definition, what one might call the paleolithic form of objectivity, left journalists, at least in theory, with nothing better to do than transcribe what others had said. So in the 1950s, trying to cope with mindless objectivity, the *Nieman Reports*, a journal of press ethics and opinion, attempted to update the definition.

By 1950, objectivity in political news reporting came to mean "accurately and completely informing readers," so that if the candidate's speech or words told the truth, one could simply pass them along—report the speech. But, "if such a simple report . . . would misinform the reader as to the candidate and his position, then it's time for the newspaper to shoulder its responsibilities and supply the missing information."[10] Such was the mesolithic definition of objectivity, a definition which seemed especially appropriate for the Joseph McCarthy era. It was McCarthy who, more than anyone, made the press recognize that the old definition of transcription journalism was simply too limited to provide for the real story.[11] But the 1960s required a new and improved definition.

George Lardner of the *Washington Post* has written what we consider to be among the best of the neolithic definitions. Lardner

---

feature film *Absence of Malice* symbolizes the new mentality about the newspaper business.

stresses a trilogy of factors that define objective journalism. Objective news: (1) relates only observable facts of an overt event; (2) cites others on matters of opinion; (3) refuses to allow one's own beliefs, principles, or inclinations—"or even his own knowledge"—to color raw, overt material for the story.[12] Objectivity includes, above all, a considerable reluctance to go beyond what was actually observed by the journalist, and an even greater reluctance to draw any explicit conclusions or inferences about the events being covered, unless the conclusion or inference comes from another legitimate source, not the journalist him/herself.

We have melded those standards that Lardner describes to test for objectivity in four different ways. To start, we gauged the extent to which CBS and UPI drew explicit and unsupported conclusions about the personal qualities of the candidates throughout Campaign '80. Second, we checked to see what, if anything, the reporters said about their personal opinions concerning the issues—how objectively the press covered questions of policy. Third, we measured the degree to which both media broke away from "description" and moved toward "analysis" in covering candidates or issues, defining objectivity here as a function of basic descriptiveness. Fourth, in order to gauge the objectivity of their prose we analyzed the verbs employed by the media, checking for the level of insinuation implied by verbs used in the reporting. In all four tests, the media behaved objectivistically.

EXPLICIT ASSERTIONS CONCERNING THE PRESIDENTIAL CANDIDATES

We checked all campaign and campaign-related stories for unsupported conclusions or inferences about the presidential candidates—conclusions coming directly from the source. Specifically, we checked for explicit, unattributable, evaluative assertions made by the journalist about the candidates' personal qualities.

In the main, we limited ourselves to explicit comments concerning the candidate's leadership ability *(competence, integrity, consistency)* and electability.* We also limited our scoring to the three most

*We also included a fifth dimension—what we call "other." This catch-all category includes practically everything else that might be said about a person running for office and that might have any bearing on his political image. For example, a statement by a journalist that a candidate was happy is an assertion about him as a person. But because characteristics like happy seem less serious than assertions concerning competence, integrity, consistency, and political viability, we have chosen

prominently featured candidates in each story. So in stories mentioning more than three candidates, we have not considered how those "minor" candidates were treated.*

What we have here is a test which relies on the one simple premise that explicit evaluations made of the candidate by the journalist may be true, but they fall outside our first rule of objectivity—a rule which holds that no assessments, other than those supported by other sources, can be considered objective.

To some this may seem too loose a test of objectivity. But if press people refrain from making explicit statements about candidate competence, integrity, consistency, and so on, then press people are meeting a very important test of objectivity—holding their fire, so to speak. Certainly, in the history of the unobjective press, those types of personal assessments were made all the time.

As it turned out in 1980, journalists made precious few explicit comments concerning any personal qualities of the candidates, other than about their prospects for winning or losing. In figure 3–1 we have graphed the percentage of stories in which there was *any* explicit, unattributable comment concerning competence, integrity, consistency, or successfulness for the principal candidate in each presidential campaign story. We scored these statements about the candidate as either neutral, positive, negative, or ambiguous. Ambiguous stories had near equal positive and negative information concerning the candidate's competence, and so forth or, in some cases, contained complex or confused wording that simply could not be called anything but ambiguous. Yet, even including all the ambiguous statements on all three *leadership* criteria combined, explicit evaluation of the principal candidate occurred in less than 5 percent of all full-fledged campaign stories.

Overall, in those stories in which at least one presidential candi-

---

ordinarily to omit the "other" category in describing our findings, at least in this chapter.

*We scored the first two candidates only until May 13. Eventually, because Anderson's candidacy made it clear that the general campaign would be rife with three-person stories, we chose to expand our analysis to the top three candidates in each story. We started on May 14, the first day Anderson, Reagan, and Carter were covered as a three-man field in a single story. We suspected that if journalists were going to evaluate anybody it would be the *principal* candidate in the story, and that there would be a clifflike drop in evaluation of the second and third candidates. We were correct. Almost 90 percent of the references to the third principal candidate made no clear statement one way or another about the candidates' skills, decency, or successfulness.

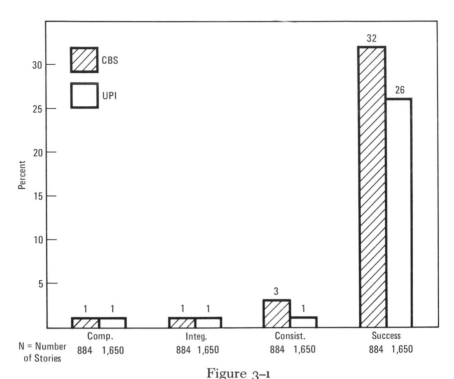

Figure 3–1
*Percentage of Presidential Campaign Stories in Which There Was Any
Explicit Evaluation of Principal Candidate's Competence, Integrity,
Consistency, or Successfulness (January 1 through November 3, 1980)*

date was mentioned, fewer than 1 percent of the stories made any
explicit assertions about that principal candidate's competence; only
1 percent of those stories said anything explicit about that candidate's
integrity; and only 3 percent made a comment concerning consistency.

For reasons of clarity, perhaps it might be a good idea to provide
an example or two of explicit evaluation. Consider these two unam-
biguous remarks, both from CBS. First, an explicitly positive comment made by Cronkite about Howard Baker early in the campaign:
Howard Baker, declared Cronkite, was "the only Republican to be
helped by Watergate, as his calm, careful reasoning won him overwhelming praise from television viewers."* On the other hand, there
was an explicitly negative assessment of independent candidate John
Anderson by Cronkite later in the year: "John Anderson was on the

*"Evening News," January 15, 1980.

campaign trail again today—in Jerusalem!—telling the Israelis, and in effect, America's Jewish voters a lot of what they wanted to hear!"* But even these examples show that the networks, and the wires, too, rarely blast or praise candidates in very heavily colored terms. As strong as these examples are in comparative perspective, they still represent relatively mild assessments. There simply is not much explicit criticism, complaint, or praise expressed by national press about candidates, *unless* it is quoted from another source.

As expected, CBS reporters showed slightly less reticence than UPI, with the "Evening News" staff providing about twice as much evaluation concerning the qualities of leadership as the wire. But this is a difference in mere millimeters. The clear conclusion drawn from figure 3–1 is that news staffs in both news organizations scrupulously avoid unsupported assertions about the candidates on those very dimensions most likely to be meaningful to voters.

Media practice a double standard however. CBS and UPI may be prudish when it comes to evaluating the man on the stump, but the media behave like libertines when judging the reaction of the crowd. Figure 3–1 makes it clear that journalists see themselves in the business of evaluating campaigns, not candidates. CBS and UPI were almost eight times as willing to draw explicit conclusions about the principal candidate's chances as about his leadership qualities!

To provide some feel for this double standard in which media avoid judging candidates but jump at the chance to judge their campaigns, we have summarized the two reports about Reagan on the eve of the election. One might have imagined that CBS and UPI would, with the final and crucial decisions still to be made by the American people, slip outside the boundaries of "Objective Reporting," and say something explicit and/or subjective about the man who at that point seemed most likely to win the election. Not so. Both Jerry Bowen at CBS and Diane Curtis of UPI followed the canons of Objective Reporting in every respect. They asserted practically nothing about Reagan the man, other than momentary mood, and they spent their last few words making inferences about what they observed on their own—the "horse race." As for last minute license, there was practically none of it here. November 3, 1980, Jerry Bowen:

> Reagan declined to make any comment on the hostage situation today except in response to one question: will it hurt him politically?. . . .

*"Evening News," July 8, 1980.

His own direct reference to the hostages was contained in a speech he taped for broadcast on the three major networks this evening. . . .

Reagan's day began on Main Street in Peoria where the candidate played to a crowd of 10,000 along with his running mate, George Bush, former President Ford and comedian Bob Hope who endorsed and upstaged his former show business colleague. . . .

Reagan displayed little emotion as he declared that Americans must consider several questions before they vote. . . .

Reagan and his advisers feel very secure on this election eve; not overly confident, they say, but confident just the same, that the candidate is near victory. This afternoon Reagan returned to the West Coast for two more campaign stops and a homecoming in Los Angeles, where he'll vote tomorrow and await the election results tomorrow night.

On the very eve of the election, the only evaluation Bowen was willing to make was that Bob Hope had drawn a bigger response than candidate Reagan. And on the wire it was much the same thing; no last-minute subjectivity whatever. November 3, 1980, Diane Curtis:

Ronald Reagan's answer to developments on the politically hot hostage issue is to tread softly in the waning hours of his 12-year quest for the Presidency.

Reagan's final day of campaigning today included rallies in Peoria and Portland, Ore., before going home to Los Angeles to cast his ballot on Tuesday.

In stop after stop before enthusiastic and large crowds in Marietta, Dayton and Cincinnati, Ohio, Sunday, the Republican Presidential candidate refused to comment first on the acceptance by the Iranian parliament of four conditions on the hostages and then on President Carter's response to the decision. . . .

He repeatedly declined to answer reporters' questions about the hostages and referred only briefly or not at all to the issue at his three campaign stops.

Reagan was beaming and obviously keyed up by the overflow crowds and cheering receptions in this final swing through voter-rich Ohio.

But his ebullience belied a concern of his aides over the uncertainty of the political effect of the new hostage developments. . . .

The campaign has prepared several commercials and speeches in anticipation of rapid-fire movement in the release of the hostages, which could prove a boon to Carter's campaign. . . .

Reagan scheduled only two events today—ending a journey that began in 1968 when he briefly challenged Richard Nixon for the GOP nomination —to allow time for the taping of three 30-minute and 20-minute commercials to be seen on the three networks tonight.

And so the very last word about Reagan on CBS was nothing more than a reference to the candidate's vote-watching plans, and on UPI, the last word was a reference to Reagan's television ads.

We might feel more anxious about declaring the national media "objective as to candidate," if we were the first to make that declaration. We are not alone. Having studied twenty American daily newspapers, three networks, and two local television stations spreading across three elections (1968, 1972, and 1976), Doris Graber found the same thing. "Explicit bias," according to Graber, "is highly unusual. Outright editorial comment in news stories is practically nil."[13]

The Consistency Hobgoblin

We are able to draw a second conclusion from figure 3–1: that consistency represents the one personal dimension where media feel any freedom to make "unsupported" claims about candidates. CBS and UPI made more than twice as many explicit comments about consistency as the other two leadership qualities combined. Part of this difference involves definitions. But the difference which exists after taking definitions into account still tells us something about objectivity, and, as important, something about print as opposed to television news.

Reporters have few, if any, objective standards for measuring competence or integrity. Consistency, however, comes with a built-in objective standard. When a candidate expresses an opinion on any topic, that becomes his or her "policy" (his own self-established position). Once he or she speaks again on the topic, the press then has an objective standard against which the new position can be gauged, that, of course, being simply the original position.

The process is historic. Writing about Campaign '76, Donald Matthews concluded:

> Judging from recent experience, a candidate's statements on public issues is most likely to be reported if it represents a change in the candidate's position. . . . Reporters place a premium on internal consistency. A politician can get away with a great deal . . . so long as he's consistent.[14]

In the last analysis, the inconsistency story has three real assets: it is inherently objective (one quotes the candidate); it is inherently critical (the candidate is shown in contradiction); it is inherently interesting (it reveals conflict between a candidate and his own record). So we have measurable amounts of explicit news about candidate inconsistency, at least in comparison with the other personal characteristics concerning leadership.

As important, perhaps, is the special affinity networks have for invoking the consistency criterion. Newspapers have morgues with old press clippings and quotations, facts on file. But networks have videotape libraries with faces and voices on file. CBS had almost two and one-half times as much explicit news about consistency and inconsistency as did UPI. Although, as a rule, we think the theory of news content determined by video is overdone (see chapter 10), we think that videotape has made the consistency criterion even more important than it was in the age of ink.

MEDIA ON THE ISSUES

It is time to define objectivity in a new way. Instead of asking how much the report or the reporter asserted about the candidates, now we ask how much did media assert about the issues. In terms of unattributed assertions, it was not even close. As reluctant as the press is about saying anything explicit concerning the leadership qualities of the candidates, the press is markedly more reluctant to assess or evaluate "the issues."

Granted, part of that stems from the fact that media cover issues much less often than candidates and their campaigns. But that fails to explain an almost total refusal by our two sources to go beyond straightforward description of the candidate's policy positions. During the last ten weeks of Campaign '80, CBS failed to draw a single clear inference or conclusion about a single issue position of a single candidate—UPI as well.

For all practical purposes, whatever the candidates or their surrogates said about the issues served as issue coverage. On television and in the wire, we did find numerous references to Reaganomics as "voodoo economics," but those comments invariably came from candidates, *never* journalists.

Consider closely the following three-part report on CBS "Evening News" (on March 20), presented as perhaps the single most comprehensive report concerning the candidates on the economy in the primary period.

[Carter quote]

CRONKITE: Just six days ago, President Carter proposed a number of measures to try to bring inflation under control, including a $13-billion cut in his 1981 federal budget. Well, how would the candidates for Mr. Carter's job in Campaign '80 handle the problem? We asked our correspondents with them for a report.

[Kennedy quote]

JED DUVALL: Senator Kennedy's alternative to President Carter's plan, a comprehensive freeze, would be temporary, time enough to put in place programs to stimulate the economy. Competition should be encouraged, he says, by deregulation, such as that accomplished in the airline industry. Kennedy proposes increasing investments through tax incentives. Overseas sales to be spurred by more agressive foreign trade policies. And a way must be found, he says, to increase American productivity. And while he supports a balanced budget, Kennedy charges that a 20 or 30-billion dollar cut in federal spending would reduce inflation by only a fraction of a point, and in the proposed Carter cuts, Kennedy sees the poor, the unemployed and the elderly hurt the most. The senator would close tax loopholes for business and the wealthy, while trying to encourage energy conservation, capital formation, and industrial modernization. And gasoline, he says, should be rationed, not taxed.

[Reagan quote]

JERRY BOWEN: That is Ronald Reagan's campaign theme; his criticism of the Carter Administration's economic policies. The Reagan solution: a 30 percent tax cut, phased in over three years. Elimination of certain taxes, the tax on savings interest, for example. Budget cuts, he doesn't say specifically where. A hiring freeze on federal employees. A transfer of programs back to the states, with taxing authority to support them. And the elimination of fraud and wasteful spending. That alone, says Reagan, will cut $50-billion from the budget. The heart of Reagan's plan is the theory of supply side economics: cut taxes to spur productivity in the private sector. More productivity, more jobs, ultimately, more tax revenue for the federal government. Reagan says his proposal is the reverse of President Carter's which he describes as the economics of despair.

[Anderson quote]

BOB MCNAMARA: The state of the American economy is the heart of John Anderson's campaign. Anderson has proposed 37 budget cuts, totalling more than $11-billion. And chief among them would be shifting the Defense budget away from the MX missile system in favor of a submarine-based missile system. Anderson says the proposal would save $200-million without jeopardizing national security. His other budget-cutting proposals include abandoning the Law Enforcement Assistance Administration to save 400-million, dropping more than $2-billion worth of federal grants to state and local governments, and eliminating the highway beautification program to save $21-million. Anderson also proposed cuts in the federal jobs program, and to slow down fuel consumption, he wants an emergency ten percent tax imposed on imported oil, a tax he believes would raise more than $10-billion in 1981.

Three things strike us about this trilogy. First, George Bush failed to be included, a stunning omission on behalf of CBS and atypical of the way the networks generally handled the delicate problem of equal treatment for the major candidates. Second, CBS proved here how issue-oriented it can be when it chooses to be. Duvall, Bowen, and McNamara each managed to summarize rather effectively the major economic programs of Kennedy, Reagan, and Anderson, respectively, in a total package 5 minutes in length. Last and most important is the absence of anything approaching subjectivity or even interpretation about the positions expressed. CBS covered these economic programs as straight as a news organization can cover anything. There are no assessments here; there are practically no inferences, and those which do exist usually relate to campaign strategy, not policy. Time after time, when CBS did "issues," CBS left its bag of assessments at home.

In both media, issue news was treated as a breed apart. Walter Cronkite did most of the issue coverage for CBS in Campaign '80, conducting interviews on the issues with each of the major candidates starting as early as November 1979. Cronkite never said anything that gave clues as to his own positions on the issues. The closest he came was an interview with Reagan on January 24, 1980, when he implied that Reagan's answer about the energy crisis was not quite rational.

> CRONKITE: You think decontrol then basically can solve the entire energy problem?
> REAGAN: I had one man, an independent in this business. . . tell me he believed we could be self-sufficient in five years with decontrol.
> CRONKITE: Let me get just one thing straight, if I may, Governor. Are you saying that U.S. federal regulations—controlling prices—are more responsible for our high prices today and our shortages than the Arab price increase, the OPEC price increases?
> REAGAN: Yes, plus our depreciating value of the dollar.

Rather than call Reagan's answer nonsense or simplistic, Cronkite merely restated the question. From the patriarch of American network news the nearest thing to an assessment of issue positions in Campaign '80 was a follow-up question.

Some press critics, and a large proportion of media theorists, regard objectivity as a charade. Yet using issue coverage by CBS and UPI as measure, we find the rule of objectivity to have almost a stranglehold over the reporters. Saying nothing about the issues, beyond what others have said, strikes us as being the first commandment in campaign news coverage. Had Reagan told Cronkite in their interview that he favored pre-emptive nuclear strikes against the Soviet Union and China, we don't doubt that CBS would have rushed out as fast as their news vans would carry them, to get the response from the rest of the candidates. But we do doubt that Cronkite would have told his audience how he felt about pre-emptive nuclear war, at least not during the interview. When it comes to issue coverage by the national media, objectivity not only rules, it practically tyrannizes.

DESCRIPTION, ANALYSIS, AND ETHICAL JUDGMENTS IN CAMPAIGN NEWS

Taken to a logical extreme, objectivity could extend beyond mere reluctance to make explicit assertions about candidates or issues. Objectivity could "objectively" be defined as news without any opinion or inference by the news source. There was a time when reporters and editors did define objectivity just that parochially. In 1860, AP correspondent Lawrence Gobright penned the ultimately stringent definition of objective reporting: "My business is to communicate facts: my instructions do not allow me to make any comment upon the facts which I communicate . . . my dispatches are merely dry matters of fact and detail."[15]

Nobody in contemporary journalism is that orthodox. But we can still use description (descriptiveness) as an indicator of objectivity. One can at least begin to quantify the level of objectivity by computing sentence by sentence the degree of "unadulterated" description coming from any news organization. This is not *the* test for objectivity; it is, among several others, *a* test.

Beginning Labor Day and ending the week of the general election, we labeled each sentence in every campaign story as either descriptive, analytical, or judgmental. Descriptive sentences present the who, what, where, when of the day's news, without any meaningful qualification or elaboration. "Reagan went south today" is a classic example of description.

Analytical sentences tell us *why* something occurs or predicts as to

49

whether it might. Analytical sentences either draw inference or reach a conclusion based on facts not observed. Reporting that "Reagan went south today to woo George Wallace voters away from the president" is a classic campaign inference.

Judgmental sentences deal in norms and values; they tell us how something ought to be or ought not to be. Judgmental sentences convey ethical standards. "Reagan went south today to put together a racist coalition that decent Americans should reject" would be a judgmental statement—a normative expression on behalf of the reporter.

In this exercise, we considered only sentences presented by the reporters, and ignored the remarks uttered by the candidates, staffs, voters, and so on. We were not, as a rule, interested in the objectivity of the contestants, only the media. And, because most analytical sentences in news stories come packaged in description, we drew our rules in such a way that sentences containing any analysis at all were considered analytical; any sentence containing any normative evaluation we considered judgmental. In essence, we have tried hard to deflate the proportion of descriptive news, because we realized from the outset that description would dominate the other two types of news.

But even with the deflated figures, descriptive sentences and descriptive stories carry the day. Figure 3–2 shows how much of the presidental campaign news between Labor Day and Election Day proved to be descriptive, analytical, and judgmental. Figure 3–2 gives only the sentence-by-sentence breakdowns for the three types of information. When we consider stories, that magnifies still more the descriptive nature of the campaign news. Almost two out of every three stories on CBS are, in majority, descriptive; just over a third are analytical; none is normative. On UPI, almost three-quarters of the news stories were predominantly descriptive. No matter which measure one uses, story or sentence, the lion's share of campaign news on CBS and UPI was given over to the most traditional four "W's" of American journalism, who, what, where, when.

As for taking positions on issues, CBS and UPI came remarkably close to total abstinence.* Neither news organization offered a single

---

*In 1982 Bill Moyers joined CBS "Evening News" and, in his commentaries, Moyers has made clear normative judgments about issues. David Brinkley, at ABC, and John Chancellor, at NBC, have also, as of 1982, begun a series of commentaries. Moyers, Brinkley, and Chancellor, as commentators, do deal in norms and value judgments, and to a degree not even approached in 1980 campaign reporting.

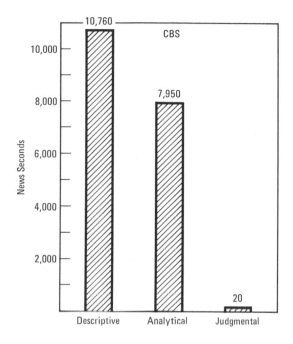

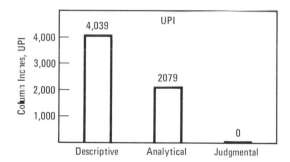

Figure 3–2

Number of Seconds (CBS) and Inches (UPI) in Campaign News Which were Descriptive, Analytical, Judgmental (Labor Day to Election Day, 1980)

story that contained a fully developed normative message—a statement about right or wrong on the issues. CBS presented only two judgmental sentences in Campaign '80, and both were, at best, tangentially related to the campaign or the issues.

The two normative sentences we did find show just how nonjudgmental national media chose to be in covering political campaigns.

The first actually involved CBS judging CBS, not the candidates or the issues. On October 8, Walter Cronkite told the "Evening News" audience that CBS had done wrong, had on the previous night made an error in news judgment. In that previous broadcast, Bill Plante had done a hard-hitting feature piece concerning Reagan's flip-flops on five major issues during the campaign. As Plante mentioned the first of the inconsistencies, CBS put a large white "X" across Reagan's photograph, implying negation of Reagan's original stance on this issue. But CBS received a fire-storm of criticism for that white "X," and Cronkite, speaking as managing editor, apologized for the visual. The second judgmental sentence came from Lem Tucker, but there too the judgment was unrelated to any issue in the campaign. It was nothing more than Tucker's attempt at wry humor.*

As removed from value judgment as CBS proved to be, UPI was even more removed. As best as we could determine, the wire covered the entire general campaign without slipping once clearly from fact to value.

UPI also behaved differently in its willingness to cross the line between description and analysis. In our definition, analytical news explains or predicts *without* benefit of quoted sources. And our evidence indicates beyond reasonable doubt that the wires do less analysis and considerably more description than television. During the general election, 38 percent of the presidential campaign stories on CBS were primarily analytical. On the wire the figure was 22 percent. Yet, clearly, both sources did much more description than anything else.

THE USE OF VERBS

UPI editor Ron Cohen told us that subjectivity is not so much a matter of unattributed conclusions or even descriptive adjectives.

---

*Tucker covered the mildly surprising endorsement by Watergate Special Prosecutor Leon Jaworski of Ronald Reagan. Tucker also noted Jaworski's announcement that he was personally establishing a political committee called "Democrats for Reagan." Tucker, noting that Jaworski appeared to be the only member of the committee, ended the piece by recommending that "perhaps the committee should be called 'Democrat for Reagan.'" Using our definition of normative news, Tucker's recommendation reads as value judgment, but obviously Tucker was not advocating values —he was having fun at Jaworski's expense.

We found one other normative sentence but it came in a noncampaign story so we have relegated it to a footnote. On November 3, Charles Osgood did a hostage anniversary report, and he made the following value judgment about the return of the hostages: ". . . Whenever that will be, it cannot be soon enough."

Objectivity: Most Objections Overruled

For Cohen subjectivity lives in the verbs. Jody Powell told us the same thing, that verbs symbolize the level of objectivity. And, according to Powell, the media always seemed to use subjective phrases such as "Carter claims," "Powell concedes," "Jordan admits." Said Powell, "The press never likes to say, 'he said.'"

But, in fact, even on this dimension, we found the media adopted verbs and syntax that are more objective than subjective. To analyze the media's choice of verbs we selected a sample of ten days of reporting and categorized all the verbs of *expression* used to describe the candidate's day on the campaign trail. We divided all "expression" verbs into three types: the *descriptive* (he said), the *analytical* (he hinted), the *insinuational* (he confessed). We then tabulated the percentage of each type in each medium.

For the most part, the verbs were of the objective (descriptive) variety. Combining results from CBS and UPI, three-fourths of the verbs were wholly descriptive, a fifth were analytical, and only about 5 percent were insinuational. As it happened, not once among the five hundred verbs of expression we counted did either source employ the word "confess," usually considered the most subjective. Although there were differences between CBS and UPI in their use of verbs (differences to be examined in chapter 5) both sources relied principally on the colorless choices: said, asked, remarked, answered, and so forth.

EXTREMISTS, MINOR PARTIES AND THE CULT OF INHERENT SUBJECTIVITY

Not all social scientists share our premise that major news media behave objectivistically, let alone objectively. Some analysts, using techniques similar to ours, find the networks and the print media to be anything but objective. Todd Gitlin is among the most recent to argue that the news media fail to behave objectively even when they try. In his *The Whole World is Watching*, Gitlin examines the role of the "mass media in the making and unmaking of the New Left" —a phrase he uses as his subtitle.[16]

In many ways, Gitlin's study of press coverage of Students for a Democratic Society (SDS) dovetails with ours. Gitlin compares CBS "Evening News" (according to him, the "best" and "first" among the news programs[17]) with what he regards as national print. (To Gitlin, national print means the *New York Times*.) Like us, Gitlin also is much more interested in content than effects. And above all, Gitlin talks about objectivity in political news. But there are differences between us as well. Gitlin does not quantify his evidence; he qualifies it. He uses examples, not proportions. And he does not discuss campaign coverage; he was interested primarily in news about social movements, specifically SDS and the "New Left."

Most important, Gitlin finds bias and subjectivity in much of what he saw on "Evening News" or read in the *New York Times*. News coverage of SDS in the earliest part of the movement was, writes Gitlin, geared toward "trivialization," "polarization," "dissension," "marginalization," "disparagement by numbers" (undercounting), and "disparagement of the movement's effectiveness."[18] Invoking the theories of Herbert Gans and Antonio Gramsci, two of the more theoretical critics of media and society, Gitlin concludes that there was no objectivity. There was "cultural hegemony." In essence CBS and the *New York Times* treated SDS as if they, the media, were arms of the state, not objective news sources.

> The news routines are skewed toward representing demands, individuals, and frames which do not fundamentally contradict *the dominant hegemonic principles: the legitimacy of private control of commodity production; the legitimacy of the national security State . . . the right and ability of authorized agencies to manage conflict and make necessary reforms; the legitimacy of the social order secured and defined by the dominant elites . . .* (italics his)[19]

George Gerbner of the Annenberg School puts it more succinctly than Gitlin. For Gerbner "all news is views."[20] Gerbner and many of his followers subscribe to the notion that there is no such thing as objectivity in American press and cannot be.

Gerbner, Gitlin, Gans, and Gramsci have a point. Our media practiced objectivity within the context of democratic capitalism. We found virtually no campaign news that questioned the political system beyond the reformist notion that primaries are too many or that the campaign is too long. The economic system, too, escaped without comment by the press. But does any of this relate to our interest in objectivity in campaign news or with our findings so far that have led us to grade the networks and the wires at minimum objectivistic? In fact, the Gitlin thesis does have some relevance and does fit loosely with our findings, not about the "moderate" candidates obviously, but about the "curiosity" candidates.

When CBS and the wire covered candidates outside the "hegemonic ideology of bourgeois culture" (the center), they did become less objective. But only marginally less. Differences in standards could be measured in inches, not yards. We start with the UPI wire, where objectivity is generally a passion and, in this case, where it teetered briefly but eventually held.

On March 27, 1980, Bruce Douglas of UPI filed a news story on Harold Covington, a man who was, in 1980, both leader of the National Socialist Party of America (Nazi) and a candidate for attorney general in the state of North Carolina. Although Douglas's piece is perhaps better labeled "unfair" than "unobjective" (Douglas never quotes Covington in the piece but cites two political opponents), it does contrast with the usual UPI style, in which innuendo and subjectivity almost never interfere with hard news reports.

> In most of the South, a Republican state primary stirs little excitement.
> But things could be different this year in North Carolina. To the chagrin of the Party, one of the GOP candidates for Attorney General is a Nazi.
> Harold Covington, stocky, bearded son of a World War II veteran rose to National Party leader . . . last December, shortly before his predecessor and founder of the Nazi splinter group, Frank Collins, was arrested in Chicago on charges of sexually abusing young boys. . . .
> State GOP chairman Jack Lee has made it clear that he disavows Covington's candidacy and will do what he can to ensure that the Nazi's opponent . . . gets the nomination.
> It is not the first time Covington has run for public office. He lost by lopsided margins in local races in Raleigh for mayor, the City Council and the State Senate.
> When Covington filed for the State Senate in 1978, he was the one Republican running in a race in which three candidates advanced to the general election. GOP leaders quickly rounded up three candidates and Covington finished a poor fourth.

For the wire, this piece moves in the direction of character assault, even drawing a weak, indirect link between Covington and an alleged sexual deviant.

CBS chose to cover a different right-wing extremist candidate, one running for federal office in California. As usual, CBS was slightly more explicit and more analytical in its reporting than UPI, but the same pattern existed here as on the wire. As an illegitimate candidate, Tom Metzger, the Ku Klux Klan boss from San Diego, received less objective, less balanced reporting than any of the centrist candidates for Congress or president or anything else.

Bob Schieffer opened the Metzger story by calling him a "curiosity candidate"; Barry Peterson followed up by linking Metzger to "racist rhetoric" and asserting without attribution that Metzger was "best known for this sort of thing—a Klan rally that turned into bloody confrontation with police and anti-Klan protesters." Peterson presented a story with less attribution and with less balance than one usually found on "Evening News."

Looking at both stories the way some analysts might, it does seem that there was in Gitlin's terminology "trivialization" and "disparagement" of the noncentrist candidates. These two reports are different in tone, construction and vocabulary from those filed about the mainstream candidates. Media do shift their news standards as they move from the acceptable to the anathematic. Distance from the political center does in part determine the level of objectivity. The farther from the pluralistic middle, the greater the subjectivity.

But in the last analysis, these examples from CBS and UPI do not put either medium far outside "Objective Reporting," only closer to the line. Barry Peterson did not say that Metzger and the Klan were wrong about racism, or even racist—Metzger called himself a racist. Bruce Douglas disparaged Harold Covington, but with facts and quotations. Neither piece took a clear position on the politics of the extreme right. In the end, our research indicates that the press does generally work within the rules of the establishment's game, but that it also works within the rules of Objective Reporting.

Conclusions

In this chapter, we have asked three basic questions about campaign news objectivity at CBS and UPI. We asked how often does the reporter make a value judgment about issues. The answer is virtually never. We asked how often does the reporter make direct assertions about the leadership quality of the candidate or the appropriateness of his policies. The answer is very rarely. We asked how often does the reporter step outside the basic description of the day's events and draw inferences from them. The answer is sometimes, but mostly to make an assessment about the candidate's chances or political game plan.

If these questions really do tap the dimension of objectivity, then CBS and UPI came close to being objective. But answering these three questions as we have raises three more: first, was our definition of objectivity a legitimate one; have we tapped the right dimension? Second, assuming these news people did behave objectively in covering Campaign '80, why did they do so? Third, and finally, was this a fluke, or does the national press always act this way?

THE RIGHT DEFINITION?

As for the first question, we reiterate a major point: we wanted to study objectivity within stories, not among stories. If one newspaper headlines with "Reagan Selects Secretary of Defense" and a second opens with "John Lennon Shot in New York," both headlines may be true, and both headlines may be objective. But deciding which of these was the day's top story is a radically subjective act—the difference in press values between a *New York Times* and a *New York Post*. But we decided to study the story, not the day's news agenda.

Had we considered what was covered instead of what was said we would have found less objective campaign coverage than we did. Take the case of Billy Carter. If one considers all stories mentioning any of the candidates in their official or campaign role, Billy Carter was the focus of 140 stories in 1980. To appreciate how hot Billy was as news copy, compare his 140 news stories with the total 19 stories given over principally to SALT II. Billy Carter attracted seven times as many news stories in 1980 as SALT II, the topic directly involving U.S.-Soviet arms limitations. What makes this even more remarkable is that Carter and Reagan were talking about SALT II; they were not talking about Billy Carter.

We are delighted not to have the job of defending this set of news priorities. One would be hard-pressed to call this news agenda very "objective." In fact, Billy and SALT II, and the press each attracted, imply that we did ask the wrong question as to objectivity. The only defense for the relative attention given Billy and SALT II is that Billy was more "newsworthy," a very subjective argument.

But we think that Billy Carter's news dominance is not a question of objectivity per se, instead Billy's news dominance over SALT II reflects on the seriousness of media, not their objectivity. To people interested in SALT II, these news priorities probably read as the essence of subjectivity; to the former Carter White House staff, the Billy to SALT II ratio must seem like blasphemy. But to us, these numbers reinforce what we have said all along about objectivity—when examining objectivity in news, it makes more sense to ask about the actual construction of each story than the architectural plan for the entire news day.

What's more, the Billy Carter case actually reinforces the original point that within stories national media do behave objectively. The majority of the Billy pieces were never linked to the election. Only 21 of the 57 stories on CBS ever bothered to mention the campaign; only 28 of the 83 stories on UPI mentioned it. Billy Carter news was handled very objectively, and certainly not as a campaign issue. Second, virtually none of the Billy Carter stories made any explicit assessments about Jimmy Carter's role in his brother's problems. Only 1 of the 83 Billy Carter stories on UPI either directly implied or concluded anything about the president, unless that implication or inference was specifically attributed directly to somebody else. On CBS none of the 57 stories drew any conclusions about Jimmy Carter based on his performance in connection with Billygate. One can go through practically every one of the 140 stories and come away with the sense that the journalists stood back, letting the descriptions and facts speak for themselves. And that is "Objective Reporting."

Reporters play scandal stories as straight as possible and Billy's press was overwhelmingly descriptive. Not surprisingly, the one thing the journalists would sometimes say is that the Billy Carter case might hurt the president's election chances—once again the liberty to assess "horse race" and nothing but the "horse race."

In the end, Billy news did not seem to hurt his brother very much, at least not directly. Although Jody Powell insisted to us that the Billy crisis in July (Billy's acceptance of loans from Libya) kept the Carter and Kennedy forces apart longer than necessary, the president actually jumped up in the polls and in delegate support after the August 4 press conference in which he denied any malfeasance on his brother's behalf. In fact, before the press conference, Kennedy had pulled even with Carter in the polls; after his prime time appeal at the press conference, Carter led Kennedy by almost two to one.[21] Even more remarkable, perhaps, was public response to a question put to them by the CBS/New York Times poll in mid-October. Asked "What worries you most" about Jimmy

Carter's possible reelection, the percentage mentioning Billy was zero.[22]

The point certainly is not that Billy Carter news helped the president. The point is that the press covered the Billy Carter case objectively. And because the coverage never proved much about the president, the reports did not mean that much in the end. As with Watergate in 1972, before the real revelations, the national press covered the case within the bounds of Objective Reporting, proving again a basic thesis—greater subjectivity in news agendas than in news items.

Because objectivity has so many definitions, it would be easy to set up criteria in which the campaign news would appear very subjective. Consider a definition that looks only at what is included and excluded within a story; subjectivity by exclusion, or by reporting out of context. In the first week of September, Jimmy Carter had the most visible week of his otherwise low visibility campaign. He gave no less than eight public speeches, statements, and interviews between September 1 and September 5. Using the *Weekly Compilation of Presidential Documents,*[23] we counted 1,135 publicly uttered sentences by the president in those five days. And as a matter of record, the press was on hand in every case, and, we assume, with cameras and pencils running all the time.

From those 1,135 sentences, CBS chose to quote Carter sixteen times; UPI twenty-two times—less than 2 percent of the total in each medium. The only "speech" Carter made that was quoted in a percentage exceeding 10 percent was his personal attack against Reagan's slam against Tuscumbia, Alabama,* the town that Reagan wrongly accused of being birthplace of the Ku Klux Klan.

One could say much about this heavy editing: that it reflects the need by all mass media to hype the most sensational quotations and play up what Colin Seymour-Ure calls clearcut issues,[24] in this case the attack on Reagan; it renders hollow the year-long editorial complaint that Carter was hiding and not giving the press a chance to get at him (when they got him they did not much quote him); it "proves" how subjective the media really are—ignoring most of what the man said and selecting quotations at subjective will.

In fact, we find all but the last point persuasive. Media ignore the overwhelming majority of public utterances by all candidates and

*This was not a speech per se. Carter agreed to answer reporters' questions while at the airport in Kansas City on September 2.

they "notice those aspects of a situation that lend themselves to storymaking."[25] But during those days in September, when CBS and UPI summarized Carter's remarks, inevitably they summarized them correctly. In short, the media either quoted Carter accurately, paraphrased him correctly, or ignored him completely. Such is the good news and bad news about "Objective Reporting."

WHY OBJECTIVE?

Assuming that the national press behaves objectively, or at a minimum objectivistically, the obvious question is why? The answer is simple, but two-fold. Journalists commit themselves to objectivity for the same reasons motorists stop on red—they're taught from the outset to do so, and it is in their own interest as well.

Few scholars ask journalists "are you objective?" or "do you believe in being objective?" This is tantamount to asking a cleric if he or she believes in the religious life. As early as 1937, when Leo Rosten broke ground with the first poll ever done of any Washington correspondents, he assumed objectivity as a value by asking reporters the following "loaded" questions: agree or disagree, "my orders are to be objective but I *know* how my paper wants stories played."[26]

In our interviews with editors and reporters at CBS and UPI, we asked the question a little more subtly. During the interviews, we told the journalists that we had failed to find a single instance in which UPI or CBS had expressed support or opposition to any candidate's position on any issue—which was true. To get at their attitude about personal opinion (subjectivity), we asked about this lack of evaluation. Among those whom we asked, the response was always the same. Journalists do not believe in telling audiences who is good or who is bad, what works or what does not, what is right or what is wrong. When, for example, we asked correspondent Bruce Morton why "Evening News" had never evaluated candidate positions on something as basic as the economy, Morton gave a response that was typical for reporters at both places.

> I don't know that journalists ought to evaluate. . . in the first place. That presumes, I guess, that some "newsie" actually knew how to solve inflation, which is presuming quite a bit.
> It's very hard [for] someone. . . to say that Kemp-Roth really is "voodoo economics"—"Folks, this is never gonna work." As it happens, that's my belief. . . But I don't think journalists ought to be (saying) that. I think what we ought to be doing is saying as clearly as we can—"And this is what this

guy says will work, and this is what the other guy says will work. And you gotta decide, folks, 'cause that's what the process is all about.'

When we asked Clay Richards at UPI the same question (why no evaluation of candidate positions), Richards put it more bluntly than Morton, but said much the same thing.

> That's not our job. We just say what his stand is. And if it's been criticized by somebody else in the race, then we say that. It's not our job to say Reagan was right or wrong and say why.

Susan Spencer, who covered Edward Kennedy most of the year for CBS, wasted the fewest words. We told Spencer that CBS had failed to draw a single inference about the candidate's positions during the entire campaign. We asked for a response. Spencer said "Good."

But beliefs are only half of the story. Journalists behave objectively in covering campaigns because they have fewer problems if they stick to that principle. Several advantages accrue to journalists who stay on their side of the story. When we asked Bill Plante about objectivity toward candidates, he concluded that "it is definitely in our professional interest never to let whatever convictions we have —and there are those who would say we don't have any convictions —interfere with the reporting of the news." Plante emphasized reputation:

> The reporter's professional reputation is at stake, in this town where reputations count for so much and appearances count for so much. No reporter wants to be labeled a partisan if he or she is involved in this kind of reporting. . . . (It) certainly would not be good for me or for any of my colleagues in this business to be known as a rabid Republican or liberal Democrat or anything of the sort.

Journalists have more than reputation on the line. Because networks and wires "sell" their news to smaller news organizations (affiliated stations or local newspapers), there is a clear advantage in staying inside the safety net of objectivity. Ron Cohen, national political editor at UPI, gave what amounts to the historical answer to the question why no personal opinion in your news copy? "We serve papers from the farthest right-wingers to the farthest left-wingers. And if we don't file something in the middle, then we're going to get bombarded from both sides."

What is true for the wires is true for the networks. The wire sells its copy to subscribing newspapers, the networks to affiliated stations.

Objective news means fewer problems for network reporters as well. Virtually every major study of network news done since the 1960s points to the need for the news division to play it straight with the news or face the affiliates, or corporate management, or candidates, or peers.[27]

One final set of advantages accrues to those who practice objectivity: a sense of professionalism and an emotional detachment, both of which allow journalism to feel better about itself. Gans, in his *Deciding What's News,* lists several psychological advantages that come with practicing objective reporting,[28] but they all come down to the same thing, that journalists maintain professional self-esteem if they follow the lessons they learned as cub reporters or in journalism school.

There are also "costs" to objectivity. When a reporter knows that the newsmaker is lying, or speaking nonsense, but can't find a way to say so inside the rules of objectivism, that reporter carries a psychological cost with him until he can get the facts or can figure out some objectivistic method of working around them.

Objectivity has other costs: "objective" stories have less punch and a lot less focus. As Bill Plante of CBS complained—"If you have somebody who's calling the president an idiot, you then almost have to have somebody who's saying, 'Well, no he's not; he's really a great statesman.'" But these costs do not begin to equal what national press would face, in the mirror or on the job, if they gave up on being objectivistic.

IS ALL NEWS REPORTING OBJECTIVE?

Is news reporting generally this objective? The answer is no, not really. Some press critics have for years been complaining that campaign news is actually too objective. James David Barber has made it a personal mission to get campaign journalism to break the bondage of objectivity.[29] Campaign '80 is not unique; what is unique is the special case of campaign news. If anything, campaign news produces the most objective reporting that national press ever provides.

Media recognize a special obligation in covering elective politics. Campaign news even gets a special name. On television it has its own very special logo: "Campaign '80" on CBS, "Decision '80" on NBC, "The '80 Vote" on ABC. In other words, media take "journalistic notice" of the democratic process. Journalists may not like the candidates, but they believe in the process and their special role in directly communicating what is going on. That was at the heart of Bruce Morton's thesis that the candidates are supposed to talk, the journalists are supposed to convey, the voters are supposed to choose.

Outside the extraordinary case of campaign news, less objectivity exists. We have already discussed the "distance principle," that candidates get less objective treatment the farther they stand from the pluralist center. But radicalism is not the only thing that allows for slippage. Foreign news has always been less objective than the domestic variety.[30] Networks and wires covered the Soviet invasion of Afghanistan less objectively than almost anything it reported in Campaign '80. And the Iranian hostage crisis pushed the networks, the wires, and all the news media beyond the brink of subjectivity on a number of occasions.

Throughout Campaign '80, Walter Cronkite was the living embodiment of objectivity: his issue interviews were classics in objectivism. But when it came to the hostages, his news reports changed perceptibly. On April 8, for example, CBS showed film of the hostages at Easter services (film all the networks bought from the Iranians at considerable expense—twelve thousand dollars). Exhibiting uncharacteristic anger in his voice, Cronkite concluded the film report by saying: "*Obviously,* the film released by Iranian television is propaganda, designed to show the better side of captivity. But there is, indeed, a dark side, of course." Without attribution, without on-the-scene information, but with total certainty, Walter Cronkite moved outside most any working definition of objectivity. Cronkite was not only drawing definitive conclusions on his own, he was also showing us that objectivity, like partisan politics, tends to diminish at the water's edge.[31]

Perhaps the most interesting aspect of foreign news subjectivity is that it extends all the way to coverage of foreign elections and campaigns. On November 25, 1981, NBC foreign correspondent Rebecca Sobel reported on an important and upcoming by-election in Britain, a campaign featuring Shirley Williams, leader of the new Social Democratic Party. In stark contrast to the treatment of the major American candidates, Sobel concluded, without attribution, that Williams was "warm," that "she listens," that "she seems to care." We doubt Sobel would have drawn so explicit a set of unattributed conclusions about Shirley Williams had Williams been an American politician.

The reduced commitment to objectivity in foreign news also extends very much into war coverage. While we fail to accept the premise, offered by so many hawkish press critics, that the national media behaved hopelessly irresponsibly in covering Vietnam,[32] we agree with much of the scholarship that shows how news coverage of the Vietnam War, after years of political and military stalemate, slipped from objectivity to subjectivity and even to bias.[33] But just as war and foreign affairs stimulate the national press to behave more subjectively than normal, political campaigns waged here at home trigger the opposite response. Once again the reason is "journalistic notice": reporters feel that when providing information to the public about the one real decision it makes in national politics, the election of a president, the press should be its most objective.

Foreign news is just one example of greater subjectivity. Once reporters leave the confines of the hard news copy or hard news programming, objectivity tends to go with them. The contrast between CBS's "Evening News" and CBS's "60 Minutes" is not as stark as that between night and day in terms of objectivity, but the difference comes close. On "60 Minutes," for example, the description of Arabs was *not* what we have come to expect from Walter Cronkite on "Evening News." In a feature entitled "The Arabs are Coming," "60 Minutes" correspondent Morley Safer began his report on Saudis living in Britain by saying: "London's been taken by storm. . . ." The city "has experienced nothing like this invasion. They come for three or four months and they come to buy anything that is not nailed down—plus an awful lot that is."[34] Combine the news magazine format with a touch of the foreign, and objectivity fades much like newsprint in sunlight.* But domestic political campaigns are handled differently, that is, objectivistically.

Perhaps the best way to demonstrate that campaign news is different, and objectivistic, is to invoke history, to look back at news coverage in Campaign '80—1880. Having already summarized media coverage of Reagan's last day on the campaign (pages 43–44), we can glance back and see how the press treated the Republican nominee on the eve of his election, one hundred years ago.

---

*"60 Minutes" consistently works outside our definition of objectivity and, as a result, is consistently under attack for its subjective style. Segments of that program have caused national debates on subjects ranging from nuclear energy to the war in Vietnam. Documentaries apparently fall somewhere between hard news objectivity and the subjectivity of news magazines. In fact, in 1982, CBS News actually had to admit publicly that one of its documentaries, "The Uncounted Enemy: A Vietnam Deception," had five editorial flaws that CBS would work to correct in future programming.

OBJECTIVITY: MOST OBJECTIONS OVERRULED

Consider the *Boston Globe*, now one of America's prestige newspapers and one of the few dailies to have lasted long enough to cover both the Carter-Reagan election and the Garfield-Hancock campaign. How did the *Boston Globe* handle their wrapup report for Campaign Yesteryear? The headlines and the lead for the final news story about Garfield tell us all we really need to know about unobjective reporting, stressing, as they do the "lies" of the Republican party and the *Boston Globe*'s delight with the prospects of a Republican defeat:

> Before the Battle
> A Review of the Situation Encouraging
> New York Soundly Solid for Hancock
> Good News from the Golden State Suffragists
> The Middle States Decidedly Democratic
> Favorable Indications in New England—Desperate Republicans
> (Special Dispatch to the *Boston Globe*)
> New York, October 31—The national Democratic committee is, today, in receipt of a number of dispatches from all sections of the country, reporting the campaign lies which are now the only stock-in-trade of the Republicans.

As it turned out, despite the *Globe*'s "predictions," Hancock lost New York, lost Massachusetts, lost much of the mid-Atlantic, and lost the election. Poor predictions still trouble the news media: in 1980, CBS had Jimmy Carter ahead as late as the last week in October. But we doubt that CBS regarded Carter's showing as "encouraging" (the word the old *Boston Globe* used to describe Hancock's situation). Try to imagine UPI or CBS claiming "lies" were the "only stock-in-trade of the Republicans" and then quoting only Democrats to prove it, as did the old *Boston Globe*. For critics who see no objectivity in the twentieth-century media, this report from the *Boston Globe* should put their criticism in historical perspective. By mid-nineteenth century standards, we evidently do live in an age of Objective Reporting. Even by absolute standards, the national press behaves objectivistically in covering major political campaigns. There are serious deficiencies in political reporting at the national level, but overt subjectivity about issues or about candidates is not high on the list. Despite outraged complaints from the left and from the right about subjectivity in the campaign media, most of these particular objections can be overruled.

Chapter 4

Access: Equal Time for Equal Actors

Thirty seconds of time on the evening news means more than anything else.

—ROBERT KENNEDY

DESPITE impressions to the contrary, the federal government does not mandate equal time or equal access to America's news media. Even the provisions that allegedly provide for equal access for political candidates involve much less than meets the eye. Newspapers, in fact all print sources, have no legal obligation whatever to furnish any access to any candidate, whether access be defined in terms of news coverage or in advertising space. The Supreme Court has specifically exempted newspapers from any such regulation or policy.[1]

Only broadcasters fall inside the legal net of the Fairness Doctrine or the "equal time" provision. But broadcasters too have great license to decide questions of access for campaigning politicians or, for that matter, access for political points of view. The "equal opportunities" law (Section 315a of the Federal Communications Act) pertains basically to *advertising*, insuring that if a broadcaster gives or sells advertising time to one candidate, the broadcaster must give or sell time to his opponents. "Equal time" has nothing much to do with news coverage.

The Fairness Doctrine, a policy mandated by Federal Communications Commission, not by Congress, does pertain to news programming, but the Doctrine generally involves coverage of "issues," not coverage of campaigns.[2] What's more, during the last twenty years the courts and the FCC have consistently interpreted both the Fairness Doctrine and the equal time provision more "liberally," giving broadcasters more authority to work around either policy.[3] It is altogether possible that by the 1984 election there will be no Fairness Doctrine or equal time provision left to be interpreted by any branch or agency of the federal government, as Congress and the FCC are seriously considering their fate. Mark Fowler, chairman of the FCC, has publicly called for repeal of both policies.[4]

But although fair access to news coverage is not rigidly enshrined as public policy, access is very much a matter for legitimate concerns. Those concerns have two roots; one political, one professional. Politically speaking, access is crucial to candidate viability. While it goes too far to claim that candidates win because of news access alone (though some have made that case[5]), it is evident that without any access candidates cannot succeed. Access to news media is a necessary but not sufficient condition for victory in a modern presidential campaign. Professionally speaking, access comes about as close to the heart of fair-minded journalism as any other concept. Public policy notwithstanding, reporters and editors believe in fair access for political candidates; "equal time," loosely defined, is a basic tenet of American press.[6]

But fair access, like objectivity, is hard to define in real terms and in real campaigns. Realistically speaking, regardless of medium, there is no absolute equality of access for candidates or for parties, nor is there anything even close. Consider, for example, the total amount of news access provided in Campaign '80 to each of those few candidates receiving any attention whatever on CBS or UPI. Despite the similarity in ranking between CBS and UPI, there is nothing here approaching equality of access even among those lucky enough to have been granted any access at all to the news. In fact, these figures understate the absolute level of inequality of access. According to the Federal Elections Commission, 156 candidates filed for the presidency in 1980. If our calculations are accurate, 90 percent of the candidates filing for president never made it to the day wire or to "Evening News." Aggregate statistics like these make it impossible to talk about equal time in literal terms.

But, because candidates themselves are not equal in any sense

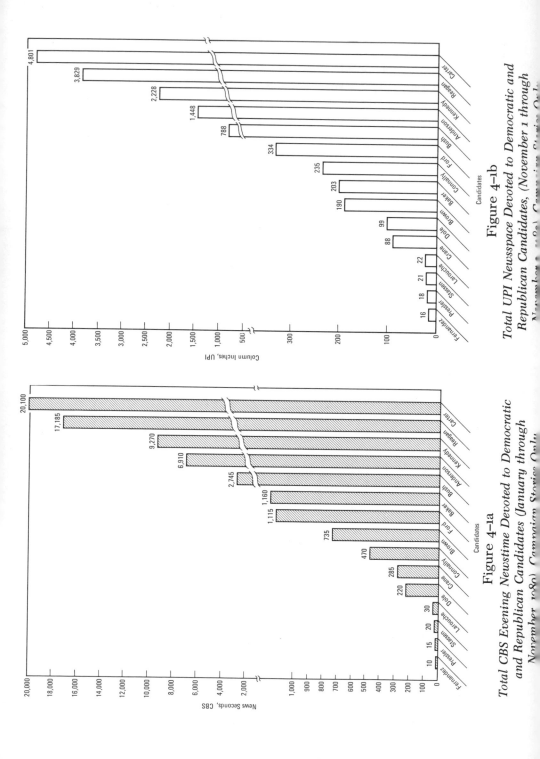

Figure 4–1b

Total UPI Newsspace Devoted to Democratic and
Republican Candidates, (November 1 through
November 4, 1980) Campaign Stories Only

Figure 4–1a

Total CBS Evening Newstime Devoted to Democratic
and Republican Candidates (January through
November 1980) Campaign Stories Only

other than legal, aggregate statistics on news access do not provide much insight for evaluating the performance of the press in terms of newsspace. In fact, evaluating the equity of access is actually more difficult than evaluating the level of objectivity. Objectivity at least has an intimate relationship with validity, and a reasonably close relationship to truth. Not so with newsspace. Equity of access is a topic practically unconnected with any real or absolute standard. And, while there is an "objective" way to cover issues, there is less objectivity to the process of doling out newstime. John Anderson's 11 percent of the total campaign newstime on "Evening News" was, after all, considered an egregious overstatement by Jimmy Carter, but less than a desirable share by the Reagan campaign.

There is no simple, clear standard for access that always applies— so, we have adopted a different strategy in this chapter from that used in the last: rather than decide *if* CBS and UPI behaved equitably in deciding questions of access, we have undertaken instead to describe how they decided those questions during each phase of the presidential campaign.

And despite the fact that we found two or three patterns of coverage special to each medium, in the end we found a set of half a dozen routines practiced by both media together. For the most part, both media granted equal access to "equal" players: dismissing the also-rans and the minor parties; giving considerable and equal attention to the frontrunners; giving extraordinary attention to anybody doing better than expected.

Similarities in Access

ACCESS FOR REAGAN AND CARTER DURING THE GENERAL CAMPAIGN: NEAR PERFECT EQUALITY OF ACCESS

If one manages to ignore the minor parties, and the mass media always do, the general campaign provides one of the few situations in which literally equal access makes any sense at all. If there is a period in which fair access means equal access, it is during the autumn campaign, when the two major party nominees contend, as equals, for the presidency.

To their credit, the national media we studied came as close to perfect equality in covering the major party nominees as could possibly be expected. According to our calculations, during the forty-six weekdays stretching from September 1 through November 3, CBS and UPI devoted identical amounts of newsspace to Ronald Reagan and to Jimmy Carter. In those nine weeks, CBS "Evening News" divided access so carefully that Reagan received 50.6 percent of the two-party newsspace, while Carter got the remaining 49.4 percent. UPI did almost as well in granting equal "time." Of the two-party total, Reagan received 48.1 percent of the column inches; Carter collected the remaining 51.9 percent. Almost as if they were doling it out with a spoon, CBS and UPI each granted identical amounts of newsspace to Carter and Reagan in the two months prior to the general election.

This is not a trivial accomplishment for the American media. For years media critics have complained that the press has employed access as a weapon against its political enemies. The professional literature bristles with studies indicating that the print medium has historically used the amount of newsspace granted to candidates to aid its friends and hobble its opponents.[7] David Halberstam concludes that for decades the *Los Angeles Times*, and the Chandler family which run it, did just that: "the friends of the Chandlers," wrote Halberstam, "were written about as they wished; their enemies were deprived of space. . . . What was not printed was as important as what was printed. . . . [The *Times*] gave its enemies no space and no voice."[8] When, says Halberstam, Upton Sinclair ran for governor of California in the 1930s, the *Times* almost neglected to mention his campaign. The very idea that Sinclair, as a Democratic nominee, deserved as much access as the Republican, was labeled by the leading *Los Angeles Times* reporter as New York "crap."[9]

Nor is inequality of access merely a problem of a simpler past. Peter Clarke and Susan Evans found that as recently as 1978 those who challenged sitting members of Congress, regardless of how serious the challenge, inevitably failed to receive equal access in the local press.[10] Although the motive was rarely as political or the bias as blatant as in the case of the *Los Angeles Times*, the result was very much the same: unequal newsspace for the "equal" candidates, with the advantage going to the congressional incumbent.

Conceivably, the Eastern establishment media might have done something similar in Campaign '80, either hype the liberal, or in this instance, hype the liberal incumbent, Jimmy Carter. But neither the wires nor the networks practiced anything approaching that sort of inequality during the general election. As it turned out, Carter received more critical press than his Republican opponent, but Carter was given precisely as much "time" as Ronald Reagan during which to make his case.

The only systematic "inequality" in access came in the ordering of stories, not in their length or frequency.* When the news for both campaigns was of comparable importance, CBS, along with ABC and NBC, inevitably put the Carter campaign story first, the Reagan story second, and the Anderson story third. The convention there was simply that Jimmy Carter, the duly-elected president, was entitled to a little courtesy in the hierarchy of news, and that Carter was first newsmaker among equals. Appearing first in the news line-up, however, was, as we shall see, one of the few courtesies candidate Carter was to receive on CBS or UPI.

ACCESS FOR THE MAJOR PARTIES: EQUALITY ONCE AGAIN

The media not only provided equal access for Carter and Reagan during the general election, they also provided equality of access to the two major parties during the course of the early campaign. Consider, for example, the period coming after the first of January but before the Wisconsin primary—the first three months of the year.

The Wisconsin primary on April 1 was a major turning point in Campaign '80. Before Wisconsin there had been a certain measure of coherence in the campaign; a string of primaries week by week and two easily defined fields of Democrats and Republicans seeking to be the nominee. But after Wisconsin almost everything changed. The primary season ended for a period of three weeks, the first hiatus since January. What's more, the field of candidates came apart: Jerry Brown quit; John Anderson moved openly toward independence; Kennedy lost any real chance of winning the nomination through the primary process.

But between January and March the Democrats and Republicans had been fielding relatively equal teams of candidates, and the media treated them as such. During the first three months of 1980 the Republicans received 48 percent of the newstime on "Evening

---

*One inequality topic did strike us. Both CBS and UPI virtually ignored Reagan's mid-October decision not to debate Carter. On "Evening News," Reagan's rejection attracted just one story. On the other hand, Carter's decision not to debate Anderson and Reagan in September received more than a dozen reports.

News," the Democrats 52 percent. On UPI, the figures were precisely the same (48 percent Republican, 52 percent Democratic). When they "could," CBS and UPI gave equal time to the two equal fields, Democratic and Republican.

Between April and August there was little month by month parity between parties in either medium. The summer months particularly produced an inequality of access for the two major parties. The Republicans, quite understandably, overwhelmed the Democrats in July during the month of the Republican convention. The Democrats, of course, came out on top in August, when they met to nominate Jimmy Carter. But by year's end, CBS and UPI had managed to make everything come out even. If Anderson is considered a Republican, which he was for half of the campaign, the total access awarded Democratic and Republican candidates from January to November approached absolute equality. On UPI the Democrats, as a field, finished up with 50 percent of the newsspace, and, of course, by subtraction, so did the Republicans. On "Evening News" the score was 51 percent for Democrats, 49 percent for the GOP. Even without a formal policy of equality the two media managed to divide access equally between the two major parties.

CBS and UPI behaved so equitably in terms of newsspace for the Democratic and Republican candidates, one ought really to ask, "Why?" As with objectivity, several factors are involved, but we suspect that there are three major reasons. For starters, the networks and wires inevitably feel pressure from the local "subscribers," pressure to play it straight, to play it equitably. Local stations and newspapers prefer not to be involved in disputes concerning access, and affiliated stations and subscriber newspapers let those feelings show, either indirectly or directly. CBS and UPI accorded equal access, in part, in order to keep their "customers" happy. Second, as for broadcasters, the Fairness Doctrine encourages equity. Although its importance is easily overstated, the Fairness Doctrine does provide psychological incentive to divide time equally among the major candidates in the field.

But both CBS and UPI could easily have gotten away with less equity than this had they wanted to. So, we suspect, the last, if not most important factor here involves craft norms, attitudes of the newspeople themselves. Media grant equal time to equal players because reporters, editors, and producers think that is the way it ought to be. To use the word of Kyle Palmer, former *Los Angeles*

Times chief political correspondent, that is precisely the sort of New York "crap" in which modern day-to-day journalism fervently believes.

ACCESS FOR MINOR PARTIES: NO NEWS IS MINOR PARTY NEWS

It made virtually no difference to the national media whether they came from the left or the right of the political spectrum: minor parties had no significant access to the news. What access they did have was so paltry that there is no point in graphing the result. Percentages were too small to register, or to be seen. Rounding to the nearest whole number, minor party candidates received 0 percent of the newstime, 0 percent of the stories on CBS and UPI.

In all of 1980, there was only one complete story on CBS weekday news about a minor party presidential candidate—a less-than-3-minute piece about Libertarian candidate Ed Clark. On UPI there were two stories featuring Clark, and two featuring Citizens party candidate, Barry Commoner. And that was it for the two most "important" of the minor party nominees. In a year's worth of campaign reporting on CBS and UPI, we analyzed over twenty-three hundred campaign stories dealing with the presidency. Fewer than ten moved outside the major party system, unless, of course, John Anderson and his National Unity Campaign is counted as legitimately outside the two-party world.*

Minor parties have not won a presidential election in the United States since Lincoln and his new Republican party did it in 1860. Given that reality, and the reality of news, minor parties have no valid claim to anything approaching equal time. But one can still wonder whether minor parties really got less media coverage than they "deserved" and whether their limited news access was based on what one might call professional news values, or, on the other hand, something not quite so professional.

Consider the two minor party candidates who did receive attention, Ed Clark and Barry Commoner. Clark, the Libertarian nominee, received well over 1 percent of the final popular vote and ran a strong third in Alaska in the general election, getting almost half as much of the vote there as incumbent Jimmy Carter. Yet Clark received nowhere near that much attention on "Evening News" (.4

*Technically and legally Anderson was an independent candidate for president, not a party nominee.

percent). And the news coverage he did receive came in late July, the dog days of Campaign '80, the period between conventions.

Citizens party candidate Barry Commoner received a quarter of a million votes but no time whatever on CBS. In fact, CBS even ignored Commoner's attempt to force the networks to cover him. In October, Commoner bought radio time to air a commercial beginning with the word "bullshit," a technique which, as the ad admitted in its opening paragraph was nothing more than a ploy to attract press. ABC "News" carried a story about the ad, a critical story as it turned out. But CBS and NBC treated the "bullshit" commercial with the same indifference they practiced in covering the entire Citizens party campaign. Neither Barry Commoner nor his platform (nor his vulgar commercial) made it to the "Evening News."

What makes noncoverage of minor candidates like Clark and Commoner more intriguing is the press history of the Anderson campaign. Anderson was a Republican until April, a nonparty independent candidate from April on. A case could be made that Anderson was viable at one point in the campaign—a possible winner. Yet nobody we interviewed ever believed Anderson would win. In the words of Peter Brown, UPI correspondent assigned to him, Anderson was a sure loser long before his press coverage ended.

> Right after the September 20th debate, Anderson became a non-story and we all knew it. All the reporters knew it. It was very obvious that once the debate was over and he hadn't done anything, he wasn't going to fly.

Anderson ended up a minor candidate if not technically a minor party candidate. Yet Anderson received more than one hundred times as much attention on UPI as Clark. On CBS, he received almost two hundred times as much. During the general campaign, when an Anderson victory was considered by the correspondents we interviewed as an impossibility, Anderson received one-fourth the news coverage given to Carter and to Reagan. In the months of September and October, as an independent and a loser, John Anderson was granted more than 2,500 seconds of news time on "Evening News," almost 700 column inches of wire copy on UPI.

Why did Clark (and Commoner) do so badly, Anderson so well in press coverage? Part of the reason is that once Anderson had earned a press entourage, the entourage took on a life of its own. Bill Peterson discusses how bizarre life was on the Anderson plane in October and how hard Anderson reporters fought to get their stories in print.[11] A press bus in motion tends to stay in motion. But Ed Clark never got his own entourage. Whatever the precise reasons for their invisibility, minor parties in general, and Ed Clark in particular, proved once again that access flows toward the mainstream candidates and away from everything and everyone else.

ACCESS FOR FRONTRUNNERS: DOING SOMEWHAT WORSE
THAN EXPECTED

During 1980, neither Ronald Reagan nor Jimmy Carter ever relinquished his status as frontrunner for the nomination. Both had, throughout the year, easy access to all the media. But the access was not quite so easy as it might have originally seemed. Between January and the first week in June, candidate Jimmy Carter had received nearly 8,000 news seconds of access on CBS, about 1,000 seconds more than Senator Kennedy; Carter also got big play on UPI, over 1,600 news inches in the first five months of the year. But Carter did not reach the end of the primary season leading in news access on UPI —Kennedy was ever so slightly ahead. As for the GOP, Reagan was so far ahead by June that it would have been almost impossible for him to have "lost" his status as most covered Republican. His preeminence in access was never in doubt. On CBS and UPI Reagan finished the primary campaign with considerably greater newsspace than Anderson or Bush. Yet, in the end, like Carter, Reagan received a much smaller percentage of the newshole in both sources than he received percentage of the primary vote.

We see several possible interpretations for this, not the least of which is that Carter and Reagan—not the press—were responsible for these differences in that both were trying to run a relatively low visibility campaign. This may be an instance in which access is "controlled" more by the major candidates than by the media themselves. A second interpretation might be that CBS and UPI chased surprises and that neither Carter nor Reagan, as frontrunners, could provide surprises. For Carter and for Reagan winning a primary or caucus vote was the expectation, so their winning was less newsworthy. A third interpretation involves something on order of manipulation or a conscious decision by the press to downplay frontrunners and play up challengers as well as dark horse campaigns.

Taking a look only at the quantity of coverage, it is almost impossible to decide which interpretation works best, or works at all. But when we consider the quality of coverage, the case for the third interpretation grows more plausible: frontrunners not only received less press in 1980 than their status merited, they also received a tougher press as well.

ACCESS FOR THE REST OF THE PACK: PERFORMING
JOURNALISTIC TRIAGE

We found that during the primary campaign, media practiced something on order of journalistic triage, dividing candidates into three basic tiers—the *hopeless,* the *plausible,* and the *likely.* Likely candidates were of course the frontrunners, the ones we have just considered. But the others merited attention too, by the media and by us.

Hopeless cases include not just the minor party candidates but the major party candidates who began the year without popular support or traditional resources. By January 1980 that list included the perennial losers such as Harold Stassen and the more contemporary also-ran people such as Benny Fernandez, Larry Pressler, Phil Crane, and Robert Dole. Coming dangerously close to the level of hopeless were John Connally and, for the Democrats, Governor Jerry Brown.

As in the traditional system of triage, it was the second tier, the plausibles, who merited disproportionate attention. In fact, plausible candidates did so well qualitatively and quantitatively in Campaign '80 we will spend the next two chapters mulling over their fate. It was, however, the hopeless cases who did the worst in terms of access, no matter how we define the term. Like the news media, we can make quick work of the back of the pack—the candidates who were never expected to win and who managed to fulfill those expectations.

Hopeless Cases

Unless or until they exceed public expectations at the polls or in the polls, hopeless cases get hopeless coverage. On "Evening News" Republicans Benny Fernandez and Harold Stassen were each featured in zero stories. Phil Crane was featured three times. So was

Kansas Senator Bob Dole. Republican Senator Larry Pressler of South Dakota was featured once (a story on "Evening News" that announced Pressler's withdrawal from the race).

At UPI the situation proved very much the same. Fernandez, the Hispanic Republican, was the focus of one campaign story; like Fernandez, Stassen and Pressler were each featured once; Phil Crane twice. Dole did comparatively well, getting himself featured seven times. All told, these five men accounted for 1 percent of the news on the day wire during the five-month primary period.

It appears as if the national media regard candidates in the bottom tier, and also the minor party candidates, as something of an obligation, *pro bono* work for journalism. Nor would we quibble much with that approach, since most of these candidacies were dead or dying as the year began. What makes the hopeless cases interesting to us is that their status not only had a bearing on quantity of coverage, but quality of coverage as well.

UPI and CBS said almost nothing explicitly bad or good about any of the candidates whose campaigns were hopeless. As we have seen, the press shies away from explicit assessments of candidates at any level of viability. But both CBS and UPI had something to say about the campaigns of the hopeless. In truth, almost everything CBS and UPI did say about these men dealt exclusively with the condition of their campaign. And, as hopeless cases, the political condition of these men was, in a word, grim. So, for example, all three pieces on CBS featuring Phil Crane focused almost solely on his standing in the race. Crane's legitimate claim to being the most purely ideological Republican was never a matter for comment (on "Evening News" Crane was noteworthy as a loser, not as a conservative). Candidates like Crane, who operate in the lowest tier, inevitably appear in the media either as losers, or at best as "responders"—those who, in a sentence or less respond to something the frontrunners have done or said.

On the other hand, both CBS and UPI refrained from saying anything at all critical about these cellar-dwelling candidates as persons. With the exception of Larry Pressler, nobody in the bottom tier had, as we measured it, any press image at all:* losers yes, but

---

*Larry Pressler actually received four positive stories on the wire—UPI giving Pressler good reviews for his nonrole in ABSCAM. Pressler was the only member of Congress who flatly refused to be bribed by undercover agents working for the FBI. But these positive stories were not campaign stories.

beyond that no news conveying anything about these men or their philosophies.

For most of the candidates in the bottom tier, media practiced a form of objectivism most accurately classified as *deathwatch*. The deathwatch generally begins with a reference to the candidate's low standing in the polls, moves on to mention financial or scheduling problems, and ends with coverage of the final press conference, in which the candidate withdraws.

Nothing and nobody typifies the deathwatch better than media coverage of Robert Dole. All the networks generally treated Dole as hopeless and moribund. Dole half-heartedly complained, in fact, about the way NBC and Tom Petit had covered him in the New Hampshire campaign: Petit had commented that Dole's car and Dole's campaign were both spinning their wheels in the New England snow, which was about all Petit had to say about Dole in that primary. CBS covered Dole more seriously than that, but Dole got classic loser treatment from all the networks. Even though Dole had been the Republican vice-presidential nominee in 1976, and even though he was serving in 1980 as ranking member of the powerful Senate Finance Committee, CBS covered Dole much the same way it covered Marshall Tito in 1980, as a continuing series of announcements concerning his imminent demise.

Between January 1 and March 15, CBS reporters spoke a dozen times about Dole and his campaign.* Not every report was a deathwatch report, but nine out of twelve turned out that way. We have included below everything CBS said about Robert Dole in the first ten weeks of 1980, classifying those comments either as "deathwatch" reporting or reporting of another kind. Consider this list of what amounts to a dozen one-liners about a man and his terminal political status.

DOLE'S DEATHWATCH

1. WALTER CRONKITE (1–21–80): Robert Dole, John Anderson, and Philip Crane do not have campaigns which are regarded as competitive with the top four leaders (in Iowa).

*We have excluded Dole's own words (words he spoke on camera). He appeared four times: to criticize Bush for not allowing all the Republicans to debate at Nashua; to criticize Carter's sense of humor; to ask for tougher wage-price guidelines; to promise to withdraw from the race soon. Total time was less than a minute.

2. BRUCE MORTON (1–22–80): Howard Baker, John Connally, Philip Crane, Bob Dole hope to survive (after Iowa).

3. WALTER CRONKITE (2–13–80): Senator Bob Dole's showing signs of pulling out of the Republican presidential race. Yesterday Dole let the filing deadline pass without entering the primary in his home state of Kansas and today Dole announced support for Senator Howard Baker in Sunday's Puerto Rico primary.

4. BRUCE MORTON (2–20–80): Longer shots have different views (on debates). (Dole quote.)

5. WALTER CRONKITE (2–26–80): A major function of the early primaries is to thin the field of candidates. Even before the New Hampshire votes were counted that effect could be seen. Senator Bob Dole openly wondered how much farther he could go. . . .

6. LEM TUCKER (2–26–80): . . . . Robert Dole has gone back to Washington where today he issued a statement admitting that his campaign doesn't have long to go.

7. BRUCE MORTON (2–27–80): The big loser here was Senator Bob Dole of Kansas who today almost sounded taps for his campaign.

8. BRUCE MORTON (3–5 80): Phil Crane and Bob Dole may be in bad trouble, but Anderson, George Bush, and Reagan are all free to fight another day.

9. BRUCE MORTON (3–10–80): Howard Baker, Robert Dole. . . . "Good Vibrations" isn't their song either. Maybe one Paul McCartney used to sing called "Yesterday."

DOLE'S OTHER COVERAGE

1. BRUCE MORTON (1–2–80): Candidate Bob Dole, after a State Department briefing linked the problem (in Iran) to the President. (Dole quote.)

2. ROGER MUDD (1–18–80): . . . . the candidate who is such a natural comedian he must guard against being too funny (is Dole).

3. WALTER CRONKITE (2–22–80): Bob Dole called for stricter wage-price guidelines with stricter enforcement.

That was Dole's coverage in toto on the weekday "Evening News" — twelve comments, nine of them deathwatch journalism. None of the comments were explicitly critical of Dole; only one was even remotely evaluative as to person; three-fourths, however, declared Dole's campaign dead or dying.

The deathwatch is not inevitable or inexorable. John Anderson in 1980 and Jimmy Carter in 1976 each proved that if a hopeless case exceeds expectations, his press will change. Media not only try to be objective about the "horse race," they also quickly respond to hopeless cases that do succeed. But what is inevitable, if not lamentable, is that media must, in a large field, cover only the morbid "horse race" aspects of the minor candidates' day-to-day campaign. Yet any other handling would certainly be a relief to those struggling candidates, and would probably provide for improved campaign reporting as well.

PLAUSIBLES

Candidates who do better than expected in the race do better than anybody else in attracting coverage. Anderson is the most obvious case. But Bush and Kennedy proved the same point: once the primary season begins, access belongs to those who beat the political odds.

Consider the attention received by each of the major candidates on CBS month by month, during the course of the primary months. Bush's attention jumps dramatically after his victory in the Iowa caucuses (figure 4–2). Anderson's jumps even more dramatically in March, after his "surprising," if unsuccessful, showing in the early New England primaries.

George Bush won the Iowa caucuses by only two thousand votes. But his press "advantage" was enormous, at least in quantitative terms. In the three weeks before Iowa, Bush had received only 45 seconds on the "Evening News," 18 column inches on UPI. In the three weeks after Iowa, Bush received 165 seconds of news time, 75 column inches of news space. Having won the Iowa caucuses by a pittance, but also by surprise, George Bush had nearly quadrupled his share of the newshole on print and television.

Six weeks after Iowa the same thing happened when John Anderson did better than expected in Massachusetts and Vermont, coming in a close second in both of those primaries. The month before, in February, Anderson had attracted 280 seconds of news time on CBS, 49 column inches on UPI. During the thirty days after his second place finishes, Anderson received 1,250 news seconds on "Evening News," 167 column inches on UPI. He, like Bush, nearly quadrupled his access by beating the odds. So too for Kennedy. Even in March there was still

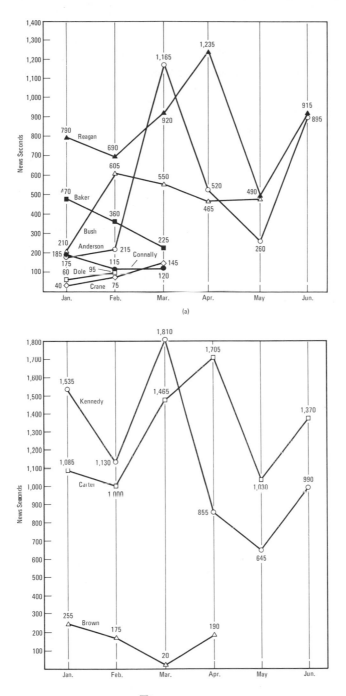

Figure 4–2
*News Seconds Given to Each Candidate During the Primaries,
January 1 through June 6, 1980*

considerable elasticity left in the newshole. When Kennedy was able to surprise the media in New York and Connecticut, and the nomination was still in doubt, he doubled his coverage from the month before. Not until May did the newshole lose its elasticity for primary surprises. George Bush received virtually no coverage for the campaign's last big primary surprise, the Republican contest in Michigan. But, it is absolute certainty that in the early part of the year access accrued most to those who surprised the press or confounded the polls, regardless of who or what they stood for, and regardless of how low in the polls they remained after the surprise.

The rush toward success is neither new nor unique to television. Thomas Patterson found the same exact pattern in the 1976 campaign, and he found it in all types of media.[12] According to Patterson's figures, in the typical week following each primary, the first place finisher received nearly 60 percent of the news coverage given all the other candidates combined.[13] So clear is the pattern that the press not only acknowledges it, but points it out. The day after Anderson's big showing in New England, CBS and UPI both did pieces that dealt with the fickleness of American journalism. On March 5 Bob McNamara made growing press interest in Anderson the focal point of his own after-the-primary news report on "Evening News":

> A fleet of chartered press planes arrived at New Haven airport with camera crews and reporters gathered. They waited for a man who not long ago was hitchhiking some of his rides. John Anderson, fresh from success in Massachusetts and Vermont, was suddenly cloaked in the trappings of a presidential contender, and he liked the attention.... Yesterday reporters who ignored him were today climbing aboard the first Anderson press bus.

By April, the press became much less sensitive to primary or caucus victories. But until mid-spring, increased access accrued most to surprise challengers.

Differences in Access on CBS and UPI

To this point we have emphasized the basic similarities between CBS and UPI; for the rest of this chapter we will consider some important differences—differences in the way the networks and print award access at the outset and during the course of the campaign. Although both "Evening News" and the day wire followed comparable rules of access, they were not identical, especially in the first six months of the year. CBS, during that time, proved to be more volatile, and more subjective than the day wire in its allocation of newsspace. And, although CBS proved more subjective and more volatile in its press coverage in general, both of these differences were particularly evident in CBS news coverage of John Anderson.

STANDARDS OF NEWSWORTHINESS IN THE EARLY PRIMARIES: NETWORK SUBJECTIVITY

Consider first the subjectivity of the newsspace awarded to each candidate at the very beginning of the year. Obviously for both media the single most important criterion for granting newsspace, before the caucus and primary voting began, was standing in the polls. Phil Crane may have been the brightest Republican and Jerry Brown may have been the most competent Democrat in the field, but neither Crane nor Brown could possibly have hoped to have had great access to news media, given their relative ranking in the polls. Support for a candidate in the polls is generally essential for attracting attention in any news medium. But as important as the polls may be for all national media, early poll results proved to be less important at CBS than at UPI.

Press Before Iowa

We imagine that Campaign '80 started for most of us on November 4, 1979. On that historic Sunday, Iranian militants stunned the American public by sacking our embassy and kidnapping our diplomats. Later that night, Roger Mudd stunned us again by presenting "Teddy," a 60-minute CBS documentary about an interview with Edward M. Kennedy, a program that proved devastating to Kennedy's chances for the nomination.[14] So, as a matter of history, Campaign '80 may well have started in early November 1979.

But as a matter of practicality, we started our research on January 1, 1980, seven weeks later. For us, the month of January, prior to the Iowa caucus vote, served as the baseline, the period during which the networks and wires (all the media) had no hard (objective) evidence other than polls to guide them in their decisions about access.

How then did CBS and UPI grant access before the returns started coming in? Table 4–1 shows the relative rankings of newsspace given each of the candidates in both media during the first three weeks of Campaign '80. The table also includes each candidate's standing in the polls prior to the Iowa caucuses.

If we use the last major survey taken before January as a measure of public support, we find that UPI comes much closer to following the lead suggested by that poll. On UPI almost everyone's share of the newshole is a mirror image of his relative standing in public opinion. But on CBS the image is consistently foggier.

Among those candidates who received any attention in both media, the UPI rankings matched the poll results in eight cases out of ten; on CBS the rankings coincide only twice. On CBS the most popular candidate was in neither instance the most heavily covered; on UPI the leader in the polls always led in terms of press. The fact is UPI made no "mistakes." Even those two candidates who seem to have been out of order (Phil Crane and Robert Dole) were actually tied for support in the Gallup survey. The CBS listing contains the real "discrepancies," with Anderson, Connally, and Kennedy very much out of line. The point, of course, is not that CBS assigned wrong

TABLE 4–1

RELATIVE RANKING OF THE CANDIDATES IN THE POLLS* AND IN NEWSSPACE ON CBS AND UPI (FIRST THREE WEEKS IN JANUARY ONLY)

	RANKING IN THE POLLS	*RANKING IN NEWSSPACE, CBS*	*RANKING IN NEWSSPACE, UPI*
Democrats			
	Carter	Kennedy	Carter
	Kennedy	Carter	Kennedy
	Brown	Brown	Brown
Republicans			
	Reagan	Baker	Reagan
	Connally	Reagan	Connally
	Baker	Anderson	Baker
	Bush	Connally	Crane
	Crane	Bush	Bush
	Dole	Dole	Dole
	Anderson	Crane	Anderson

*The most immediate poll for Democrats coming before January was Gallup in mid-December. For Republicans, it was CBS News–New York Times poll, November.

news values to those candidates, but that CBS assigned very different news values to them.

This might be dismissed as accidental, the mere consequence of having analyzed so limited a number of news days. Martin Plissner, political director at CBS, made very much that case, emphasizing the difficulty in scheduling network news coverage in such a way that everybody gets his share of access in a day-by-day routine. And, in fact, Baker led in coverage on "Evening News" in large part because it was during these three weeks that CBS chose to do their lengthy interview with the Senate Minority Leader.*

These findings might also be considered as evidence that the networks really do practice partisan (liberal) bias during the earliest phases of the competition: the liberals (Anderson, Baker, and Kennedy) all did comparatively well in news time, and the conservatives (Reagan, Connally, Carter, and Crane) not so well. To the degree that there was circumstantial evidence in support of the theory that the "liberal" networks hyped liberal candidates in 1980, this was most of it—a news agenda that in the early going did appear to benefit the more liberal elements within both parties. A third interpretation might be that Carter and Reagan were hiding in January, and that the networks, tied as they are to film and videotape, were forced to cover the more "visible" candidates in the field.

For any number of reasons, each of which we will consider later on, we choose none of these interpretations as our own. Instead we see these news preferences at CBS and UPI as reflecting the purer form of objectivity usually associated with the wire, and a more wide open brand of journalism that comes from network news.

NEWS DECISIONS AFTER THE IOWA CAUCUSES: NETWORK VOLATILITY

Polls, punditry, and seat-of-the-pants assessments determine access before Iowa has voted. After the balloting, the criteria shift notably in favor of "the returns." Returns from the early primaries and caucuses are the most "objective" measure of viability, hence the most important standard for access to news. On the night of the Iowa caucuses, both Walter Cronkite and Roger Mudd pointed out that now the press would finally have "more than polls and opinions," and would, in Mudd's words, "have our first real test" in Campaign '80.

*We consider the timing and tone of this interview in chapter 5.

We have already considered how CBS and UPI rushed to cover Bush after Iowa and jumped toward Anderson after his unexpected successes in the New England campaign. But, in fact, CBS jumped higher and quicker than UPI, not just toward Anderson, but toward almost anybody who did better than expected in any of the primaries coming the first four months of the year. And the process was two-way: CBS not only moved more spryly to cover surprise winners, it also moved away more quickly from surprise losers (candidates who did worse than expected).

Standard deviation is a straightforward statistic measuring the amount of variance (volatility) in an array of numbers. The greater the standard deviation, the greater the variation (the greater the spread or dispersion among those numbers). Using as a measure of volatility each candidate's month-by-month access, we found that candidates consistently received a more volatile press on "Evening News." In eight out of ten cases, the standard deviation was greater on CBS than UPI. In other words, winners gained space more quickly, losers lost space more quickly on CBS. CBS generally moved quicker in changing the level of access it awarded candidates as the primary season wore on.

In the course of an election year all media tend to rush toward surprise winners and slide away from surprise losers. But some media move and slide more quickly than others, and CBS was almost always a step ahead of UPI. Whatever the reasons—different size in news-hole, more aggressive news reporters, a more competitive news medium, a richer news budget, a more sensational orientation—CBS proved measurably more volatile in its news coverage than the wire. It was, we suspect, just one more instance in which network journalism seemed more energized, exercised, and sensationalized than traditional print.

Anderson Access in Campaign '80

By the end of Campaign '80, John Anderson had received just about as much of the newshole on CBS as on UPI. But that fact masked a more important reality: Anderson's access came early on "Evening News" but late in the campaign on UPI.

Consider the first three months of the campaign (figure 4–3). In relative terms, Anderson received about twice as much coverage on "Evening News" as on the day wire. By mid-February, despite his incredibly poor showing in the polls (1 percent support in the November CBS poll), and despite the fact that UPI produced twice as many campaign stories, John Anderson had been featured in two fairly lengthy news reports on "Evening News" but had not as yet been featured at all on UPI.

Even after Anderson had arrived politically, after his moral victories in Massachusetts and Vermont, he appeared more frequently on the "Evening News." While Anderson's percent of the newshole tripled on UPI in the three weeks after those primary successes, on CBS his news time quintupled. So sensitive was CBS to "the Anderson Difference" in terms of access, the correspondent assigned to cover Anderson was himself surprised by the amount of attention

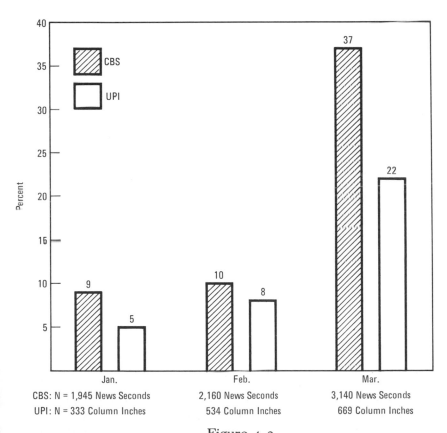

Figure 4-3

Percentage of Republican Newshole Given John Anderson in January, February, and March on CBS and UPI, (Gerald Ford not Included)

given Anderson the day after the balloting in Massachusetts and Vermont.

As the CBS reporter assigned to Anderson in the early going, Bob McNamara might have been expected to appreciate the decision to give Anderson extra heavy coverage after his showing in New England. In fact, McNamara wound up expressing his own reservations: "There was," McNamara told us, "one instance that bothered me. I didn't see any reason for it and that was the day after the Massachusetts primary. The "Evening News" did a two-way (interview) between Cronkite and Anderson and I did the standard day-after-the-election piece. . . . I was surprised they had gone that heavily with him, especially for a guy who came in second place." During Campaign '80, no other candidate received so much access for so little success in a primary campaign.

Toward the end of the campaign season, CBS and UPI covered Anderson in nearly equal proportions; in fact, during the general campaign, the day wire gave Anderson more newsspace than did the "Evening News." But Anderson was, without doubt, the most heavily covered minor candidate on CBS in the crucial first three months of the year. In the next chapter, we treat the Anderson coverage at considerable length, offering an explanation for what proved to be, throughout the year, one of the most intriguing differences between CBS and UPI.

At the very least, "Evening News" coverage of John Anderson's campaign in January, February, and March shows just how much more sensitive the networks are to surprise winners and new faces in politics. Whether Anderson's extraordinary access represents something more than that remains to be seen.

Conclusions

The Anderson case represents an important exception in 1980. For the most part, the media behaved responsibly and equitably, granting access to the major political actors involved. Carter and Reagan got equal time and equal space during the general campaign; the Democrats and Republicans wound up with equal access over the course of the year. Even during the primary season when media had a dozen candidates and scores of states to cover the general rule was equal space for equal actors.

One might also conclude that CBS and UPI behaved "objectively" in granting access, if by objective we mean nothing more than providing newsspace as a function of electoral success. Again, with the exception of Anderson, both sources began by using the polls as a major criterion for covering anybody's political activities. And, as the primary votes became available, both sources shifted from polls to returns as a measure of newsworthiness. Finally, both sources wound up using the predicted delegate counts to determine who deserved coverage in the final stages of the primary campaign, when delegate count had become the most objective test of success and viability.

One can justifiably find fault with all this movement from polls, to returns, to delegate score cards as the standards for access. Patterson found, for example, that in their desire to designate a clear winner, the media granted access to the victor of the week in proportions that wildly exaggerated his actual success.[15] That sort of exaggeration (what we call "surprise journalism") took place in 1976 and in Campaign '80 as well. In those early primaries when the winner, or the runner-up, turned out to be a surprise, CBS and UPI granted newstime to the victor that obviously transcended his real success.

But as a question of news policy, one can look at "surprise journalism" in two very different ways. As a question of validity, the rush toward the unexpected obviously contradicts the reality of the political situation; surprise winners have only marginal support in the polls.

As practiced by the national media, surprise journalism does tend to violate somewhat the "objective" circumstances concerning popular support for frontrunners and challengers. Yet if one raises the question slightly differently, the hypersensitivity of the press seems a plus, if not for frontrunners, then for the "little guy" in the campaign. With no backing to speak of from the party, and with stringent limitations on the kinds of contributions they can legitimately accept, challengers have only the media to sustain them, or catapult them, from obscurity to plausibility.

But one might raise a larger question concerning surprise journalism. One might ask why, to begin with, journalists use successfulness as the only real criterion for establishing newsworthiness or granting access. Why not competence or decency or the ability to answer questions with fact and reason? The answer, of course, is that none of these criteria are easily made objective, and none reflects so directly the people's choice. Access goes not to the best or to the brightest, but to those who win, or who appear to win, public support. So it is in free press. So it is in democracy. When the League of Women Voters had to decide if John Anderson deserved access to their prospective televised debate, the League used the polls as their only guide, not his credentials. It is the Objective—and the American —Way.

Ironically, the present system for awarding access discriminates most against both those with the greatest chance of winning and those with the least. Minor party candidates receive no coverage to speak of in any of the national media. And because minor party candidates do not compete in state primary elections, they have no real opportunity to stage any sort of electoral surprise.

Frontrunners, too, have some problems in terms of access. Frontrunners do receive more access than challengers, but generally less than their initial support in the polls merit, and less than their primary victories might otherwise predict. However, frontrunners can, if they choose, get themselves on television or into the wire. As we will see very shortly, frontrunners wind up having more trouble with the tone of their coverage than with its size.

Access, after all, is only one dimension of press coverage. Surprise candidates who enjoy advantages in the size of their coverage profit from it only so long as their press remains favorable, or at worst, neutral, in tone. Carter in 1976 and Anderson in 1980 both did well politically in the primary and postprimary season, but they did so only as long as their press stayed positive. Access is a necessary but not sufficient condition for getting "good press." Access is a necessary but not sufficient condition for getting nominated or elected. So before we conclude that the media hinder frontrunners or benefit the challengers—or, for that matter, before we conclude that the media treat Democrats and Republicans equally—we need to transcend the simple notion of access and look at the qualitative side of media coverage as well. We need to shift from the starkness of press access to the subtlety of press tone.

Chapter 5

Fairness: Network Fear of Flacking

If there's anything good about the guy, fuck it, the press officer will get it out.

—RICHARD REEVES, FORMER *NEW YORK TIMES* CORRESPONDENT

AS the length of this chapter implies, fairness may be the most important press value of all. In its most recent formal statement concerning press ethics, The American Society of Newspaper Editors (ASNE) listed but six fundamental values of journalism, and two of them specifically deal in notions of fairness in content—"Impartiality" and "Fair Play."[1]

Fairness in content is so important it is the only single news value which the federal government chooses to enforce, or at least to regulate. Broadcasters are not required to grant access to candidates at the state or local levels, only to candidates for federal office. But broadcasters must, under terms set out by the FCC and upheld by the courts, treat all candidates and issues fairly, if broadcasters choose to cover them at all.[2] In fact, the FCC has a host of guidelines requiring that if the broadcaster steps outside the normal boundaries of news reporting in covering a political candidate, the candidate has a right in the interest of fairness to reply.[3]

Our research in this chapter does not address the legal issues involved in fairness. Instead our work focuses on the empirical question, how "fair" in terms of quality of content was the coverage on CBS and UPI? Unfortunately, with the possible exception of "responsible press," fairness in content conjures up perhaps the most subjective press value there is.

To measure fairness or really to reach an *approximation* of fairness, we have borrowed liberally from the federal government's own definition: that fairness and *balance* are approximately one and the same. Public law, case law, and federal regulation all treat balance and fairness as nearly synonymous, and that holds both in terms of quantity and quality of coverage.[4] The Fairness Doctrine, which the FCC has labeled the "sine qua non" of licensee responsibility, is wholly predicated on the notion of balance.[5]

We have already treated the quantitative side of the issue. Now we judge the qualitative dimension of fairness by checking to see how balanced each candidate's news coverage was with respect to *tone*. In chapter 4, we asked if candidates receive equal "time"; in chapter 5, we ask if the candidates received equal "tone."

Tone pertains not simply to the explicit message offered by the journalist but the implicit message as well. Tone involves the overall (and admittedly subjective) assessment we made about each story: whether the story was, for the major candidates, "good press," "bad press," or something in between. "Fairness," as we define it, involves the sum total of a candidate's press tone; how far from neutrality the candidate's press score lies. But before deciding whether a candidate's coverage, or coverage of the fields was balanced (fair) in tone, we need to agree on a definition of good and bad press.

Good Press/Bad Press: Implicit Messages

"Good press" and "bad press" are themselves problematic terms. News people tend even to dispute the idea that there is good press or bad in political reporting, stressing that what the candidates themselves do (and what others say about those candidates) is simply news and reality, not good or bad press. But somewhere between reality and blatant subjectivity lies the gray area of tone. And tone carries with it the concepts of good and bad press. There was, after all, some explicit evaluation of these candidates. And, most important, there was innuendo; there was the indirect conclusion; there was the story with quotations out of balance. Combining into one measure all the innuendo, all the indirect conclusion, all the stories with one-sided quotation, we have come up with a measure of tone, hence a measure of good press and bad.

Here, for instance, is a short Cronkite lead-in to a lengthy news feature report by Lesley Stahl—a lead-in which made no explicit evaluation concerning Jimmy Carter but which clearly includes tone. As for the direction of the tone there is, we argue, precious little room for imagination:

> It's been called the Rose Garden campaign—Jimmy Carter's nontraveling bid for reelection. Ostensibly it is dictated by concern about the hostages in Iran. But has it been above the fray of politics? Well, Lesley Stahl reports . . .

Even if correct in its implicit message that Carter was hiding behind the hostages for political advantage, we consider this introduction a good example of "bad press." We do not consider this remark and its implications to be irresponsible or even wrong. We do, however, regard this lead-in as "bad press."

To support our point we offer a hypothetical situation. Instead of Cronkite, we suggest that John Chancellor of NBC serve as anchor. Instead of Jimmy Carter, we make Cronkite the subject of the lead-in report. The issue changes also. Our hypothetical case deals not with Carter's campaign style but with something more objective, Walter Cronkite's real-life decision in 1981 to join the Board of Directors at Pan Am.*

> JOHN CHANCELLOR: It's been called nothing more than an honorary appointment—Walter Cronkite's decision to accept a position on the Board of Pan Am. Ostensibly the appointment still permits Cronkite to report objectively about science news for his new series, *Universe.* † But is objectivity possible in these conditions? Well, Chris Wallace reports . . .

There are no conclusions, no explicit judgments in this hypothetical lead. But we suggest that had NBC chosen to cover Cronkite's ap-

---

*In March 1981, Walter Cronkite accepted a position with Pan American Airlines. Cronkite has since resigned from the board.

†The "Universe" series was cancelled in late 1982.

pointment in this way, Cronkite and CBS would have regarded this as an example of "bad press."

Defining the Terms: Formal Rules for Good and Bad Press

We have taken special pains to argue the existence of "good press" and "bad press" for two reasons. First, such proof allows us to work outside our much tighter definition of "objective press" and allows us to consider tone. Second, by expanding our research to include tone, we produced the basic building block in a measure of approximate fairness. With evidence on good press and bad press we can gauge how much of each went to all candidates, either party, or each political philosophy during the course of the campaign.

We considered a story to be "good press," if after excluding "events," and excluding information too partisan to assess, the story has three times as much positive information as negative about the principal candidate involved. We considered a story "bad press," if after excluding events, and excluding information too partisan to assess, the story has three times as much negative information as positive about the candidates.* And in almost all circumstances, we excluded all explicit references made by the journalist as to the candidate's chances of winning.

EXCLUDING EVENTS

"Events" per se have no place in our notion of good press or bad. When, in late April, CBS and UPI reported that Carter's commandos failed to free the hostages and that eight of the commandos died in the attempt, that story was not necessarily considered bad press. We considered it bad press only if the source said something critical or presented critical comments about the mission in an unbalanced (one-sided) way. We are, after all, evaluating *press*, not Carter's foreign policy. In our research, good press/bad press did not include

*If the information goes in both directions, but fails to meet the test of three to one, we consider the story "ambiguous." If there is no directional information whatsoever, we consider the story "neutral."

hard news events, unless the journalist drew or implied a conclusion from those events. Coverage of Reagan's ethnic joke, Carter's brother Billy, Anderson's suspicious trip in the summer to see Kennedy, were not regarded as bad press per se.

EXCLUDING POLLS

When a candidate wins, that may be good news but it is not necessarily good press. We exclude from our measure of good press/bad press practically all references to winning or losing. As with events, polls and electoral success do not tell us much about the way in which the media treat the person running for office. In the past, most content studies have considered news about winning as "good press" and news about losing as "bad press."[6] But we think that seriously confounds the issue of how well a candidate is doing with his press image.

EXCLUDING PARTISANS

We also set aside comments about candidates made by partisans. We set aside comments by Carter's campaign director, Robert Strauss; Reagan's campaign director William Casey; and comments by anyone else who had made a political commitment to one of the candidates. We set aside such remarks because we felt that voters as well as reporters tend to set them aside.

EXCLUDING CRIMINALS AND ANTI-AMERICANS

Also disregarded were statements by criminals* or individuals whose remarks have consistently been considered inimical to the interests of the United States, such as those made by Castro, Brezhnev, the Ayatollah, and so forth. Our feeling was simply that Khoemini's comments concerning Carter as Satan were not relevant to Carter's press score. So comments by militants, communists, or terrorists were set aside.

EXCLUDING THE CANDIDATES THEMSELVES

Finally, we held out from our analysis statements made by the candidates themselves. We considered candidates' comments to be

*During the course of the year there were stories about murderers who attributed their crimes to Reagan or Carter.

the purest sort of partisanship and we considered their comments irrelevant to the fairness or tone of the story involved—the story as offered by the news organization.

INCLUDING NONPARTISAN SOURCES

Excluding events, polls, partisans, and the Ayatollah does not solve our problem completely. A story could easily be considered good press if the source said nothing positive about the candidate but incorporated other politically unaffiliated spokespersons who did.

Consequently, we have measured fairness and tone by adding together two sets of comments: first, the comments and words presented by the source; and second, the remarks made by independent observers, those unaffiliated with any party or presidential campaign. In other words, we considered in our assessment of good press/bad press what the reporter and the person on the street appeared to be saying about the candidates involved.

In the end, then, we have a measure of tone within each campaign story, hence a measure of tone for each candidate in his entire year's press. Balance in tone, story by story or month by month, may not be the best measure of fairness, but it is reasonably close to the one that the government itself relies on and is one that the press can understand, if not share.

Good Press/Bad Press: Similarities Between Media

THE GENERAL ABSENCE OF TONE: MORE BALANCED THAN UNBALANCED REPORTING

CBS and UPI both showed much greater balance in their news reporting than imbalance. Neither news source came close to providing more stories that were out of balance than within. Even if we include information about winning and losing, during the course of the entire year there were far more stories that turned out to be neutral or ambiguous in tone than turned out to be either good press or bad, what we term "directional" press.

As figure 5–1 indicates, if explicit references to a candidate's electoral strength are excluded, the percentage of news items without clear direction (i.e., neutral or ambiguous) rises to something on an order of 80. And although there were differences between media, the fact remains: the overwhelming majority of the news stories, and news space, fell within our precise definition of balance and fell within our approximate definition of fairness. Even Jimmy Carter, who received the most "colorful" coverage of any candidate, still received more balanced press than directional. In the end, about three-fourths of Carter's campaign press was neither good nor bad, but was ambiguous, or neutral.

For two reasons this large dose of "fairness" did not come as much of a surprise. First, having already discovered in the earliest stages of our research that the lion's share of the stories made no explicit evaluation concerning the candidates, we did not anticipate that the implicit evaluations would make much of a difference. Adding together all the implicit evaluations did cause a three-fold increase in the amount of evaluation uncovered, but we expected that implicitness would not, on its own, change the fundamental "nature" of press coverage.

But there was a second factor that made it unlikely that these

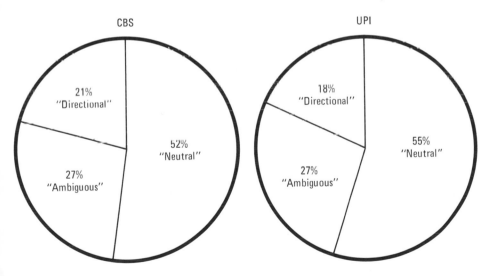

Figure 5-1
Percentage of Stories Judged as Neutral, Ambiguous, Directional (CBS and UPI, January 1 Through November 3, 1980), "Horse Race" Assessments Excluded*

*Figure includes data only for the principal candidate mentioned in each story.

figures would be surprising. Most everybody who has systematically studied campaign journalism in the last two decades has found the press to be essentially neutralist in its reporting. Richard Hofstetter, in what still remains the most exhaustive analysis ever of network news coverage of a presidential election, concluded that "most news stories cannot be coded (considered) as favorable or unfavorable to a candidate, a political issue or party."[7] In fact, after combing through more than four thousand news stories from all three networks during the 1972 election, Hofstetter found that "by far the largest proportion of candidate stories. . . 77 percent for the Republicans and 78 percent for the Democrats. . . were neutral or ambiguous." Doris Graber in her assessments of the 1968, 1972, and 1976 elections found very much the same sort of thing, not just with network news coverage, but with print too.[8] Only Edith Efron, the most vocal and visible of all network news critics, found evidence that the networks consistently treated candidates in an unfair and unbalanced way.[9] And even her data, on reanalysis, proved that most campaign coverage is not unbalanced or unfair.[10]

THE NONPARTISAN NATURE OF TONE: LITTLE LIBERAL ADVANTAGE HEARD OR SEEN IN 1980

So far we have spoken mostly about tone in either direction. Now we pick up on our concept of good press and bad press in order to test what must surely be the single most discussed topic concerning fairness in media: the extent to which the national media behave partially toward the Democrats or the liberals.

The Eastern press is liberal. According to the most recent evidence, two out of three members of the Eastern press establishment think of themselves as liberal.[11] On average, the Eastern press has voted Democratic 85 percent of the time in presidential elections during the last twenty years.[12] And the history of press criticism in the last twenty years contains a goodly share of analysts who believe, and claim, that those progressive attitudes spill or, at minimum, drip into the press coverage of political campaigns.

Edith Efron has remained for the last decade something akin to a household word among network news people for the conclusion she drew concerning television coverage of presidential elections. "It is clear," wrote Efron, "that network coverage tends to be strongly biased in favor of the Democratic-liberal-left axis of opinion, and strongly biased against the Republican-conservative-right axis of opinion."[13] She went on to say that "the networks [in 1968] actively favored the Democratic candidate, Hubert Humphrey, for the Presidency over his Republican opponent," and that "the networks actively opposed the Republican candidate, Richard Nixon."[14]

We have already considered the question of access and found, outside the Anderson case, precious little evidence of liberal hype. Now we consider the qualitative side of the topic directly by looking at the good press and bad press given to the parties and major candidates during the ten months of the election campaign.

By year's end, whatever partisan favoritism in the press did exist was, apparently, flooded over by other factors. Consider first the two major parties. If we add together all the bad press about the Republicans (events and "horse race" assessments excluded) in all campaign stories on CBS, the figure comes to 15 percent of the total news time. If we add together all the bad press for the Democrats, the figure is 19 percent. On UPI, the bad press for the Republicans amounted to 7 percent of the news space; for the Democrats, the figure was 9 percent. Not only did the Democrats attract more bad press over the wire than did the Republicans; on network television, regarded by many as the epitome of liberal news bias, the Democrats did even worse than on the wire.

So far we have looked only at the bad press. What about the good press? What little there was wound up fairly evenly distributed between Democrats and the GOP: On CBS, the Democrats received 6 percent good press, the Republicans 7 percent. On UPI, the percentages were identical, (9 and 9).

Obviously these figures combining all Democrats and all Republicans mask a great deal: coverage of the individual candidates, and coverage as it shifted "up" or "down" during the length of the campaign. But these grand totals reflect a real equality. Table 5–1 contains the list of "Worst Press of the Month" recipients from January through October. The entries represent the one candidate who, in that month, had the worst press index among those receiving any press at all.*

What is very clear is that there was no great favoritism shown to Democrats, and not all that much shown to the liberals either.

*The index represents nothing more than the percentage of bad press subtracted from the percentage of good press. A candidate who had, in a month's time, 20 percent bad press and 10 percent good press would have a score of minus 10.

TABLE 5–1
WORST PRESS OF THE MONTH, CBS AND UPI

MONTH	CBS	UPI
January	Carter/Kennedy tied	Kennedy
February	Baker	Anderson
March	Carter/Kennedy tied	Reagan
April	Reagan	Anderson
May	Carter	*
June	Anderson	Kennedy
July	Anderson	*
August	Reagan	Reagan
September	Carter	Reagan
October	Reagan	Anderson

*Nobody received a negative press index during these months on UPI.

Kennedy makes the list four times, Anderson five times. Carter made the list four times, Reagan six times. These entries conspicuously contradict the thesis that the press is biased in favor of the "left-liberal-Democratic axis." Liberals and conservatives, Democrats and Republicans divided up "worst press" honors in near perfect equality.

GOOD PRESS FOR CHALLENGERS: TRACES OF "HYPE"

We have already noted that the media seem to practice their own special form of triage, dividing candidates into the hopeless, the plausible, and the likely. That apparently holds for the quality as well as the quantity of press coverage. If we assume that, as of January in Campaign '80, the plausible challengers (the middle tier candidates) were Bush and Baker (and that Kennedy, as a Democrat, was a special case), the middle tier did very well in its press during the earliest stages of the race. It is the plausibles who represent our immediate concern.

George Bush

Nobody, except John Anderson, received great press during the primary months, but in January, George Bush did well. After disregarding almost all traces of explicit comments concerning his electoral successfulness, we found that Bush had a slightly positive press on CBS and a positive press on UPI. In January, Bush was the only candidate who was able to get more good press than bad from both news sources. It was UPI that gave Bush his best press in the weeks just following Iowa, the weeks during which Bush posed the most serious challenge to the expectation of a Reagan certainty. Clay Richards filed this good press report:

> George Bush acts like a frontrunner, talks like a frontrunner, campaigns like a frontrunner, but he says he doesn't want to be called the frontrunner in the Republican race.
>
> He won in Iowa and he won in Puerto Rico. . . .
>
> There is a gleam in his eye and a spring in his step and when he talks, one remembers the happy warrior campaign style of Hubert Humphrey.
>
> One week before the crucial New Hampshire primary, the Bush campaign is one of enthusiasm and optimism.
>
> The candidate's energy seems limitless.*

CBS was not so explicitly positive toward Bush, practicing something closer to benign neglect. After Iowa, however, CBS did begin to portray Bush more positively. The day after the caucuses, Cronkite treated Bush to a breezy and pleasant lead-in, one which implied that Bush was both vigorous and serious in his continuing campaign and that he was a smart winner.

Not until late February (February 23 to be exact) did Bush's good press evaporate. Anybody who followed the campaign closely should remember that it was on that day that Bush refused to allow Anderson, Baker, Crane, and Dole to join the debate he had scheduled earlier with frontrunner Reagan in Nashua, New Hampshire.

We will consider that blunder and the press response in short order. For now, the clear implication for Bush's early media coverage is that serious challengers do get more favorable press than the frontrunners.

Howard Baker

In January, using polls as a guide, Baker, not Bush, was the "real" challenger in the Republican party. On CBS, he was clearly regarded seriously in early January, getting more news attention than any other Republican, including Reagan, during the first three weeks of the year.

On January 15, Cronkite did a 6-minute interview with Baker on

*UPI, February 19, 1980.

"Evening News," an interview which aired ten days before Reagan's on-the-issues interview.* That Baker was given this interview before the Iowa vote, while Reagan's came after the fact, is interesting in and of itself.† But we are more concerned with the tone than the timing of Baker's interview, especially when compared with the Reagan interview that followed.

CBS never once in Campaign '80 expressed real enthusiasm for any active candidate. But when Cronkite began the Baker interview, he came about as close to praising a candidate as he did at any point during the year. Baker was, in Cronkite's words, "perhaps the only Republican to be helped by Watergate, as his calm, careful reasoning won him overwhelming praise from television viewers." In comparison with what Cronkite said about Reagan, prior to his January interview, his introduction of Baker borders on outright commendation. Compare this introduction for frontrunner Reagan with the one we have just read for challenger Baker.

> Although his loss to George Bush in Iowa has caused Ronald Reagan to reconsider his strategy, there's no sign yet that it has affected his stand on the issues of Campaign '80. . . . It is Reagan's third shot at the Presidency and some of his opponents like to say his ideas haven't changed in a decade. [1–24–80]

Even in terms of film selection, the Baker feature looked better than the Reagan piece. CBS began the Baker story with a clip of the senator expressing his emotional support for making politics "honorable" again, and began the Reagan interview with a film clip of Reagan contradicting himself.

UPI also gave Baker good press. One week before the New Hampshire primary, on February 18, Steve Gerstel reinforced the image of Baker as the man who could lead Congress, if not out of the desert, at least better than anybody else. According to Gerstel:

> The candidate with the best prospects for a partnership with Congress is almost surely Howard Baker.
>
> Baker gets high marks from colleagues, who also seem to like him personally, Democrats as well as Republicans.
>
> More important, Baker is known as a consensus politician who has

*Cronkite had conducted such interviews with Anderson in November and Bush and Brown in December 1979—interesting choices in timing, given their status as middle tier candidates.

†Martin Plissner, political editor at CBS, says that the timing was logistical, not political.

always argued for Congressional participation prior to submission of legislation. Such an approach would surely endear him to members of Congress.

What may be even more revealing about Gerstel's press analysis is that it directly implied that Baker would have been best at congressional relations, that Bush would have been next, and Anderson third. In Gerstel's column, frontrunner Reagan came in fourth in prospects for handling Congress.

John Connally

Connally was the only serious challenger among the Republicans to lose out in terms of press quality. He did badly in terms of newsspace, and not much better in tone. His final press index for the first three months was ever so slightly negative: zero on UPI, minus 8 on CBS.* Like most candidates, Connally from the outset just did not receive all that much good or bad press coverage, yet what he got was not great. The last evaluative comment came on CBS when Bruce Morton quoted a South Carolinian who described John Connally as a "Texas show horse [who had] been gelded." In terms of both access and tone, Connally was the only Republican challenger who entered the race as plausible but failed to receive anything approaching good press.

Jerry Brown

Setting aside the Kennedy challenge, only one other person who qualifies as middle tier was Jerry Brown. But the Brown challenge, unlike Kennedy's in 1980, was less than plausible. The CBS/*New York Times* poll in January indicated that only 4 percent of the Democrats were supporting Jerry Brown for the nomination. At best, Brown straddled the line between the hopeless and plausible. Worse for Brown, he was going down in public approval, not coming up. As Bernard Goldberg would cleverly conclude in the earliest days of Campaign '80, the Brown campaign was following "the path of Skylab," crashing haphazardly to earth. As it turned out, Brown was the

*These statistics do not include press references to Ada Mills, the only delegate Connally was able to win during his abbreviated, but very expensive (thirteen million dollars) campaign. Using our own definitions, we did not consider media references to Mills as bad press, but, in fact, the way in which the media used the phrase "13 million dollar delegate" to describe her could easily have been construed as belittling to Connally.

only candidate to completely contradict everything said so far about challengers getting the benefit of the doubt. On CBS and UPI, Brown's press coverage was slight and in the direction of negative. On "Evening News," Brown had 25 news seconds of bad press in January and February. For Brown, there was no good press whatsoever in 1980.

First came the Skylab analogy [1–7–80]. Later in January, Roger Mudd pictured Brown as "the candidate who rarely tells jokes about himself but is frequently the butt of them." Even after Brown had long since dropped out of the race, Bruce Morton in a feature story on the strange world of presidential campaigns referred to Brown as "the only candidate who spent money to appear on television with holes in his head," a reference to a television commercial in which bad video work had produced gaps in Brown's superimposed profile.

UPI showed practically no interest in Brown. Outside the death-watch, Brown hardly existed on UPI. But in late March the wire did quote Brown's multi-media advisor, Francis Ford Coppola, who called Brown's Wisconsin primary campaign, "an act of desperation." In the stories we read, even Brown's supporters sounded like detractors.

Was It Really Hype?

Anderson, Bush, and Baker represented the most plausible challengers to Reagan in the first few months of 1980 and their press, at least when compared with Reagan's, was on the border line of outstanding. Connally and Brown fail to fit the theory but neither of them ever came close to being surprise winners in the primaries or to being personally popular with the press people themselves. There was no justification for hyping either Connally or Brown. But there was opportunity and reason to hype Baker, Bush, Anderson, and of course, Kennedy. And the media did, at various points of the campaign, seem to be hyping one or more of these candidates.

But there are two important qualifications about hype. The first qualification involves events: what challengers do with their press advantages when reality changes. We found that good press for challengers lasts only as long as events merit, only so long as the challenger does his part. Take the classic case of Howard Baker, a man who in January received good press from Walter Cronkite, but who, three weeks later, would undergo the single most negative news feature done on any challenger throughout the entire year.

On February 8, Betsy Aaron, then working for CBS, offered what amounted to an exposé on Howard Baker. This special feature was a six-minute hard-nosed investigative report concerning Baker's role in the production of a television commercial that he had used in his Iowa campaign. Aaron centered her investigation on Baker's decision to use film footage of a dramatic confrontation he had had publicly with an Iranian citizen studying at Iowa State—a student who expressed something on the order of sympathy with the seizure of the hostages. The confrontation had taken place weeks earlier in an auditorium at Iowa State, where Baker had given a campaign address. But Baker had not told his university audience, or the Iranian student, that his advertising people were filming his address or planning to use the audience's reaction as a backdrop for his ad. Nor had Baker ever asked permission from the Iranian student to use that portion of the film which had included him.

On CBS, Aaron explained all this and presented interviews with Baker and with the Iranian student. Aaron also pointed out several inconsistencies between Baker's statements and what the films themselves revealed. According to Aaron, Baker's own aides and campaign consultants disputed some of Baker's recollection of facts. Aaron never explicitly charged Baker with anything, but she implied that Howard Baker had been insensitive, inaccurate, and unethical in his use and construction of the Iowa State commercial.

Having seen both the Aaron exposé and the Cronkite interview with Baker, we concluded that CBS behaved in both instances the way national media generally behave toward challengers: that serious challengers do get something like the benefit of the doubt, until the challenger does himself in. Media tend less to hype strong candidates than to extend them extra rope.

The second qualification centers not so much on events, but on political conditions—what happens to challengers who come close to being the new frontrunner. In 1980, George Bush's press symbolizes the problem.

When George Bush decided on February 23 not to allow any Republican candidate but Reagan to debate him in Nashua, New Hampshire, he triggered an extraordinary amount of press. By the following night, the network evening news shows chose to devote 13 minutes of airtime to the fight over the Nashua debate (20 percent of the news total). Merely by covering the story that heavily, regardless of the level of balance, the media could not possibly have been seen as hyping George Bush at that point. This was not good news for Bush. On the other hand, when we consider precisely what the media did say in those few days, the Nashua coverage reinforces the notion of better press for challengers.

Although the story broke on a Saturday, our evidence, as always, comes from the weekday news reports. As far as the Monday and Tuesday reports are concerned, Bush failed to get any bad press, not, at any rate, by our definition. CBS and UPI in those two days offered four stories in toto concerning Bush's performance in Nashua and all of them were "in balance," and none met the test of being bad press.

Compare that with the way CBS and UPI covered Reagan's major blunder in New Hampshire—an ethnic joke he told reporters about Poles, Italians, and the mafia. Reagan's gaffe merited five stories on CBS and UPI and two of the five were out of balance and fell decidedly in the direction of bad press. In other words, "Evening News" and the day wire followed a pattern of perfect balance when covering Bush's political faux pas, but expressed implicit criticism in covering Reagan's verbal miscue.

We interpret the size and the shape of the Nashua coverage to mean three things. First, that once a challenger really challenges the frontrunner, the press shifts toward a more critical posture, one more in keeping with the posture afforded frontrunner status. Had Benny Fernandez engaged in a political misstep such as that taken by George Bush, the press would not have been there to notice or, if in the room, would not much have cared.

Second, as with Baker, Bush's coverage following Nashua indicated that press advantages are ephemeral. George Bush, having tripped over his own political lead, paid a price.

Press after Nashua suggests finally that it's not so much the hype for challengers as the albatross of being at the head of the pack. As bad as the news was after Nashua, Bush's press score stayed in balance. Not so for Ronald Reagan, whose ethnic joke did produce, by our measure, "bad press." Challengers look good in the media only in comparison with frontrunners, not in any absolute sense.

Why Hype?

If this is so, the inevitable question becomes why so: why do the media shade toward challengers. We see two major interpretations, one of which centers on the impishness of the press, and one of which emphasizes its traditional role as watchdog. As for the first, media critics have for years been speculating that the press has good reason to hype challengers during the course of a very long primary and general election campaign. The motive is that hyping challengers makes for exciting copy and makes just possibly for a tighter race. In Campaign '80 this notion might well have been called the new Peters principle, named this time for Charles Peters, time-to-time critic of the Washington press corps.

Peters, himself a journalist, charges that the press likes to cause trouble and excitement by aiding challengers. Peters draws his evidence from his experience in journalism and his argument from sports:

> Unless [my team is] involved, I root for the team that is behind—until it moves ahead . . . switching sides as often as the lead changes. The reason for my deplorable inconstancy is that, above all else, I want the game to be interesting. And that is just what I think reporters want from a political campaign. . . . when it seemed that Kennedy would blow Carter out of the park, they became sympathetic to the president, and when Carter won in Iowa, they were ready to discover that Kennedy was reborn.[15]

But Peters appears, in our view, to overstate the impishness of the press and to understate their attitudes about their mission and role. Although our reporters would not say that they sympathized with challengers, they were remarkably candid about their mission to subject frontrunners to a double standard, and to agree that scrutinizing most thoroughly the lead candidate was a part of their trade.

CBS media critic Jeff Greenfield* specifically combines these two factors, titillation and role of watchdog, to explain challenger hype. Writing about Bush's fall from grace in the press, Greenfield concluded "that with higher visibility comes a higher standard. Now the press is not looking for a glimmer of excitement surrounding a candidate, now they are looking with more critical and skeptical eyes at a figure who may well hold the power of life and death over the world."[16] In short, Greenfield sees what we see, a built-in advantage for challengers predicated not merely in excitement but also in the media's assumed role of watchdog.

POLITICAL OBITUARIES: WINNING FOR LOSING

CBS and UPI shared a fourth characteristic in terms of fairness. Both called off the watchdog immediately, once any candidate had

*In April 1983 Greenfield joined the staff at ABC news.

quit the race. Almost everybody who quit wound up getting good press. Kennedy's case is vintage; but Bush, Baker, Connally all prove the rule. When media cover the campaign's fatalities, Shakespeare's dictum is reversed: the good these men did lives after them, and the evil is oft interred with their political bones.

When Baker dropped out of the race on March 5, CBS correspondent Lem Tucker did not offer a eulogy or anything that could be read as overt praise. But Tucker did describe Baker as a man "with no bitterness" and at peace with himself. The Tucker piece also supported Baker in one more way. It gave Baker literally the last word. Most campaign stories on television have a *closer*—a sentence or two explaining the political meaning of the featured events, usually the hidden meaning. This time CBS let Baker make his own best case and then let Baker's emotional words stand pat—there are no closers at political funerals.

Bush's press after "death" resembled Baker's. UPI's Bruce Nichols filed this piece about Bush the day following his withdrawal from the race.

> Tears glistened in the eyes of his wife, Barbara, but George Bush appeared at peace, joking his way through what might have been the hardest news conference of his presidential campaign—the one that ended it. [May 27, 1980]

On the March 10 wire, even John Connally got a break when he quit: Steve Gerstel called Connally "a proud Texan," a man who to his credit ". . . didn't decide to hang around and pout. . . he went to the podium and cut out clean."

None of this is surprising or unwarranted. The reason seems plain enough—compassion. Having removed themselves from the race, "dead" candidates get press coverage that accentuates the positive. When we asked Martin Plissner at CBS whether good press inevitably follows the funeral, he replied, "Of course. . . in effect, it's an obituary. The campaign's dead—what's the point of dumping on them?"

That media provide death benefits for candidates may not surprise, but the implications of those benefits are less than trivial. First, obituary press implies that context, as well as events, determines press tone. Reporters seem less willing to admit that the press grants a honeymoon for the winners than to admit that the press writes eulogies for the dead. But if context influences press coverage for people on the way out of the campaign, it might also influence coverage on the way into office.

Press eulogies also suggest something that transcends news context and reaches all the way to public opinion. The press benefit candidates get for quitting may seem perfectly harmless. After all, the candidate is gone. But, in fact, there may be a significant side effect to all this. Frontrunners get worse press than challengers while the challengers survive. And as challengers drop off, *their* press improves even more. The result is that the frontrunners look even worse after their competitors lose out, because those competitors did lose out. Media eulogies help to convey the notion that only the good die young in presidential campaigns, and we are left with a Hobson's choice between wretched frontrunners.

PRESS HONEYMOONS: CONTEXT COUNTS AGAIN

Finally, both the wire and "Evening News" gave Ronald Reagan a honeymoon press, at least for a time. Even with the news about his victory distilled out from his press coverage, Reagan's press score in November jumped thirteen points on CBS, and four points on UPI. What makes all this intriguing is that most of Reagan's good press in the early honeymoon centered on his niceness, his openness, his decency—things which went virtually unreported during the campaign. Given all the early attention to his gaffes and misstatements, Reagan himself was surprised by how much good press he received simply for visiting the nation's capital and dining with its black leaders during the third week of November.[17]

What Reagan's postelection press symbolizes, once again, is that all media, to some degree, do share a fear of flacking*—a need to address the bad news about frontrunners until the voters have made their choice and relieved the press, for the moment, of its watchdog detail.

Bill Plante, as a function of postelection circumstances, could, after November 3, more easily report that "from his first appearance on Tuesday [November 18] everyone. . . did indeed seem to enjoy Reagan's week in the capital. . . . This city's local establishment, many of whom are black and most of whom are Democrats, was flattered and astonished to be invited to dinner and told by the Reagans they

*Flacking is journalistic slang. A flack is one who serves as a mouth piece more than a watchdog, one who is tied too closely to his or her news source, either formally (as a public relations employee) or informally (as a reporter).

wanted to get to know their neighbors." Overnight, Ronald the Frivolous had become Ronald the Humane—decent, in part as a function of reality, in part as a function of context.

But the national media, especially the networks, do not go in for long honeymoons. By the end of November, Reagan had given the media something to report critically—a series of political miscues ranging from leaks at the transition office, to Nancy's remarks about owning "just a little gun," to Reagan's inability to make his own cabinet appointments on schedule. By mid-December, CBS political correspondent Diane Sawyer would conclude that "both sides say that the (mistakes) have already soured Mr. Reagan's traditional honeymoon even before it began." And, to be sure, on CBS things had soured: Reagan's press index on CBS slid from +9 in November to −13 in December. Things did not sour nearly so quickly at UPI. They barely soured at all. Reagan's press index on UPI in December stayed positive. Broadcast journalism had found the problems more quickly than had the wire. Yet honeymoon coverage was only one of several important differences between CBS and UPI in their qualitative treatment of the candidates and the campaign.

Good Press/Bad Press: Differences Between Media

TONE DIFFERENCES: "COLOR" TV

As balanced as the press may have been in tone, the fact is hundreds of stories were directional. And, as expected, CBS had more tone, more "message," than the wire.

We look first at the total amount of newsspace which we scored as either good press or bad press, or as "ambiguous" press, the "nonneutral" combination of the two. If we add all this together and exclude "horse race" assessments, CBS turned out to be substantially less neutral.

There was in both sources a large proportion (one-fourth) of "ambiguous" news coverage; a result, in part, of our insistence that the ratio of good to bad press had to be three to one before designating the story either way. Combining the ambiguous stories with the good press and bad press, the nonneutral press on UPI represented 37 percent of the total; on CBS, the figure was 50 percent. In essence, the network turned out to be more colorful, more directional, more subjective, than traditional print.

Differences in color also appear when we shift away from good press and bad press toward syntax and rhetoric. In chapter 3, we divided verbs of expression into three types: descriptive, analytical, and insinuational. Descriptive verbs involved words such as "said," "told," and so on. Analytical verbs included words such as "hinted" or "implied." Insinuational verbs represented the most colorful forms of expression: "confessed," "admitted," and so on.

As noted before, both sources relied mostly on the descriptive verbs. But CBS used the analytical and insinuational verbs more frequently in the ten days of reporting that we sampled. In fact, although neither source chose very many insinuational verbs, CBS used almost three times as many. Overall, UPI relied on descriptive verbs in precisely four out of five instances. CBS chose the descriptive, colorless verb in two cases out of three.* Regardless of how one defines tone, either thematically or rhetorically, the network proved more colorful than the wire.

NETWORK NEGATIVISM: MAJOR DIFFERENCES IN TONE

Despite the fact that most stories in both media were balanced, CBS had a much smaller percentage of positive reports.

So far in this book we have talked about differences between media measured in single digit percentages. For the next few pages we talk about differences measured in double digits, if not multiples. In all these instances, the differences run toward network television as the decidedly more critical, sometimes hostile, information source.

Consider first the candidates in the aggregate. If we exclude "horse race" assessments and comments by political partisans and rely, once again, on our good press or bad press measures, we see just how much more critical the network proved to be. Focusing on the principal candidate in each story, we found that the ratio of bad press to good press on "Evening News" was almost two to one negative—65 percent of the *directional* press on CBS proved to be bad press. For UPI, the ratio was just under four to three positive—56 percent of the directional press proved to be good press. Among those stories with any coloration, CBS reported news that was, in percentage terms,

---

*This is one instance where direct comparison between network news and wire copy is possibly misleading. Networks can show the person talking; consequently, television has less use for the basic verb "said."

twenty points more critical. If we consider each candidate separately, every candidate receiving good or bad press in Campaign '80 got a higher percentage of bad press on CBS than UPI (figure 5–2).

Nine of the ten candidates receiving any tone whatever in their coverage on CBS wound up with more negative press than positive. On UPI, the press images were equally divided; half those evaluated came up with a positive press ratio, half came up with a negative balance. Most important of all, if one computes the amount of bad press presented about all the candidates as a total of all the coverage

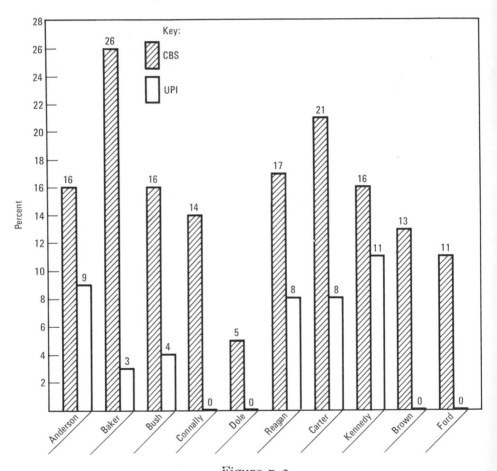

Figure 5–2
Percentage of Bad Press Given Each Candidate (January 1 through November 3, 1980, Presidential Campaign Stories Only)

available, CBS presented two and one-quarter times as much critical news as did UPI (18 percent vs. 8 percent). And these figures inflate the level of criticism coming over the wires as news, including as they do the formal and more colorful commentaries on UPI. (CBS "Evening News" used only five commentaries in Campaign '80). Even John Anderson, who did so well in attracting favorable attention on CBS during the first few months of the year, ended the year with a bad press image on CBS, slightly more negative in fact than his press image on UPI.

The argument so far involves statistical analysis. But the case evidence moves the same way. Consider first the case of George Bush, the only candidate to lead three press lives in 1980: challenger, loser and vice-presidential nominee. The setting involves Bush's July 17 press conference at the Republican convention, the day he was offered the chance to return from the politically dead and become Ronald Reagan's vice-presidential nominee. Covering the press conference for UPI was Diane Curtis, and covering for CBS were both Diane Sawyer and Richard Roth. Curtis covered the story almost without tone, certainly with too little tone to have the following piece considered as bad press.

> Ronald Reagan today declined to characterize his handpicked running mate George Bush as a second choice to Gerald Ford. . . .
> Bush appeared at a nationally broadcast news conference and said, 'We're delighted . . . I'm very pleased to have been selected. . . .'
>
> Bush, reminded by several questioners how he had differed on many issues with Reagan during a sometimes bitter primary campaign, reacted sharply saying he did not intend to stand on the podium and 'be nickled and dimed to death' over differences with the former California Governor.
>
> Bush, who clashed with Reagan in the primaries on abortion and the Equal Rights Amendment, said the big issues this fall will be unemployment in the economy and foreign affairs. . . .

By our measure, this was a neutral story, neither good press nor bad, essentially colorless.

On CBS, the Roth story had considerably more tone. Using *eight* edited videotapes of Bush from the early campaign, eight tapes in which Bush denied he would ever accept the vice-presidential spot on the Republican ticket, Roth began very colorfully indeed:

113

Unambiguously, unequivocally, relentlessly, repeatedly. Through months of campaigning George Bush insisted the Vice-Presidency didn't interest him. . . .

Time and thinking, he said, had changed his mind. . . .

And by the time he met with reporters today it was as if the past had never happened. . . .

But if Roth was colorful, Diane Sawyer was vibrant. Sawyer's report not only played upon, as theme, Bush's ideological differences with Reagan, it also painted the entire arrangement in a Machiavellian hue:

Nothing like a shot at the White House to clarify perspective. Today the new George Bush tried hard to dismiss the old George Bush—the one who made all the fuss about the crucial differences with Reagan. . . .

Bush likes ERA; Reagan doesn't. Reagan urges a constitutional amendment to ban abortion; Bush resists. . . .

So Ronald Reagan and George Bush have signed their treaty on the issues. Bush yielded most of the territory on the theory that it may have been embarrassing today, but if it gets the Republicans to the White House, it doesn't matter.

Having left the presidential campaign in May, Bush had gone into retirement with a press image that was favorable. Having returned this day from the dead, he was slapped twice with bad press, but only on the network news, not on the wire.

So much for George Bush. What about the rest of the field? The following piece by Roger Mudd stands as perhaps the best single example of the comparative negativity of network campaign journalism—criticism of all concerned.

In what proved to be the first feature story of Campaign '80 concerning the whole array of candidates, Roger Mudd presented one line summaries on the wit of each. In rapid succession, Mudd criticized every presidential candidate he mentioned:

Ronald Reagan: "The candidate who recycles the old punch lines."

Edward Kennedy: "The candidate who tells the same story almost everywhere he goes."

George Bush: "The candidate who cracks a joke and doesn't quite know it."

Howard Baker: "The candidate who is forever the small town country boy."

Jerry Brown: "The candidate who rarely tells jokes himself but is frequently the butt of them."

Mudd found one candidate whose humor was apparently rather good, but Mudd did not exactly say so. Instead he described Robert Dole as "the candidate who is such a natural comedian that he must guard against being too funny."

That Mudd could find nothing good to say about anybody's style as a public performer, including the very apt Ronald Reagan, struck us as representative of a pattern we found operating in network news all year long: if the correspondents could not say something critical about the active candidate, they tended to say nothing at all. Network news does not say or imply all that much about the candidates: most news is neutral or ambiguous, but when the networks do paint images, the sketches suggest the cynical caricatures of Daumier, not the ennobling portraits by David.

FEAR OF FLACKING: A NETWORK DOUBLE STANDARD TOWARD FRONTRUNNERS

We have already seen that the most serious challengers generally profit from their status. CBS and UPI both treated strong challengers slightly better than most other classes of candidates in 1980, at least at the start of the campaign. What is particularly interesting, however, is that CBS and UPI did not make frontrunners pay equally for their status as leader of the pack. While many wire reporters told us that they do treat frontrunners more harshly than challengers, it did not quite work out that way in the actual copy.

On UPI, the frontrunners did not do nearly so badly as they did on CBS. In fact, because Reagan did so comparatively well on UPI in the last few months of his campaign, the two consistent frontrunners did slightly better in their press index than all the challengers combined. On the wire, Carter's index was zero and Reagan's was +4. All challengers wound up the year with −1. CBS, on the other hand, produced vivid differences between Reagan and Carter, and the rest of the field. On "Evening News," Carter's combined press index was −17; Reagan's was −14. All their challengers, taken together, had a press index of −4, which was one-fourth as low as the frontrunners. The double standard which applies generally to most of the press, applies doubly to the networks.

CBS also displayed its special penchant for criticizing frontrunners in its campaign exposés. "Evening News" presented five exposés in Campaign '80, stories which went beyond 4 minutes in length and represented clearcut instances of investigative reporting. One, as we have already seen, involved Howard Baker and his conduct in connection with his television ad campaign in Iowa. The other four involved frontrunners: two dealt with Carter, two with Reagan.

Even the mid-length features about frontrunners were tougher on CBS. "Evening News" correspondent Bill Plante produced the first mid-length report about Reagan in early January, ten days before the Iowa caucuses. Plante's report dealt directly with Reagan's frontrunner problems, using Reagan as example, if not object lesson, in the perils of being ahead in the polls. With film, video, and voice-overs, Plante pointed to several of the inherent problems of being frontrunner: being too cautious; putting one's foot in one's mouth; not being able to be two places at once. Plante and CBS provided examples of each problem using footage of the Reagan campaign, footage that was always less than flattering to frontrunner Reagan. Plante did not mention in his report that frontrunners also face a tougher press but the piece made that point on its own.

We asked Plante about his report, why he had done it and whether it confirmed our point that frontrunners get tougher press on television. In eloquent cadence, Plante acknowledged to us that "The degree of scrutiny a candidate receives increases in direct proportion to his standing in the polls." Our evidence suggests that Plante's thesis about double-standards is accurate, but that the thesis holds tighter for television than traditional print.

The Press of the "Final Four"—Kennedy, Anderson, Carter, Reagan

Kennedy, Anderson, Carter, and Reagan were in a class of their own. The "Final Four" consumed 89 percent of the presidential campaign newstime on "Evening News"; 87 percent of the newspace on UPI. As newsworthy as they all proved to be, the press of each of the Final Four deserves some special consideration. We start with Edward Kennedy, the man who ended the year with the third greatest amount of copy in both media, but who was also the first of the Final Four to go.

KENNEDY: FRONTRUNNER; ALSO-RAN; HERO

Kennedy's press odyssey in 1979 merits a short historical review. Although we started our study in January of 1980, Kennedy's campaign press had already begun at least as early as November 1978, when he, not Carter, addressed the midterm National Democratic convention in Memphis. From that point until November 1979 all the media gave Kennedy enormous play, and play is the correct word. The national press joined a cat-and-mouse game with Kennedy concerning his intentions about running.

Although there were exceptions, the bulk of Kennedy's press prior to his announcement that he would run had been favorable. But on November 4, 1979, Kennedy's press took a historic turn for the worse. That night, CBS and Roger Mudd presented "Teddy"—a now legendary special devoted to analyzing and interviewing the last of the Kennedy brothers on the eve of his formal bid for the presidency.

Mudd's review of Chappaquiddick, and the senator's fumbled responses to easily anticipated questions, helped to change the way the press corps viewed Kennedy. By mid-November, two weeks after "Teddy," press treatment of Kennedy had become a story in its own right. Charles Seib, then serving as press ombudsman for the *Washington Post*, asked theoretically if "the press [is] leaning over backward to the point where it is now unfair to the man it was accused of favoring."[18] Television critic Tom Shales accused CBS and Mudd of what Shales called "willful Mudd-slinging."[19] He also concluded that "Teddy's Torment" was in part "another case of the press sensing its role in having created a legend, trying to break it down again."

Kennedy's bad press in November of 1979 did not improve come December. His infamous accusation in December that the shah's regime in Iran was "one of the most violent . . . in the history of mankind" and that the shah had stolen "umpteen billion dollars" from his people could not have come at a worse moment. The *New York Daily News* headlined that comment by Kennedy with "Teddy: the Toast of Tehran," a snide allusion to the popularity Kennedy's remarks enjoyed among the militants and mullahs holding the hostages in Iran. The *Washington Post* editorial staff, sometimes supportive of Kennedy, said that his allegation "wasn't right. . . wasn't responsible, wasn't smart."[20]

Because none of this happened in 1980, all of it fell outside the immediate scope of our study: in essence, this information is, so far as we are concerned here, "prehistoric." We have no good press or bad press figures for Kennedy in 1979; we have qualitative assessments of what the national media were doing. But that evidence strongly suggests that Kennedy's press in late 1979 proves the rule: that frontrunners get the worst press of all.

By January, Kennedy was no longer the frontrunner; he was now the challenger. As the principal challenger, Kennedy should have, as of January, started to receive benefits in that role. But despite this theory, he did not do well during the first few months of the year (see figure 5–3). He did, as we shall see, do better than Jimmy Carter, however, and that at least implies that he had comparative press advantages as challenger.

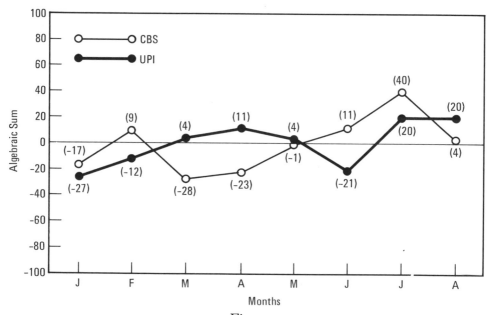

Figure 5–3

Kennedy's Month-by-Month Press Index, CBS and UPI (Presidential Campaign Stories Only)*

Each number represents the algebraic sum of Kennedy's bad press and good press for each month of the campaign.

Kennedy's press in Campaign '80 also implies one more time that to the media and in the media, a statesman is a dead politician—that the press reports the good side of the candidate after the candidate has lost, withdrawn, or become a nonfactor in the race. In the words of UPI political editor Ron Cohen: "Ted Kennedy is a classic case. . . . As soon as he was not a threat any more, people started saying wonderful things about him." Jeff Greenfield at CBS also feels that Kennedy's standing in the race played a big part in his shifting image from "Klutz to Class."[21]

Statesmanship came slowly, but by May, Kennedy's press began to show signs of resuscitation, if not resurrection. In June, July, and August, Kennedy received the "best press of the month award" on CBS.* On UPI, he had "best press among all candidates" in July and August.

Dean Reynolds, who covered Kennedy for UPI, and Susan Spencer, who followed Kennedy for CBS, stress events and Kennedy's turning his campaign around as the reason for the increasingly positive tone. But the reports they filed suggest that context, not just reality, influenced the tone.

Let's start with Reynolds at UPI. On April 22, Kennedy won the Pennsylvania primary. He was at that point still clinging to plausibility. A week later, Kennedy, as public official, was visiting Mexico and Dean Reynolds filed this less than flattering report:

> His 24-hour trip to Mexico City clearly was (tailored) to his home audience. The Massachussetts Democrat literally campaigned in the foreign capital. . . .
>
> It was all billed as "Senate Business" and Kennedy brushed aside a suggestion he was really trying to curry favor with Hispanic voters in Texas.

Kennedy was at that point a politician.

But six weeks later, Kennedy had been all but mathematically eliminated from contention and the same Dean Reynolds had a different message to convey. Writing on June 2, Reynolds failed to call Kennedy a statesman, but did label him a hero:

> As it waited out the final 48 hours for the judgment of the voters in 8 states, the campaign of Senator Edward Kennedy seemed enveloped by a good natured serenity. . . .

*The best press of the month designation goes to the candidate with the highest percentage of good press.

Then Kennedy, somewhat like the movie hero who rides into the sunset, said "It does not matter whether they are popular today or whether they will be popular tomorrow, I will stand for the values I believe in."

Susan Spencer's reporting over the course of the spring suggests the same thing (good press for political basket cases). On June 4, Spencer did a wrapup (campaign obituary) report on the senator. "If," began Spencer, "it proved anything, the Kennedy campaign proved that Kennedy was a man not easily discouraged." Then Spencer took us back to April, with film of Kennedy campaigning in Michigan before that state's primary:

A biting wind, a driving sleet, no overcoat [for Kennedy]. But the sight of a few more possible votes at the fence was enough for Kennedy to brave it all, whirl himself and his gargantuan press corps around and greet the folks."

In June, Kennedy was portrayed as a brave and determined campaigner, with footage taken from his April campaign. But in April, there had been no such report, nor any piece commending him for his political style with the folks. This film clip taken in April apparently proved more appropriate after Kennedy had lost in June.

When it was finally over, the day after he withdrew from formal contention, Kennedy received this conspicuously upbeat report from CBS political correspondent Jed Duvall:

While other dropouts are suddenly ignored and alone in the world there is still a mob around Kennedy as there was today at lunch.

He dines—the mob waits—and dashes—as he and his wife Joan walk back to their hotel.

Kennedy's press during 1980 indicates that, within the limits of Objective Reporting, a statesman is a dead politician. And his press before the year began suggests that the national press corps had an especially deep-seated anxiety about appearing to flack for somebody they knew or liked, what Tom Shales labeled the "Petty for Teddy" bias.[22]

Reporters may reject or resist the premise that Kennedy, as a function of his politics, his friendship, his viability faced a media-based double standard, not just once, but twice. But despite what reporters may think, despite what all this up and down press may have meant to the Kennedy campaign, it seems clear to us that the media, liberal and partial to the Kennedy clan as they may be, did treat Kennedy with hostility when he was the frontrunner, and with sympathy in the end. As students of free press, we would be much less happy had it been the other way around.

"THE ANDERSON DIFFERENCE": FRESH FACE, AND LIBERAL TOO

Once it became clear that Anderson would run as an independent and would pick up reasonable support, Jimmy Carter began to complain that Anderson was a creation of the news media, that if the networks pulled the plug on his candidacy it would cease to exist. This was a bizarre accusation from a man who had himself won a nomination in 1976 from outside his own party, a man who had put together a string of his own media events beginning in Iowa and extending on through Super Tuesday '76.[23] But Carter was right about Anderson in two ways. First, Anderson had no real campaign outside the media. His was a series of appearances, not political rallies or meetings. Peter Brown, UPI's man on Anderson, corroborates the point:

> The thing about Anderson. . . he only campaigned on college campuses . . . media appearances. . . press conferences. . . . That was it.

> There was one ten day period when all he did was to go to college campuses, do "Good Morning L.A." types of shows. But he couldn't get appearances any place else. . . .

Second and more important for us, Anderson really was, at the outset, the network news candidate. Recognizing that our formal evidence has only to deal with CBS, but knowing too that we conducted checks on ABC and NBC as well, we found consistent support for the idea that Anderson was a television story, at least in comparison with traditional print.

We have already considered Anderson's early advantage in access to "Evening News." But access was just the beginning of the "Anderson Difference." Anderson also got good press on CBS during the first dozen weeks of the year. So good, in fact, one might say that the coverage he got in "Evening News" was almost in perfect keeping with his own political strategy of painting himself as a solitary statesman. None of this "Anderson Difference," however, showed up in the wire stories.

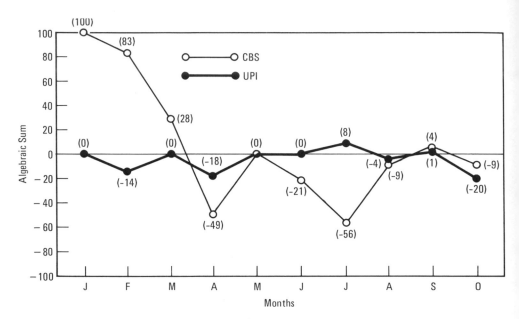

Figure 5–4
Anderson's Month-by-Month Press Index, CBS and UPI (Presidential Campaign Stories Only)

Figure 5–4 makes the point vividly. As usual, these numbers represent the percentage difference between the good press and bad press accorded the candidate during a set period of time. And for Anderson on CBS, the numbers for these first few months represent a real press bonanza. In the first three months about half his press was favorable! On UPI, his press index for the first three months was −3 percent.

Obviously, in the first few months of one campaign, his score was based on traces of directional news. But, despite that qualification, nobody in Campaign '80 received anything approaching so positive a press index as Anderson did early on with CBS. In January, his press score was +100 percent. He was featured for 125 seconds of news coverage, all of it meeting our test of good press.

Anderson's good press in January came on the tenth of the month in a feature story about the "lost" candidate who had been "found" at the Iowa TV presidential debate. With the help of a videotape borrowed from "Saturday Night Live" (a clip of Jane Curtin declaring Anderson missing in a bulletin on "Weekend Update"), Walter

Cronkite introduced the piece. Jim McManus then went on to discuss how well Anderson had done in the Iowa debate.

The McManus report was not a puff piece, but it was decidedly upbeat for and about Anderson. Not only did McManus use the word "articulate" to describe Anderson, he also did something very unusual for "Evening News," he let Anderson and his staff go almost wholly unchallenged in all their assertions about how well everything was going in the campaign.

What made the McManus piece particularly intriguing is that the implicit conclusion, that the debate had been, in Iowa, a political plus for Anderson, was probably wrong. The Iowa poll, released the morning after the piece had appeared, indicated that Anderson had gone from 0 percent to 1 percent in the Republican race for caucus votes.[24] If Anderson's performance in the Iowa debate had been a coup of any sort, it had been a *media* coup. But media coup though it may have been, it was a coup unique to the prestige press and television. The wire gave Anderson's performance in the Iowa debate but 2 column inches of flat reporting.

CBS also gave Anderson good press in mid-February, just before the New Hampshire primary. At a forum of New Hampshire gun owners, Anderson had come out in favor of gun registration; all the other Republicans at the meeting dutifully, and predictably, came down hard against it. At UPI, this confrontation between Anderson and the gun owners got but a passing reference. On CBS, it became the lead-in to Anderson's second full-length news story in as many months. Cronkite began the piece by pointing out that Anderson's favoring gun control "was not surprising. John Anderson has often found himself standing apart from the crowd." The piece went on to make Anderson look not just different, but courageous, too. Bob McNamara noted that Anderson had been labeled the candidate who can't win, but McNamara also said that Anderson was the one man voters "see as the most articulate, honest, and best candidate in the field." McNamara then defined the Anderson campaign like this:

> Anderson has no endless bank of phone solicitors—no computers automatically printing pleas for money. His small army of volunteer students write, address and stuff envelopes by hand. Still this low budget, loosely organized, amateur run campaign is collecting cash.

But that was the beginning of the year. By July, Anderson was getting bad press from "Evening News" that explicitly involved Anderson's character. The same Bob McNamara who had spoken so warmly about the Anderson Difference in the winter months had cooled off his prose for summer. Summing up Anderson's day tour around Israel on July 10, McNamara wrote:

> This is the image John Anderson's media strategists are trying to project —Anderson with a top Israeli general on a West Bank mountain—the candidate getting foreign policy schooling through his own eyes.

> Portrayed as a serious fact-finding mission, Anderson's foreign trip is still an image-building campaign tour, designed to show him with famous faces and orchestrated to sell credibility, particularly to Jewish voters who might see Anderson visiting Israel's memorial to the victims of the holocaust—a sight he has seen before, without cameras.

The wire copy that day about Anderson's Israeli visit contained none of this. And as his press line indicates (figure 5–4), news coverage of Anderson on UPI was as monotonous as a relief map from his home state of Illinois. The peaks and valleys of Anderson's press in the first seven months of 1980 existed only on network television.

Explaining Anderson

Clearly, the most important question about Anderson's press year involves the first few months. Whether the dimension is access or tone, John Anderson did better than any other nonfrontrunning candidate on "Evening News" during the winter months, and did much better on CBS than on UPI, at least until spring. Why so much good press and so much access up front, especially on TV? Here are four plausible interpretations of the Anderson story.

1. Political Bias. The most obvious explanation is political: the liberal press hyped the liberal Republican. And because the networks are even more liberal than print, Anderson was simply the beneficiary of ideological press bias. Two things are fairly certain. First, Anderson was the liberal Republican, and second, CBS News is liberal, too.

We have no hard evidence on the political ideology of the people who work at UPI, but through the research of S. Robert Lichter and Stanley Rothman, we do know something definite about the political ideology of CBS News. In 1979 and 1980, working under the auspices of the Research Institute of International Change at Columbia University, Lichter and Rothman interviewed scores of reporters in the most prestigious of the eastern news organizations, CBS News among them. Although the CBS sample was small (about 20), the findings are hard to dismiss as anything short of incredible. Since 1964, among those responding and voting, CBS news people have voted Democratic 90 percent of the time![25] We have no figures for 1980, but as late as 1976 Jimmy Carter received 87 percent of the two party vote at CBS. We doubt that UPI is quite so Democratic or, by implication, quite so liberal. But whatever the ideology at the wire, the political philosophy of the CBS news staff more than suggests that Anderson did as well as he did in the early campaign because he was the most liberal Republican.

Yet was ideology really an issue here? We think yes, somewhat. Still, we believe that there are far more powerful influences at work in news reporting than partisanship or liberal hype, even in the case of John Anderson.

The theory of partisan network journalism suffers from everything that happened to Anderson after the March 11 Illinois primary, the point at which Cronkite and Morton declared Anderson a "big loser" and the point after which his press slid downhill. To understand Anderson's press, one needs to begin with ideology, not stop there.

2. Personal Appeal. Most reporters liked the early Anderson. Although Bruce Morton qualified his feelings, saying that reporters felt "the more you know John Anderson, the less you liked him," practically everybody we interviewed expressed enthusiasm for the Anderson of January, February, and March, particularly the reporters assigned to him. Peter Brown at UPI:

> I think it is clear to say that the press corps generally liked John Anderson. . . . Yes, reporters liked him. He's a politician, but he's a humane one.

Mark Bisnouw, Anderson's press secretary during the outset of the campaign, stressed personal style as well, claiming that the reporters who covered him early on considered Anderson to be "quite a remarkable person."

> I think (media) people saw Anderson as being very noble, and in a sense innocent. . . . I think there was a genuine sympathy. . . . And you had people like Bob McNamara at CBS—I think he's a fine reporter—I wouldn't be surprised that he developed a certain admiration. . . which came across, consciously or unconsciously in his reporting.

That the press approved of the early, original Anderson is beyond question: as late as April a National Press Club poll conducted in

Washington among newspaper people who attended spring meetings found Anderson to be the heavy favorite for president. He led his closest competitor, Edward Kennedy, by a margin of two to one.[26]

Not just liberal, but cerebral, and open, John Anderson was appealing to almost all the boys (and girls) on the press bus. No doubt that helped him get good press, at least until April. But why would network reporters and editors be more vulnerable to Anderson's charm than wire reporters?

The answer probably lies first and foremost in the realization that network journalists, when compared with wire reporters, will let more of their interpretation come through. But almost as important is the way in which CBS and UPI covered candidates in the early field. Networks traveled more closely with Anderson than did the wires. In fact, in the early campaign UPI relied almost solely on stringers—reporters who covered Anderson, locally, and one day at a time. Anderson, as a personality, did well with the boys on the bus, but UPI had nobody on Anderson's bus full time until late in the campaign, not until late summer.

The networks covered Anderson in a man-on-man strategy; the wires did more zone coverage. Anderson's low-key charm would work more effectively against man-on-man coverage, which is what CBS provided.

3. Structural Bias. This last point, concerning the way in which reporters were assigned to candidates, smacks of "structural bias" in news, a tendency to report the news in keeping with the structural design of the news organization.[27] Stringers will, in other words, report somewhat differently from correspondents who travel on the press bus.

Although we consider this structural/organization theory of news in greater detail later on, for the Anderson case the theory seems to hold. Hypothetically, the networks hyped John Anderson because he fit the needs of television, providing as he did a fresh face, and above all, good visuals. In short Anderson was offering and the networks were buying political drama, publicly confronting as he did virtually every other Republican in the field. As odd-man-out Anderson was the candidate tailor-made for television. In the end, then, this comes down to the special relationship between "confrontational politics" and the television news system.

This particular theme, that the network news business looks harder for the curious, the odd-man-out, was very popular among our respondents in both media. No doubt some of this took place. But the structural interpretation explains Anderson's share of the television newshole, *not* his disproportionate amount of good press. And the structural thesis assumes that the networks were, with their need for video and conflict, the only news source showing disproportionate interest in and appreciation for Anderson. That was not the case. In the beginning Anderson did not play well or long on the wires, but he did play very well in the prestige print press.

4. Networks Following Prestige Print. The wires ignored Anderson but the prestige print press did not. In fact, the *Washington Post* had in mid-November of 1979 already done an extraordinarily flattering news story about Anderson, calling him "handsome, bright, articulate. . . honest and outspoken."[28] A week later CBS did a 7 minute interview with Anderson, an interview in which Cronkite used some of the same flattering phrasing to describe the Illinois Republican.

While it goes too far to say that the networks relied wholly on the *Washington Post* and the *New York Times* for campaign news, with the Anderson story it appears that the networks did rely on the prestige print press for campaign cues. In other words, Anderson probably profited from the early hype from the eastern dailies which filtered eventually into the evening news shows. Martin Plissner at CBS instructed us that Anderson was more a *Washington Post* story than a story for "Evening News."

Eventually we return to the premise that the networks use the prestige dailies as their bellwether. For now it is safe to conclude that the early Anderson was not so much a television story per se as he was a story for the eastern press, networks included. And clearly his liberalism and his style helped to get the ball rolling both in prestige print and in network news.

But what does that say about our theories of impartial press? The answer lies in a comforting point made by Peter Brown at UPI. Brown concluded that "had Anderson been stronger" (politically), it would "have been a different story." In other words, had Anderson been in serious contention at the outset, his press would not have been so good. When he was still implausible in January and February, Anderson's style, his uniqueness, and to a degree, his politics could gain for him some press advantage. The network reporters knew him, liked him, liked what he said, and saw him as Bruce Morton described him, "cute and catchy." It cost reporters little to be nice before Anderson had moved into contention. But by March he had moved there, and when he lost in Illinois the press trumpeted his defeat as major. By late March, when he became a possible contender, CBS began sounding taps for Anderson. By summer, prestige print and network news were dumping on Anderson.[29]

Which leads to our final conclusion about Anderson's press in 1980. In the past, we have criticized the press, and particularly the networks, for making too much of the early primaries and too much of the surprise showing of men like Eugene McCarthy, George McGovern, and, most recently, Jimmy Carter.[30] But the fact is the national media, particularly the networks, have been "correcting" for this deficiency by growing tougher on candidates they perceive themselves as having helped, either in terms of access or in tone. The Anderson case suggests very clearly that those who do well in the news media in the beginning of the year pay for it as the calendar moves on. If the press helped build an Anderson bandwagon, by March the press was helping to break spokes off its wheels. If 1980 serves as a model for beyond, we should expect hard times for the original frontrunners and even tougher times for the surprise candidates who, on the crest of the news media, move ahead in the pack —even if those candidates are liberal, even if nice.

CARTER: THE ULTIMATE IN FRONTRUNNER PRESS COVERAGE

Among the major candidates, certainly among the Final Four, Jimmy Carter reached election day with the worst press image of all. On UPI, after subtracting his bad press from the good, his press index was zero. On CBS, his press index was −17 (21 percent negative, 4 percent positive). In both media, Carter received worse press than Ronald Reagan; and on CBS, where candidates always did worse in terms of press scores, Jimmy Carter's press index never once went above zero in any of the ten months of the campaign (figure 5-5).*

Figure 5-5 actually understates Carter's problems with press. Almost a third of his coverage on "Evening News" we deemed "ambiguous," but in Carter's case, about nine out of ten ambiguous stories shaded toward unfavorable. If we had added together his "question-

---

*Christine Schultz, working with John Petrocik and Sidney Verba, also found Carter's press to be much more unfavorable than Reagan's. Her figures include all three networks. See "Choosing the Choice and Not the Echo: A Funny Thing Happened to the Changing American Voter on the Way to the 1980 Election," paper presented to the American Political Science Association, New York, 2 September 1981, pp. 26–28.

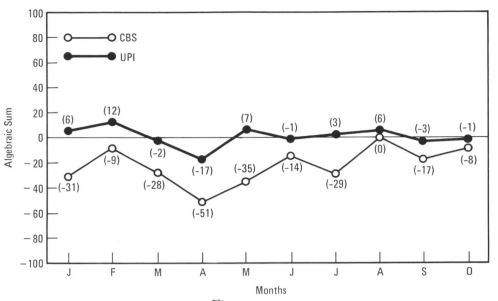

Figure 5-5

Carter's Month-by-Month Press Index, CBS and UPI (Presidential Campaign Stories Only)

ablc" coverage to his bad press score, half of the newstime given Carter in stories not evaluating the "horse race" would have proved unfavorablc toward him as person or a president.

Before we try to explain why it was that Carter became the press fall guy in Campaign '80, we make one very important distinction. Much of what we claim to be true about Carter's press in this chapter pertains mostly to CBS, and by implication, the other two networks covering him.* Carter did do badly on the wire, ending up with just about as low a press score as any candidate in the field, but, by November, his wire press was no more negative than positive. It was on CBS, which is to say network television, that Carter led everybody in terms of bad press, and on CBS that he received five times as much bad press as good.

From the beginning of the year, CBS painted Carter as a poseur, a practitioner of political symbolism. Consider these examples from just the first three months of the year, before Carter left the Rose Garden.

*Our analysis of Carter's coverage in a ten day sample from ABC and NBC indicates that his press was about equally bad across the evening news broadcasts.

Cronkite on January 18:

In 1976 Jimmy Carter campaigned as the common man, the outsider. He ran on trust and made a lot of promises. . . . Now this film is being distributed by the Carter campaign stressing the President's experience in Washington, showing off the symbols of power.

Mudd on February 12:

These are photographs showing Jimmy Carter *actually campaigning.* The pictures are less than four years old but he is clearly in such far away places as Maryland, and Michigan, and Indiana.

Stahl on February 25:

The Olympic athletes said they did not think they were being used by the President to help his political campaign. But none disputed that the timing was fortuitous. With the economy gloomy, and the hostage situation in Tehran tenuous, what better for the President on the eve of the New Hampshire primary than to be seen on television surrounded by a group of young, happy and victorious American heros.

Morton Dean on March 19:

Cynics might say that today's news about a White House invitation for Sadat to visit Washington could have something to do with the New York primary.

Stahl on the same day:

There was some skepticism in Washington about the reasons for the meeting. . . . Others on the Hill say they feel the timing of today's announcement without any fixed date was an attempt to get the word out before the New York primary next Tuesday, where roughly 30% of the Democratic voters are Jewish.

That Carter received a worse press than any of the Final Four is certain; the reasons for his bad press are much less clear. Four theories stand above the rest.

Reality

As usual, reporters and editors we spoke with saw Carter's press as a fair-minded assessment of fact. Reality was, for them, the best explanation of Carter's poor press.

Bruce Morton covered Carter in Campaign '80, not on the road or at the White House, but as the CBS correspondent handling much of Carter's feature press on "Evening News". Having pointed to Carter's low press scores we asked Morton to explain. His response was, plain and simple, reality:

> We ran stories that said Carter was a manipulator. Well, one of these that I happened to do said that the average amount of federal aid to Maine was, say $100 a month, except that two months before the Maine caucuses, it went up to a million a month. That's true. Carter was pouring money in there as if there was no tomorrow.[31]

Lesley Stahl suggested an interesting corollary to the reality thesis. It was not only the facts that were at issue, it was the criticism the other policy makers expressed which the media dutifully reported. In essence, Stahl claimed that policy makers, especially on Capitol Hill, served as the source of the news river about Carter. The press reflected what the Hill said about the president.

Stahl's thesis may explain why President Carter got much of his bad press, but news flow from the Capitol does not explain fully why candidate Carter did as poorly as he did. It was Stahl, after all, who reported that candidate Carter was posing and posturing on the campaign trail.

Reality must play a part in the press image, unless the media behave dishonestly or irresponsibly. But the fact remains that there was almost no "good news" about Carter whatever on "Evening News"—something which might be hard to reconcile with reality. (On CBS, nobody mentioned, for example, how well briefed or prepared Carter always seemed to be—he was Jimmy the Manipulative, not Jimmy the Informed.) What's more, reality on CBS meant newstime that was 21 percent negative—only 8 percent negative on UPI. Even in an objective press, reality is a necessary, not sufficient, condition for understanding media images.

Style

Near the opposite end of the spectrum of explanation comes style: the idea that Carter received bad press not because reality was bad but because his personal style was bad.

We asked several of the principals involved about the idea that personal bias was at the bottom of Carter's press. Whether it was Jody Powell or whether it was Lesley Stahl, the answer seemed to be a qualified "yes"—Carter's press suffered from his own personal style.

Helen Thomas, the dean of White House reporters, told us that Carter's problem was not so much personality as it was skill.

> I think that Carter had a big communication problem. I think there was a lack of understanding of what President Carter was all about. And this kind of befuddlement . . . put the reporters in limbo. . . .

> And he seemed to be much more of a loner, and so that might have contributed to what they might have considered as some hostility. . . . I didn't feel that way . . . but he did have a lack of rapport.

As cool toward Carter as this remark may be, it was warmer than most. Only one person in the twenty that we asked expressed positive personal feelings for Carter. Reporters of every kind seemed to dislike almost everything about Carter and his family. In the words of Diana McLellan, gossip columnist for the *Washington Post*, the Carters were "boring and dreary and small town and always have been and always will be."[32]

But how much weight does style per se deserve as a factor in Carter's press image in 1980? Stahl acknowledges that style did explain some small part of it: "Well this is something I'm very interested in myself and talk about it whenever I give a speech . . . I do think that interpersonal chemistries play a part and we really don't deal with it enough."

As for the relative importance of style and personal bias in news relationships, Stahl concluded "certainly it is a greater problem than political bias." We concur: the theories of Dale Carnegie help us understand more of Jimmy Carter's problems with media than any of the theories associated with Edith Efron.

Incumbency

In their book *Portraying the President*, Michael Grossman and Martna Kumar argue persuasively that all presidents go through a press cycle, one which corresponds to the phases of almost any prolonged social interaction such as marriage, friendship, job. According to Grossman and Kumar, press and presidents begin their relationship in a phase called "alliance," move quickly toward "competition," and eventually end up in "detachment."[33]

Alliance, of course, comes close to the traditional concept of press honeymoon. Competition begins when the press moves from stories about the new first family (usually puff pieces) and starts to cover the conflicts among personalities and controversies over policies within the administration.[34] Finally, in the detachment phase the antagonisms which have begun earlier lead the president to withdraw from the press and lead the press to look to other sources of information about the president such as the Congress or the bureaucracy, people more likely than his family or staff to be critical of the president.

If this near deterministic picture is correct (and we believe that essentially it is), then the fourth year is inevitably one of strain between an incumbent and the White House press corps. In that interpretation, Carter's bad press was a by-product of his first three years, with familiarity breeding its usual share of contempt.

The history of recent presidents fits almost precisely with the theory. Johnson, Nixon, and Ford all went through the three phases. And so did Carter.* Starting on a press "high" in February, March, and April of 1977, his press image fell quickly. By the fall of 1977, Carter, having experienced the full force of the Bert Lance affair, was in his detachment period, moving away from the press and using Powell more and more as his emissary. David Broder wrote as early as fall 1977, that the same press which said in the summer that Carter could walk on water, now says he's drowning.[35]

We see this as a major factor in Carter's press problems in 1980. After three years in close proximity, the press inevitably had more information about Carter on which to base their news coverage. The first reason Powell gave to explain Carter's press miseries was the idea of "blood in the water"—that more bad press goes to those who have just had bad press. Almost nobody in main-stream politics is as likely as a fourth-year incumbent to have just come off a stint of bad press.

The Ultimate Frontrunner

Were we to choose one explanation which transcends the rest, perhaps even reality, it would be that Carter faced the double standard in double. Not only was he the incumbent, he was regarded by the press as being the real frontrunner, not just in the primary season, but in the general campaign as well.

Reporters, in Jody Powell's phrasing, "see the Presidency as having these mystical powers upon which he can call . . . that the incumbency is a bigger factor than it is." Just as Carter lost a point or two

*Reagan's case is virtually identical.

with press for being the frontrunner, he lost a point or two for being the frontrunning incumbent.

We think Carter's problem went even further because the press had come to believe that no matter how far back in the pack he appeared, Carter always seemed to pull it out. On Labor Day, the opening day of the general election campaign, with Carter behind by at least ten points in the polls, Lesley Stahl wrapped up her nightly news report with a prediction of sorts: "Ronald Reagan," she concluded, "is about to learn what Senator Kennedy found out during the primaries—that Jimmy Carter has learned how to use the advantage of incumbency." As of September 1, Stahl was suggesting that Carter was the favorite.

Stahl was not alone. According to David Morgan's figures, as late as 1979, even among the Washington reporters who believed that Reagan would be the Republican nominee (a minority of those interviewed), the overwhelming belief was that Carter would beat Reagan.[36] Our point is not that the media guessed badly about Carter's political magic—although they did—but that their perception made it easier to be hard on Carter from start to finish.

Jody Powell is not a disinterested party, but he made the point:

> People covering us . . . would even admit when you talked to them about it, that they were being tougher on the President than the people on Reagan were on him.
>
> They thought in a strange sort of way that they had that leeway since he [Carter] was going to win anyway.

No unidimensional explanation can account for Carter's press in 1980. We think his style, his incumbency, and his behavior melded together in such a way as to invite bad press. But beyond all that, Carter suffered from one more malady. Having come from nowhere in 1976 (and, in the process, having confounded the media), having come from oblivion again in 1979 (having confounded the media once again), the press was not going to be surprised a third time. The press was ready for Jimmy Carter in 1980.

REAGAN: SEPARATE IMAGES IN TV AND PRINT

In early October, the Carter political team began calling around Washington complaining about the "free ride" that Ronald Reagan was getting in the press. According to Jonathan Alter, who analyzed

Reagan's press during the campaign, it was not exactly a free ride: "It was more like half-fare."[37]

Alter's thesis has become part of popular wisdom that "Reagan emerged with his hair in place and teeth gleaming for the camera,"[38] that Reagan was somehow able to get good press in 1980, despite his long standing status as Republican frontrunner.

In fact, that assessment is mostly wrong, at least as far as CBS is concerned. On "Evening News" Reagan received the worst press designation three times in ten months. Excluding "horse race" assessments, 17 percent of Reagan's newstime was bad press; only 3 percent was good press (figure 5–6). One liberal television critic even felt the need to condemn coverage of the GOP nominee as the "Harassment of Ronald Reagan" and subtitled it "TV's Assault on a Candidate, 1980."[39]

Reagan did, however, come through to election day with a smaller press deficit than Carter, 3 points less. And Reagan did something Carter could not do in either medium. He actually wound up with a positive press index on UPI!

What then does Reagan's press tone tell about fairness in the

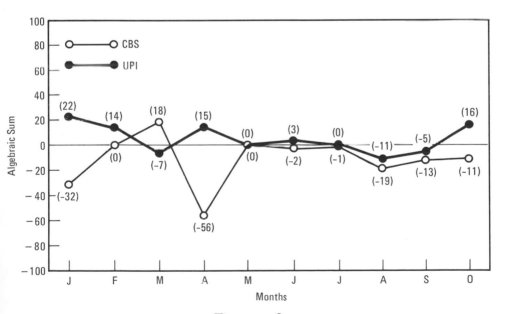

Figure 5–6
Reagan's Month-by-Month Press Index, CBS and UPI (Presidential Campaign Stories Only)

media? First, his press coverage suggests one of our earlier assumptions: that media go a bit easier on challengers than on frontrunners, assuming of course that one considers Reagan the challenger, not the frontrunner. Second, Reagan's less negative press coverage suggests ever so slightly a form of bias we have not yet considered, a bias in which the reporters promote the challenger at the expense of the incumbent, not for reasons of excitement but in order to promote their own professional careers.

In his provocative essay, "Rooting for Reagan," Jonathan Alter claims that Reagan did well at press because the correspondents assigned to him knew that if "their" man won they might well be covering the White House for the next four years. Alter builds a theory around the not too implausible thesis that there were *personal* incentives to be less harsh with Ronald Reagan. Alter's thesis argues that reporters who follow a winning challenger will wind up covering a new President, not get sent back to a boring beat.[40]

Despite its intrinsic appeal, the Alter thesis has its problems. Most of the network reporters covering Reagan did not immediately wind up serving as chief White House correspondent for their network. And the one network reporter who did move quickly from the relative obscurity of general assignment to the White House lawn was Bill Plante of CBS. Yet it was Plante who, as Alter points out, gave Reagan the toughest coverage he was to receive throughout 1980. It was Plante who early in April asked the rhetorical question as to whether Ronald Reagan was too dumb to be president. It was Plante who showed in early October how Reagan had blatantly contradicted himself on welfare, taxation, labor law, the Chrysler bailout, and aid for New York City. If a young reporter were to use 1980 as his or her reference point, Plante's performance in that campaign suggests that it pays to be tougher, not softer, on the front-running challengers.

Alter's thesis also suffers from its original premise. Ronald Reagan did *not* get good press on network television or in prestige print. As far as the networks are concerned, Reagan got nothing approaching a free ride; he only managed to do slightly better than Jimmy Carter.*

*In some instances, the press did seem to be softer on Reagan than it might have been on Carter in comparable circumstances. For example, on October 28, the *Wall Street Journal* broke a story charging that Richard Allen, serving at the time as a Reagan's campaign manager, had peddled influence between the Nixon administration and Japanese business associates. But between the day the story broke and the

Why did Reagan do slightly better than his principal opponent? As usual, reality played a role. We heard over and over again that Reagan simply directed a better campaign.

But reality is almost never the whole story. Lyn Nofziger, Reagan's campaign press secretary, reiterates a theme we have already considered in analyzing Carter—style. When we asked about Reagan's comparative press victory, Nofziger mentioned first Reagan's style: "First of all, Ronald Reagan, whether you like him or not, always comes across as a nice man. Carter does not come across as a nice man. And I think that has to have a subconscious effect over reporters."

Then there was the notion that Reagan had an easy act to follow. One of the great press advantages that Reagan had was not being a poorly regarded incumbent and not having a checkered, national record to defend. Uninterested in reviewing Reagan's record as *governor*, the press simply had less to complain about. It was easier in almost every respect to report Carter's White House critically than to say anything negative or hostile about what Alter called Reagan's "tarmac strategy"—a technique based on a short quip and a good-bye as Reagan climbed the stairs of his campaign plane.

We remained convinced that Reagan's less-than-rotten press needs to be considered in light of his simply not being the incumbent. Obviously, Carter's record as incumbent cannot be dismissed as irrelevant the economy sagged, the Soviets advanced, and the hostages remained in Tehran during the Carter years. But television particularly needs a theme in its campaign reporting and one perennial theme is the manipulative incumbent. Reality notwithstanding, Reagan, as nonincumbent, was less vulnerable to that theme.

---

day of the election, "Evening News," on its weekday programming, gave the scandal only two stories. In its weekday coverage, the wire gave the Allen scandal only one story.

As it turned out, Allen received a very healthy dose of scandal news coverage in November and December of 1981, after the White House admitted that Allen had received a one-thousand-dollar honorarium for an interview he had arranged between Mrs. Reagan and a Japanese magazine. But the pre-election scandal did not take hold the way the Billy Carter story had taken hold throughout 1980, or the way the Hamilton Jordan story had taken hold.

We suspect that the media chose not to cover heavily the original Allen controversy, less out of sympathy for Reagan but out of a sense of fair play. Without the real evidence likely to surface between October 28 and November 3, the media concluded that heavy coverage might have been unfair in a most fundamental procedural way. We also suspect that the press covered the second Allen controversy much more forcefully because he had gotten off the hook in 1980. The press remembered full well what it had and had not done with Allen on the eve of the election.

Content research can never tell us exactly why content was as it was. Reality, style, incumbency, and in Plante's words, "position in the polls," all played a role in Reagan's press "victory." What content research does prove, however, beyond reasonable doubt, is that Ronald Reagan had much better press on UPI than CBS. In fact the bigger story may be not that Reagan slipped by Carter in press image, *but that both did about equally badly on television.* While Reagan had a considerable amount of good press on UPI—comments to the effect that Reagan "enthralled audiences," that he was "a man under control," "relaxed," a man who knew how "to poke fun at himself"—only once, in a commentary by Bill Moyers, did CBS really say anything unambiguously positive about Ronald Reagan.

In its treatment of Ronald Reagan, "Evening News" proved one last time that networks play by different, tougher rules than those associated with traditional print. In short, when it comes to frontrunners and to incumbents, network television makes no presumption of innocence. Unlike traditional print, networks have a presumption which shades perceptibly the other way.

Conclusion: Fairly Fair

It would be ludicrous to conclude that the press in 1980 was basically objective and then conclude that the press was fundamentally unfair. We draw no such conclusion. Using our definition of "fairness," the majority of stories were neutral or in balance. Both CBS and UPI were fairly fair in their treatment of the individual candidates, and of the field.

We did discover that the press treats some candidates "more fairly" than others. Candidates who are personally popular tend to get a slight break, unless they happen to be frontrunners. Challengers, too, enjoy marginally better press. The only other type of candidate to benefit inherently from press seems to be the president-elect. There *was* a honeymoon press for President-elect Reagan but, of course, it ended very quickly, particularly on "Evening News."

As for the disadvantaged, in 1980 frontrunners and the incumbent consistently experienced the least balanced, least favorable new coverage. Being at the head of the pack almost always means lots of access but lots of bad press as well; being the incumbent may almost inevitably mean the toughest press of all.

Remarkably enough, a candidate's press was more easily predicted by his position in the polls than by his party or philosophy. As far as we could determine, a candidate's political ideology had little to do with his press score, at least not over the long haul of a year's campaign. If CBS stumbled a bit with Anderson in the first few months, giving him better press because he was the liberal, CBS more than corrected for its "errors" by late spring. Nobody, not even Anderson, wound up the year with a press advantage predicated on his political point of view.

Finally, we return to that robust difference in tone between the wires and the networks. CBS produced a news image of Carter and Reagan that was almost twenty points lower than that which came over the wire. From start to finish, "Evening News" always covered candidates more critically than UPI. Yet despite conventional wisdom, it was the frontrunners and the incumbent that CBS sought to pummel, not the Republicans or the conservatives, or any other ideological group.

Chapter 6

Seriousness:
More is Less

What's TV news all about? It's about two minutes.

—BRUCE MORTON, CBS NEWS

The national press is entirely concerned with "horse race" and popularity. . . if thermonuclear war broke out today, the lead paragraph in tomorrow's *Washington Post* would be, "In a major defeat for President Carter . . . ."

—FORMER CONGRESSIONAL PRESS
SECRETARY

FORTY years ago in the movie *His Girl Friday,* Cary Grant played the part of a devilish but lovable newspaper editor named Walter Burns, a man out to save his failing newspaper and his failed marriage. Rosalind Russell played Hildy Johnson, Burns's estranged wife and the newspaper's in-house feminist reporter. By accident, Burns and Johnson scoop every other newspaper in town by discovering the whereabouts of an innocent man who has been condemned to die for a murder he had not committed.

It sounds serious, but it was really late 1930s comedy, based on the original Broadway hit *The Front Page.* So it was farce when Burns, both editor and publisher, called his copy desk demanding that they hold page one for him and give him a list of stories he could kill to make room for his scoop. In rapid succession, he kills news items about the "European War," a "Chinese earthquake" with a possible one million dead, and Nazi movement along the Polish corridor. Burns decides, however, to leave in "the story about the rooster. The rooster," says Burns, "is human interest."

So too, four decades later, on CBS "Evening News" in 1980: fowl news—only this time it was news about a turkey instead of a rooster. In fact, "Evening News" had two news stories about a turkey. First came the original, by Lesley Stahl, who described how a wild turkey had somehow found its way onto the White House lawn. Then came the more politically relevant follow up in which CBS tried to get to the bottom of the mystery: how had the wild turkey come to inhabit the White House grounds?

The question for us is not what did the turkey know and when did he know it. The question is, instead, were those two wild turkey stories on CBS typical of network or wire coverage in Campaign '80? Fortunately for us all, the answer is no.

Neither CBS nor UPI presented a continuing stream of in-depth, comprehensive news stories about issues in Campaign '80. Nor did they break their string of consecutive campaigns in which "horse race" news dominated "substance." Nor did they pass up many opportunities to season their political coverage with human interest. CBS not only did a follow up on the turkey item, it also did a report on Carter's first female chauffeur from his Secret Service detail. UPI covered such stories too. Still, as the campaign moved on, and as we reached the last two months, CBS and UPI also provided a sampler of issues and substance, not enough perhaps to satisfy their traditional critics, but enough to meet what has been the traditionally low standard of issue coverage in presidential campaigns.

The "Issue-Issue" in Historical Perspective

Press critics often complain about the limited historical perspective of journalism, especially television journalism. But media critics also lose track of history. For example, consider the issue-issue dispute as to the amount of issue coverage different media offer during national campaigns.

Much of the modern press criticism insinuates that television journalism has been at the root of issueless campaign coverage, if not, in fact, at the root of the issueless campaign. Most media theorists assume that television inherently fails as a serious mass medium. Some of the most distinguished analysts have made the inherency claim. Paul Weaver is one of a dozen major critics of American press who considers television, if not issueless, at least uninformational:

> Finally, television news differs from newspaper news in the vastly greater importance that TV attaches to spectacle. . . . In practical terms, this emphasis on spectacle is revealed in the television news organization's preoccupation with film. . . The emphasis on spectacle tends to make TV journalism superficial in the literal sense of being fixated on the surface sights and sounds of events.[1]

As for campaign news specifically, Thomas E. Patterson, of the Maxwell School at Syracuse University, has probably done more systematic research in this area than anyone else. And, having studied the content of network news or print news or both in the 1972 and 1976 elections, Patterson has complained that network television works against issue coverage in presidential campaigns. At least that was his argument in *The Unseeing Eye,* his first book about television. In that study, Patterson and Robert McClure concluded that "networks downplay election issues," and that "hard issue information is the victim of television journalism's preference for pictures. . . . When the networks report anything about issues. . . the coverage is so fleeting and so superficial that it is almost meaningless."[2]

But in his latest book, Patterson is not quite so certain. In the *Mass Media Election,* a study which compares the three major networks with the two major newsweeklies and with four local newspapers as well, Patterson does not find much evidence to support the premise that network journalism is that much less issue-oriented than print. For example, in their coverage of the presidential debates in 1976, the networks according to Patterson were just as interested in covering the issues raised in the debates as the *Erie Times* and the *Erie News,* the *Los Angeles Times* and the *Los Angeles Herald-Examiner,* and also *Time* and *Newsweek.*[3] Patterson has not exactly retreated from the original position that television news has an innate antipathy for serious issues. Instead, he points out that networks shun policy issues and emphasize "campaign issues," issues which generally "develop from campaign incidents, usually errors in judgment by the candidates."[4]

But before there was Thomas Patterson there was Thomas Jefferson. And even though one generally cites Jefferson for his defense of a free press, Jefferson also helps us understand that issuelessness did not start with television. For Jefferson, it was the weekly newspapers that were inherently worthless as a source of political information. Writing without benefit of content analysis, Jefferson was able to reach the following conclusion as to the issuelessness of press:

> I really look with commiseration over the great body of my fellow citizens who, reading newspapers, live and die in the belief that they have known something of what has been passing in the world in their time.[5]

"The man," lamented Mr. Jefferson, "who never looked into a newspaper is better informed than he who reads them."

For Jefferson it was the six penny press that was issueless and baneful. For de Tocqueville it was the penny press. Writing in the 1830s as the Jacksonian revolution was fundamentally reshaping the contours of American political process, de Tocqueville paused to compare the American newspaper and journalists with their French counterparts:

> In France the space allotted to commercial advertisement is very limited and the news intelligence is not considerable. . . . In America three-quarters of the enormous sheets are filled with advertisements. . . or trivial anecdotes. It is only from time to time that one finds a corner devoted to passionate discussions.[6]

After de Tocqueville comes Walter Lippmann, and then H. L. Mencken, men who regarded daily newsprint as an issueless, superficial medium.

It was not until the advent of radio that communications research found newspapers to be the inherently substantial political medium and radio to be inherently deficient. Paul Lazarsfeld, in his *Radio and the Printed Page*, concluded in 1940 that "because radio has to please a much larger number of consumers than the newspapers without giving the different groups a chance to select the parts of the news that are of most interest to them," radio inevitably seeks "the lowest common denominator through the dramatic and the emotional."[7] Remarkably, Lazarsfeld came to that conclusion after finding that radio provided twice as much international news as local newspapers, something we usually take to indicate seriousness in press.[8]

Lazarsfeld's thesis, coming as it did during the age of radio, makes us wonder about the general quality of criticism as much as the general quality of news. The fact is if one goes back through the history of press criticism, a distinct pattern emerges: the most modern medium is always regarded as the most issueless, the most frivolous—first, print, then daily press, then radio, then television. It is, of course, possible that there is a causal relationship between modernity and superficiality, that the newest news medium inevitably behaves the most superficially. On the other hand, just as plausible is a causal relationship between modernity and criticism, the assumption that the newest medium inevitably attracts the loudest complaints. And with these conflicting interpretations in mind, we try to answer the major questions that, taken together, those interpretations imply.

First, how much issue coverage is there in the national press, in absolute terms, during the course of a modern, year-long presidential campaign? (How serious are the mass media as a whole?) Second, are networks less serious than other forms of national media, in our case, the wires? (Do the media vary much in their commitment to or treatment of the "substance" of the campaign?) Third, have the media become less serious in their concern for issues during the age of television? (Has there been a real decline in substance as campaigns have passed through the age of print and the age of radio?)

At the outset of this research, we had expected to find the answer to each question to have gone badly for the modern mass media, especially television. But the results, particularly the historical comparisons, have forced us at least to consider the notion that the mass media change their emphasis and behavior less than the critics change theirs and that television behaves neither more nor less seriously than other mass media do, or have done.

Issue Coverage in Campaign '80: Absolute Standards

POLICY ISSUES

To most critics, "issues" mean policy issues. Policy issues have come to symbolize seriousness in campaigns. So we start with policy issues. Policy issues involve major questions as to how the government should (or should not) proceed in some area of social life, such as taxation, welfare, foreign relations, and so forth. "Policy issues" separate the parties, or the candidates as to how the government should behave, while "candidate issues" separate candidates as to how they should behave.

Seemingly, the media also accept the notion that policy issues are some sort of romantic ideal in campaign coverage. So, for example, it was an embarrassed Walter Cronkite who led the "Evening News" report on Reagan's ethnic joke about cock fights, Poles, and Italians, with Cronkite making it perfectly clear that he would just as soon have let this item pass:

> It seems that every political campaign at some point gets involved with peripheral matters that excite great attention but have nothing to do with the issues of the campaign.
>
> In New Hampshire, Ronald Reagan finds himself in the center of such a situation because of an ethnic joke he told on the press bus.*

Because reporters and press critics regard policy issue coverage as so important, we have used issue coverage as our first test of seriousness and we have also measured issue coverage in two ways: story by story and sentence by sentence.

The first measure asked is if the story is in plurality an "issue piece" —is most of it about policy issues? But given that most stories meld the "issues" into the day's events, that technique understates policy news to some degree. So we relied on a second method, measuring newsspace devoted to policy issues sentence by sentence. This second method involved culling through each campaign story, line by line, and deciding if the sentence at hand dealt predominantly with: an issue (any disputation about public policy among candidates); a candidate (any information about the person); the "horse race" (any consideration as to winning or losing).†

Some sentences fit into two categories—"horse race" and issues were, on several occasions, blurred together beyond recognition. Some sentences fit all three basic categories; some fit none. But the majority of sentences were fairly easy to classify as one form of news or another.

For both CBS and UPI, the totals for policy issue coverage were not

---

*CBS "Evening News," 18 February 1980.

†We had a fourth category, and it was a large one. We called it "other" and it contained miscellaneous historical information: lists of government activities; news about campaign people other than the candidates; "dead air"; information not about the campaign but which appeared in campaign-related stories.

impressive. On the darker side of the issue-issue, we found that 59 percent of the full-fledged presidential campaign news on CBS failed to contain even one issue sentence. On UPI, 55 percent of the news items made not a single meaningful reference to any one of the ninety-odd policy issues we identified during the course of Campaign '80. Using our less precise measure of general issue coverage, story by story, on CBS, 20 percent of the news items emphasized issues. On UPI, the figure was 18 percent.

The more detailed measure of issue coverage, line-by-line assessment, widens the gap between CBS and UPI ever so slightly. Excluding sentences pertaining neither to "horse race," to issues or to candidates, "Evening News" wound up spending 25 percent of its campaign news time on policy issues. UPI followed at 20 percent (one-fourth versus one-fifth). In toto, considering all stories concerning the campaign between January 1 and November 3, CBS managed to present 331 news minutes of hard news or features concerning public policy, either as candidates addressed the issues or as CBS described them. On UPI, the wire cranked out 355 news feet of policy information in all stories linked to or featuring the campaign.

Admittedly, news minutes and news feet sound like measures that only social scientists would concoct. But the measures take on a more common meaning when we work them through on a day-to-day basis. CBS gave us about 90 seconds a day of policy issue coverage, if we consider all levels of campaign coverage. The wire carried about 15 column inches of policy issues on the average news day. The average news day, in other words, gave over somewhere between 20 and 25 percent of its campaign news coverage to "policy," or as one might say, substance. As a batting average, those percentages are passable. As a quiz score they represent failure.

But there was some substance, and even signs of greater attempts at substance. In 1972, Patterson's big complaint was that issues were never treated as anything other than frosting for stories almost inevitably baked in hoopla or "horse race." But since 1972 all the networks have begun to use extended interviews with the candidates to make their issue coverage less vestigial than before.

The night of October 20, "Evening News" began its week-long candidates-on-the-issues final reports with five lengthy interviews, with Reagan and Carter appearing "together" on split screen answering Cronkite's questions about the issues of the campaign. In this one week, CBS and Cronkite did over 1,800 seconds (30 minutes) of policy reporting, more than any other month, and 10 percent of the entire year's issue news.

Perhaps the most interesting thing about the final set of Cronkite issue interviews (those coming in late October) was their scope—not depth so much, but breadth. In fact, Cronkite's late-in-the-campaign interviews with Carter and Reagan show how self-conscious national media have become about covering "the issues." In one split-screen interview with Reagan and Carter, Cronkite was put in the embarrassing position of having to ask each man about esoteric problems concerning strategic metals—surely one of the year's nonissues. Reading from a questionnaire with which he seemed neither familiar nor pleased, Cronkite asked whether or not either man would use military force to defend: (1) our access to chrome from Zimbabwe and South Africa or (2) our access to tin from Malaysia and Thailand. Having finished the questions on strategic metals, Cronkite, looking sheepish, told Carter, "if your answer is the same to each (metal), if you say it is, we can dismiss this." But despite Cronkite's embarrassment, somebody at CBS News had felt the need to push Carter and Reagan on "issues" as exotic as chrome and tin.

"HORSE RACISM"

Press critics usually complain more about the presence of "horse race" journalism than the absence of issues, perhaps reflecting the greater ease at defining "horse race" than what one means by "issues." But whatever the reason, critics are right: media are "horse racist." They all discriminate in favor of fast-moving news about the game and against nonmoving background stories and issue reports. Almost nobody disputes it; most everybody complains about it. Cronkite regularly bemoans it:

> Well, I was disappointed again this year [1976] in our ability to come to grasp the issues on the daily broadcasts, on the evening news. We say this every four years, and every four years we determine that. . . we're not going to be swept up by the panoply of campaigning and stick to the substance.
>
> And I wonder, maybe, what is possible with daily journalism. Maybe there wasn't any substance to cover but I don't think that's quite true.[9]

To our knowledge, no systematic study of any national medium has ever uncovered a campaign in which the modern press, during the course of an election year, emphasized anything more heavily than it emphasized "horse race." (Despite Patterson's estimates that newspapers in the 1940s gave more space to substance than "horse race," his figures deal only with the months just prior to the election, not the full campaign.[10]) Our study of Campaign '80 proves no exception. At every level, in every phase, during each and every month, CBS and UPI allocated more newsspace to competition between candidates than to any other aspect of the campaign. Compared with time provided for news about policy or news about the candidate per se, "horse race" wins (see figure 6–1). "Horse race" permeates almost everything the press does in covering elections and candidates. We found that in our wire copy and videotape about five of every six campaign stories made some meaningful reference to the competition but, by comparison, well over half of the same stories made no mention of issues.

"Horse Race" Vs. Issues: Some Explanations

Try as hard as they did (in Susan Spencer's words, "we knocked ourselves out to make issues interesting"), neither CBS nor UPI came close to making policy issues as big a story as winning and losing. So, at the risk of asking questions as banal as why candidates make campaign promises, we ask ourselves why did "horse race" news do so well, while policy news did so poorly in Campaign '80, at least in absolute terms?

In fact, the reasons are not all quite so obvious as it at first might seem. Clearly "horse race" news has the advantage of being more interesting to audiences. (Note that Spencer said that they knocked themselves out to make the issues interesting, not necessarily to cover them more fully.) Competition tends to produce interest, and, of course, interest produces audiences. So "horse race" has its greatest advantage in its commercialism.

But there is more to "horse racism" than simple-minded calculus of improved ratings or advertising rates. A large part of the problem is definitional. For a host of reasons, objective journalism has, for a century and a half, defined news as *events*, as happenings. "Horse races" happen; "horse races" are themselves filled with specific actions. Policy issues, on the other hand, do not happen; they merely exist. Substance has no events; issues generally remain static. So policy issues, or substance, have been traditionally defined as outside the orbit of real news.

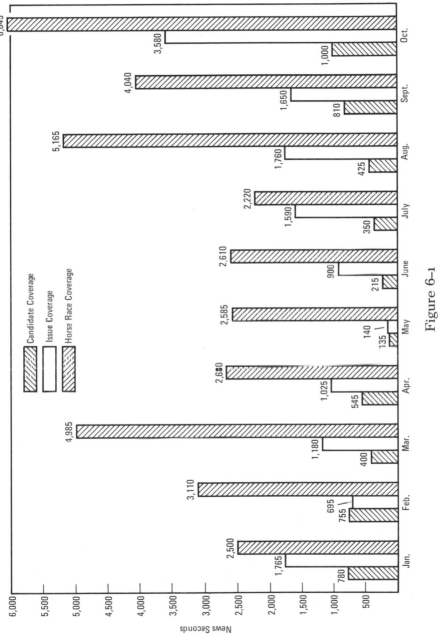

Figure 6-1

News Seconds Devoted to Policy Issues, Candidate Information, and "Horse Race" on "Evening News" (January through October, Presidential Level Stories Only)

Richard Roth spoke not just for CBS or the networks, but for his profession as well, when he offered what he considered the major reason for the inevitable triumph of "horse race" over substance:

> I think there is a feeling that once the issues have been explained or explored they become a reference point. And rather than be repeated . . . they [issues] are used. . . to introduce some other aspect of the story, in which case, the biggest aspect would be the horse race.
>
> [The issues] have long since become non-news for most of us. So you look for something a little different.

Given the definition of hard news especially, substance and issues are written out of the day's top story, unless, of course, the candidate has changed his position on the issues during the course of the campaign day. Given the static nature of issues and policy, a case could easily be made that the media did well to include as much substance as they did in 1980. Most of the substance has to be added on to the day's hard news events, if not as afterthought, then as something on the order of a feature report.

Yet if journalism defines issues as outside the normal definition of newsworthy, candidates often define issues as outside the terms of their own campaign. Candidates, on occasion, would just as soon not talk about issues. Some candidates always prefer homilies; some clearly prefer to discuss the nonissues in their campaign. George Bush in 1980 invented a novel approach to stump speaking—he chose for the first two months of the year to campaign by talking about the campaign. Acting almost like a reporter himself, Bush seemed to relish analyzing the "horse race" and seemed to find boring any discussion of the issues.

But Bush was not the only candidate who made issue coverage a real chore during Campaign '80. Having personally observed Ronald Reagan's September 15 address—an address presented with great fanfare from the steps of the Capitol and dedicated to the principles of Republican party unity—we came away a bit sympathetic to the usual defense offered by campaign reporters who dwell on the "horse race." Some days there are just no issue statements out there to cover.

There are several other factors that encourage "horse racism." We have already considered in chapter 3 the first professional advantage reporters have in covering "horse race" instead of issues: reporters can find several objective measures for evaluating a candidate's standing in the race, yet can find few, if any, objective standards for analyzing a candidate's stands on the issues. But, in fact, the "horse race" has a second professional advantage as well: it gives reporters a chance to measure the candidate by measuring his campaign.

Bruce Morton made the point this way: "I think people vote on what they think of the candidate as a person. And that's partly a defense for doing horse race stories. Candidates don't control very much. . . . What the candidate does have control over is his campaign." In Morton's opinion, campaign stories let the voters know how well the candidate guides the one thing over which he has full authority, his own campaign organization.

Reporters also feel that without the sugar coating that "horse race" news provides, readers would never swallow any of the policy news that is available. John Russonello interviewed several major political correspondents on this "issue"—why so much hoopla and "horse race." And in the words of one nationally prominent print reporter, "the issue coverage must be couched in the horse race coverage in order for it to be read."[11] "Horse racism" is, in part, a promotional technique employed by journalists and their editors.

Finally, the campaign *is* a "horse race," a personal contest. So, in some part as a function of reality, "horse race" coverage becomes the backbone of any campaign news medium, print or television. Academic and professional criticism notwithstanding, for all these reasons, the "horse race" inevitably becomes the major element in coverage of any political campaign.

Comparing Television and Print

ISSUE NEWS

If we use policy issues as the test, CBS actually did more issue coverage than the wire (as we've seen in terms of newsspace about 5 percent more—20 percent vs. 25 percent). That statistic alone makes it hard to defend the conventional wisdom that network television news is inherently less interested than print in issues and substance. What makes the conventional wisdom even harder to defend is that when the types of stories receiving the biggest play in the two media are considered, CBS comes up as more likely to emphasize types of stories which emphasize issues.

During the course of Campaign '80, we identified more than 100 "types" of campaign stories, types which included stories about preference polls, stories about the news media, stories about debates, and so forth. These are *not* topics in the normal sense, but again, types of stories: unemployment is a story topic, but a traditional day's account of the candidate speaking about unemployment while on the stump is a type of news story as well.

When we look at the ten most frequently used story types in Campaign '80, we find that CBS, more than UPI, used types of stories that stress issues (see table 6–1). Three of the top-ten story types on CBS stressed issues—story types involving statements concerning the issues; a candidate's response to President Carter on a particular issue; the issues as treated in the party platforms (see table 6–1). But on UPI two of the top-ten story types focused on issues and substance. The same message comes through when we look at table 6–1 qualitatively. The third most frequently utilized story type on "Evening News" was that involving candidate recitation on the issues, and that type of story actually came close to being number one. But on UPI those candidates-on-the-issues pieces came in a very distant fifth on the list.

This list of top ten story types in the two media also confirms some of the conventional thinking about the more subtle differences between traditional print and network news. Consider first the importance of the charge and countercharge style of journalism that is usually associated with network television, the kind of network reporting Robert Kaiser of the *Washington Post* labels "fluff."[12] On "Evening News," the fifth most frequently occurring type of story was, in fact, the sort in which CBS presented some candidate responding directly to a position taken by President Carter. But on UPI this sort of story, with Carter saying one thing and the opposition responding in kind, never even made the list of top ten.

One other difference that comes through is the much greater reliance by the networks on preference polls. On "Evening News," stories involving preference polls came in ninth as a type of story, but on the day wire, polls failed to make the list. We could interpret this as an indicator that CBS was more "horse racist" than the wire, but it may really indicate nothing more than the fact that CBS News has an in-house polling unit and that UPI has none. Nonetheless, CBS did

TABLE 6–1

TYPES OF STORIES EMPHASIZED BY CBS AND UPI IN PRESIDENTIAL CAMPAIGN REPORTING ("TOP TEN TYPES" ONLY, JANUARY 1 TO NOVEMBER 3, 1980)

CBS		
Top Ten Types	News Seconds	Stories
1. Candidate(s) on the stump	6,905	58
2. Candidate(s) campaign assessment by source	6,655	67
3. Candidate(s) on the issues	6,630	54
4. Candidate(s) campaign strategy	5,085	48
5. Candidate(s) respond to Carter on the issues	2,845	30
6. State/regional analyses (general campaign only)	2,830	14
7. "Open convention" developments	2,065	21
8. Party platform and its issues	1,930	22
9. Nomination preference polls	1,520	23
10. Humor and human interest	1,290	8

UPI		
Top Ten Types	Column Inches	Stories
1. Candidate(s) on the stump	1,591	105
2. Candidate(s) campaign strategy	1,469	92
3. Candidate(s) campaign assessment by source	1,403	79
4. State/regional analyses (general campaign only)	1,358	57
5. Candidate(s) on the issues	825	55
6. Party platform and its issues	628	41
7. Vote returns assessment by source	545	36
8. Nonsource, noncandidate speaking about a candidate	515	40
9. "Open convention" developments	482	27
10. Candidate endorsements	393	34

emphasize polls—part of the new politics; UPI emphasized endorsements—a major part of the politics of yesteryear.

But the big story here remains the relative seriousness of CBS compared with the wire. Both media did go overwhelmingly for the "horse race" types of stories: stories about the proposed Democratic "open convention,"* stories about the political implications of the primary returns in the various states, stories about predictions in the electoral college vote. But CBS went slightly *less* overwhelmingly in that direction.

We had not expected CBS to spend more time on substance. Neither Patterson nor Doris Graber, the two most widely recognized experts in this regard, found television to be more substantial when compared with print. Patterson's comparisons for 1976 showed neither television nor print turning up clearly more substantial. But Graber's research from the 1968, 1972, and 1976 campaigns shows newspapers consistently more interested than television in policy and issue coverage.[13] We have no simple explanation other than pointing to the possible differences in elections or between newspapers and wire. But by 1980, without much question, UPI did not treat the campaign more substantively than "Evening News."

We might make more of this finding were we not somewhat anxious about our own methodology. Having excluded the weekend news, and the night wire too, we cannot claim with complete certainty that CBS did "better" than UPI. But we can claim, with near certainty, that "Evening News" did at least as well. Given all our findings concerning substance and hoopla throughout Campaign '80, we can conclude that, in a cadence borrowed from former President Gerald Ford, there is no network domination of "horse race" news.

"CANDIDATE NEWS"

Policy issues are not the only form that "substance" can take. News and information about the candidate per se (his background, family, staff, and so forth) qualifies as substance in almost anybody's thinking. And, there has been a long-standing assumption that television has an inherent tendency to cover the personal side of the campaign, that the networks make much of the candidates, at least in comparison to print.[14] In reality, this is only a half truth. We found CBS to

*Democrats trying to deny Carter the nomination after the primaries had ended fought to establish an "open convention," one in which delegates would not be bound to vote for the candidate who had won their state's primary or caucus.

be somewhat more crisis oriented in its coverage of the candidates, but not altogether more personal.

If we look at that part of the campaign news which deals directly with the candidate's life, background, personality, family, or character, we come up with almost no coverage of candidates in either medium. According to our calculations, news about the candidate per se accounted for less than 5 percent of total newsspace, on both CBS or UPI. As for what the journalists said explicitly about the presidential candidates, they restricted themselves for the most part to physical descriptions: Carter was ashen gray; Kennedy was jovial. There was virtually no personality assessment going on in either medium, unless it came from one candidate speaking about another.

In a recent study of Washington correspondents, Stephen Hess asked national reporters whether they felt that "personalities journalism" was a serious problem; almost three-quarters said that it was not.[15] By our count, the reporters were completely right. Neither the wires nor the networks did anything that came close to personality reporting, let alone psychojournalism in Campaign '80.

CANDIDATE ISSUES

Not all issues involve policy or background, however. Some of the issues involve personal behavior—Jimmy Carter's alleged meanness was one of the main behavioral issues in Campaign '80. Press critics usually refer to these sorts of issues as campaign issues,[16] implying that Jimmy Carter's meanness is only relevant to one particular campaign. Some campaign issues are so short-lived they last only for a week or two. Chris Arterton calls these issues "press crises"[17]—blunders is the traditional name.

We consider blunders, press crises, and campaign issues to be all of one type, and we call all three "candidate issues"; issues concerning the personal behavior of the candidate during the course of his or her campaign.

Candidate issues, as opposed to candidate background, get considerable coverage in both media, but regardless of the measurements involved, candidate issues always receive considerably more attention on TV. In September and October, for example, we classified each story as either a policy-issue story, a candidate-issue story, or a nonissue story. Policy-issue stories emphasized information about government behavior: what the government should do about inflation, for example. Candidate-issue stories emphasized information about candidate behavior: Carter's refusal to debate Anderson or Reagan's confusion over facts. On "Evening News," stories about candidate issues accounted for 27 percent of the newstime during the last two months of the campaign. On UPI, the figure was 16 percent.

The same thing happens if we look directly at the *topics* covered throughout the campaign. We kept track of the major topic in each story throughout 1980 and, for the most part, topics divided themselves neatly between policy issues and candidate issues. A story about SALT surely implies policy; a story about Billy Carter just as assuredly implies candidate.

During the course of the year, CBS and UPI covered scores of topics from ERA to ABSCAM, from Polish strikes to Billygate, from Tito's funeral to Tim Kraft's resignation. Despite the range, and in part because of it, there was little depth to the coverage. On CBS, only a dozen of the seventy-three topics covered between January and election day produced as many as eight stories. On UPI, only thirteen topics attracted eight or more reports. But by restricting ourselves to the "top twenty" topics, we learned how much attention each medium gave over to candidate issues.

We gave the label "topicless" to campaign stories that had no real topic other than "horse race." On CBS, 53 percent of the campaign news was "topicless"; on UPI, the figure was 51 percent. But if we exclude the topicless news reporting, we come up with the statistics in table 6–2.

Looking at table 6–2 three things stand out. First, as before, both media have considerable interest in candidate issues. Among the year's "top forty" topics (CBS and UPI combined), eighteen topics emphasize candidate issues, almost half the total. Second, topics covered both by CBS and UPI were generally the same in both lists. Even the sequences followed fairly closely. Six of the top ten policy issues on "Evening News" also made the top ten at UPI.

Third, CBS proved again to be more interested in candidate issues. On the wire, eight of the top twenty topics stressed candidate issues; on "Evening News," ten of the top twenty. And CBS had the more personalized candidate issue coverage. While the wire covered lots of speeches about problems in "leadership," CBS was covering the Stealth security breach, and, to a surprising degree, also covering the

156

Carter administration's controversial vote against Israel in the UN Security Council.

CBS was also more interested in the debate-debate—the issues surrounding acceptance and rejection of the various invitations extended by the League of Women Voters to Carter, to Reagan, and to Anderson. Only in the instance of the issue of Chappaquiddick did UPI show a measurably greater concern for a candidate issue than did CBS. As a general rule, "Evening News" proved slightly more interested in candidate issues and candidate blunders.

Have the Media Grown Less Serious?

Perhaps the most intriguing argument Patterson makes in his *Mass Media Election* is that press has grown less serious in the age of television. Patterson points to estimates he made from studies done in the 1940s, but those estimates seem less than directly comparable with his findings from 1976.

We have tried to make direct comparisons between the modern media and the press from Campaign Yesteryear by looking at the same three local newspapers which we have already relied upon in chapter 2. Using the resources at the Library of Congress, we looked back at Campaign '40 and Campaign '60, as they were reported in the *Boston Globe*, the *Columbus Dispatch*, and the *Seattle Times*, and compared that reporting with the reporting of Campaign '80 in those same three papers. And having compared the press coverage across four decades in three newspapers, we also compared that historic coverage with issue coverage on all three networks and both wire services in Campaign '80. Using the same definition of issue coverage throughout, we found no quantitative evidence for Patterson's thesis that the press has grown less issue-oriented over time. If anything, the evidence shades in the other direction: the media seem slightly more "serious" in the 1980s than in the 1940s or the 1960s.

To do these comparisons, we adopted a different method from that used so far. In order to include extra years and extra media, we sampled, taking one day each month for the ten months of each

157

TABLE 6–2

TOPICS EMPHASIZED BY CBS AND UPI IN PRESIDENTIAL CAMPAIGN REPORTING (TOP TWENTY TOPICS ONLY, JANUARY 1 TO NOVEMBER 3, 1980)

CBS			UPI		
Top Twenty Topics	News Seconds	Stories	Top Twenty Topics	Column Inches	Stories
1. Issues concerning general economy	4,075	30	1. Issues concerning general economy	591	36
2. General national defense	1,505	10	2. Hostages as *policy* issue	353	25
3. Anderson, Carter, and Reagan on proposed three-way debate	1,410	12	3. The Equal Rights Amendment or women's issues	344	22
4. Hostages as *policy* issue	1,400	22	4. Anderson, Carter, and Reagan on proposed three-way debate	246	15
5. Inflation	1,390	13	5. General national defense	222	14
6. Carter, Reagan one-on-one debate	1,220	15	6. Chappaquiddick	218	11
7. Race relations	1,200	8	7. Carter, Reagan one-on-one debate	197	14
8. Taxation	990	10	8. Reagan's confusion over China policy	179	11
9. U.S. vote against Israel in U.N. Security Council	895	9	9. Hostages as *candidate* issue	169	10

10.	Hostages as *candidate* issue	740	8	10.	Taxation	133	9
11.	The Equal Rights Amendment or women's issues	685	8	10.	Issues concerning leadership	133	7
12.	Reagan's confusion over China policy	610	5	12.	Grain embargo	127	8
13.	Security breach over development of Stealth bomber	590	6	13.	Race relations	124	8
14.	General social welfare programs	465	2	14.	Problems with big government	111	6
15.	Carter's charge that Reagan was running racist campaign	445	4	15.	Public funding of the arts and letters	110	6
16.	Domestic energy supplies	420	4	16.	Labor	106	8
17.	Chappaquiddick	385	4	17.	Domestic energy supplies	92	6
18.	Howard Baker's controversial TV campaign ad	370	2	18.	Carter's warmongering charge against Reagan	90	5
19.	Reagan's slur against Tuscumbia, Alabama, as home of the Ku Klux Klan	335	4	19.	Reagan's slur against Tuscumbia, Alabama, as home of the Ku Klux Klan	82	5
20.	Unemployment	325	3	20.	Abortion	71	5

campaign year (January through October). In essence, we selected the same ten dates for Campaign '40, Campaign '60, and Campaign '80, and then analyzed the coverage for each of those thirty days. For the ten days in Campaign '80, however, we expanded the search and included in our sample ABC, NBC, and the Associated Press coverage as well.

For each medium in each year we computed the percentage of campaign stories that were about policy—that were issue-oriented.* In figure 6–2, we present those percentages for each campaign and break Campaign '80 coverage down into its three major components: local press (the *Boston Globe, Columbus Dispatch,* and *Seattle Times*); the wires (AP and UPI); and the networks (ABC, CBS, and NBC).

Concerning the print during the last four decades, we find almost mind-numbing stability. In Campaign '40 in the local press the ratio of "horse race" to policy was five to one; in Campaign '60 the ratio was five to one; in Campaign '80 the ratio was five to one. To be sure, there was much more campaign news of all kinds in 1980 than 1940 —on the order of double! But in these three papers at least the press was almost precisely as uninterested in policy then as now (figure 6–2).

Just as interesting is the comparison among media in 1980. The wire was a trace more interested than the locals in policy news, but the percentages are close enough to render these differences meaningless. Even with the prestigious *Boston Globe* included, it appears as if traditional print is traditional print is traditional print. Somewhat unexpectedly the networks turned up most issue-oriented of all the media, at least on these ten days in this campaign by a percentage point or two. Of course, these percentages also prove one more time how "horse racist" all the mass media are, and have historically been. But these findings also fly directly in the face of the premise that we have been regressing in terms of seriousness. If anything, the media have made a little progress, if one insists on defining issue coverage as a step in the right direction.

Qualitatively the same things hold true. Local news coverage of Campaign '40 included, among other banalities, personal letters from grammar school kids to FDR asking him to please run again.

---

*In these comparisons we compute percentages only for those stories which were in the main "horse race" or issue stories, excluding stories about candidate background, etc, or "other" stories, miscellaneous sorts of reports. "Horse race" and issue stories represent the overwhelming majority of all stories in each election.

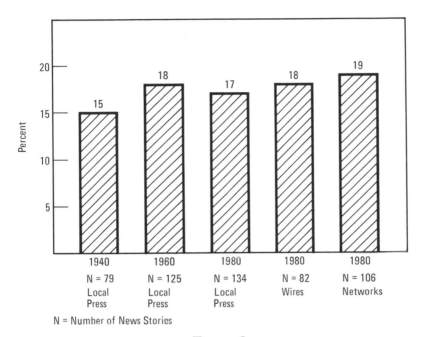

Figure 6–2

Percentage of News Stories Dealing With Policy Issues in Three Local Newspapers (1940, 1960 and 1980), the Two Major Wires (1980), and the Three Networks (1980), "Horse Race" and Policy Issue Stories Only, January through October

Nor did the less-than-serious "candidate issues" begin with television journalism. In 1940, the biggest "issue" of the campaign, at least in the press, was not the war in Europe or the lingering depression. It was Roosevelt's decision to seek an unprecedented third term.

In 1960, the big issue in the days sampled was the issue over Quemoy-Matsu, two insignificant islands off the coast of China— then, of course, Red China. The issue was whether the United States should defend the islands against the Chinese by force. But because Richard Nixon and John Kennedy had somehow managed to square-off on the topic of Quemoy-Matsu during one of their televised debates, it became a major concern in the press. In so many ways, the 1960 press debate over Quemoy-Matsu shows how much the press has not changed in several decades. The press made about as much of this as it did over Gerald Ford's statement declaring a free Poland in Campaign '76. And in neither case was the issue much more than a media event—a press by-product of a nationally televised debate.

In short, the last forty years of campaign coverage does nothing for the theory that the media or the local press have become less serious in the age of television. We did find that the hard news seemed much less critical of authority in Campaign Yesteryear, but it was certainly no less trivial than in Campaign '80.

Conclusions

Walter Cronkite has on occasion apologized for television news, saying it is basically a headline service. He is wrong. "Evening News" was more than a headline service in Campaign '80.

Following Campaign '80 over the wire or on television, a voter would have learned at least something about a candidate's style, something about his background. A voter would have learned more about candidate blunders and problems however, especially if the voter had been following on television. Voters would have learned most about who was ahead, who was behind. But voters would also have learned something about issues. Issues were covered the way Cliff Notes might handle them in an introductory course on public policy—Candidate X says this; Candidate Y says that; Candidate X says Candidate Y is wrong about that. But if policy issues are the test of seriousness, both CBS and UPI passed in Campaign '80, if with very mediocre marks.

We refuse to line up with the purists or the lunatic fringe of media critics, people like R. Emmett Tyrrell, who calls network news "always factless and fanciful," nothing more than "euphonious blathering" from "TV wisenheimers like 'Dr. Cronkite,' et al."[18] "Evening News" invested about 25 percent of its campaign newsspace to issues; most of it factual, little of it fanciful.

But with so low an absolute percentage in policy news, why not line up with critics like Tyrrell; why not fail the media, particularly the networks? Part of our reluctance stems from our earlier observation that issues get considerable coverage outside the campaign news. When Jimmy Carter, as president, announced a grain embargo, that was policy news, even though the announcement may not have been covered in Campaign '80 news reports. Campaign news is not the only place "the issues" are covered, nor is it the only place that issue coverage should count.

We have a second reason for refusing to condemn press coverage outright. Using newspapers as our guide, we found print coverage of campaigns overall went up by more than 75 percent between 1940 and 1980. For every four stories we found in Campaign '40, we found seven in Campaign '80. And despite impressions to the contrary, stories are longer now than they were then. In absolute terms then, the amount of issue coverage has gone up dramatically over the last four decades—a fact most modern press critics seem willing to forget. It is true that the substance is every bit as invisible in proportion now as then, but as far as the print media are concerned, the base has expanded to a point we had not anticipated.

But what about the networks? We went back to CBS and sifted through their files from 1960. No videotape then. And, because reporters and producers have been rifling their own film files for documentaries and such, there is practically nothing left from Campaign '60 as it appeared on the "Evening News." But the trace evidence indicates that in Campaign '60 it was not just the issues that seemed invisible, it was virtually the entire campaign. Compared with 1980 we found almost nothing in the way of campaign coverage from the 1960 Kennedy-Nixon election. Part of that stems from the short broadcast used by all three networks at the time (the now quaint 15-minute evening news show). But the fact is networks did not do much campaign reporting twenty years ago. In fact, network campaign journalism barely existed twenty years ago. So if absolute standards are to be invoked, CBS News, like the print press, has grown more serious, using 1960 television, or we imagine, 1940 radio as the point of comparison.

We offer one final reason for seeming to go easy on the media, networks particularly, in their most obvious weakness. The networks are right—seriousness does not sell. Complaining about the issuelessness of the media, without considering the issuelessness of the audience, is to beat a dead horse, if not a dead "horse race." The usual ratings for the most serious news programs almost always prove the point.

Consider, for example, the morning news programs on network television. Unlike the evening news programs, which are so similar in almost every respect, the morning programs differ in several ways; for example, in their commitment to seriousness. ABC's "Good

Morning America" has generally been regarded by critics as the lightest of the three. NBC's "Today" has been considered the middle program, and CBS's "Morning" has usually been seen as the hardest —the news show for news junkies.[19]

For the most part these critical perceptions hold. We studied two weeks worth of all three programs during the last phases of the campaign, dividing news time into three separate categories: general political news, hostage crisis news, light information/entertainment. CBS's "Morning" presented the highest percentage of substance (64 percent). ABC's "Good Morning America" presented the least (41 percent). NBC's "Today" wound up in the middle with 60 percent.

Nielsen ratings for these three programs run the opposite direction: "Good Morning America" came in first in 1980 with an audience "share" of 29; NBC's "Today" stood at 27; and CBS's "Morning" came in a distant third with a 17 percent share of the early news audience. This ranking in the Nielsens in 1980 was not a simple function of personality, at least not at the level of anchorman. In terms of ratings, Charles Kuralt, who anchored "Morning" in 1980, actually has done better than Dan Rather when subanchoring the "Evening News."* Until CBS chose in 1982 to make the program softer, "Morning" was perhaps the best evidence for believing that seriousness in news programming does not sell and that networks probably cover politics and campaigns more seriously than the audience would prefer. We are *not* suggesting that networks should follow the lead of public response and become less serious in their campaign reporting. We suggest only that, given the audience, any improvement whatever in coverage, compared with other media or with earlier campaigns, is improvement indeed.

We have our list of quarrels with all commercial news media, television news among them. But in fact, most of our complaints are only partially related to content. Salaries for network "talent" (the name used for on-camera reporters) are, by any criterion other than market forces, indefensible. Before receiving his own million dollar plus salary, Dan Rather complained that million dollar contracts had begun to jeopardize the integrity of network news.[20] Yet if rumors concerning his contract are accurate, Dan Rather will be an eight million dollar man between 1981 and 1986.[21] From Cronkite on down,

*In 1982, Charles Kuralt was replaced as anchorman by Bill Kurtis.

almost nobody at the networks even tries to defend greater-than-Hollywood-size paychecks as appropriate to journalism.*

If network salaries are lamentable, the ads for television news are worse. News ads in Campaign '80 were little more than hucksterism, and sometimes contradicted the news itself. CBS ads for the nominating conventions were promising excitement and thrills while the news reporters were predicting (wrongly, as it turned out) mass boredom and nothing more than a media event. In Campaign '72, NBC produced perhaps the worst news ad ever: a short spot saying that NBC News was "All You Need to Know." Even if the decisions about news commercials fall outside the news divisions, the themes and claims of the campaign news ads demean the news organizations and personnel in whose name they appear.

Network news also falls victim on occasion to its own immediacy —its own "live" broadcasting. And that is especially so during campaign news specials and special events. One of the lows in Campaign '80 came on July 16 at the Republican National Convention when Ronald Reagan and Gerald Ford agreed that Ford would not be the vice-presidential nominee, despite what the networks were predicting. Network reporters who had been claiming that Ford would be selected fell all over themselves to be the first to announce that George Bush would be the nominee, now that Ford was out.†

As the Republican Convention coverage implies, the networks on occasion are worse than unserious, they become irresponsible. Not surprisingly, the irresponsibility almost always involves "horse race" coverage, not issues or personalities. The toughest complaints in Campaign '80 were hurled against ABC News for its "surprise" phone-in poll conducted immediately after the Carter-Reagan debate. The poll, done by Louis Harris, was, as ABC said, "unscientific," but ABC did not say it was inherently biased in favor of Reagan in its construction.‡

*When asked whether any newsman is worth eight million dollars over five years, a reference to Rather's contract with CBS, Cronkite responded, "Compared to a rock and roll singer, yes. Compared to a teacher, no."[22]

†On this occasion, CBS has been singled out for the harshest criticism because it treated Ford's nomination as a certainty with no real confirmation. In covering the illusory dream ticket of Reagan and Ford, says media critic Frank Greve, CBS was "first and wrong."[23] Even CBS News producer Don Hewitt admits that his network was used by Jerry Ford.[24] But a week later, CBS ran a full-page ad in the *Washington Post* about its own performance in covering the dream ticket: "On top of the story. Just where you'd expect us to be." Jeff Greenfield, media critic at CBS, found both the ad and the entire affair to be among the year's worst moments for CBS.[25]

‡The entire print press responded hostilely to ABC's surprise poll. And one colum-

And the list goes on for all the networks, and all the media: loaded questions; sensationalism through quotation; shouts at candidates by journalists on the campaign trail; the intrusive microphone shoved indelicately into the newsmaker's face or car. Anyone who reads this chapter as a blanket endorsement of network news coverage of presidential campaigns is skimming.

But networks deserve an objective evaluation as to overall seriousness. And when the issue is issue coverage, the networks did as well, if not better, than the wires, and even a trace better than history.* Slightly more personal in their coverage of candidates, and slightly more aggressive in the coverage of blunders and gaffes, the networks behaved as we had supposed. But when it came to issues per se, the networks behaved more seriously than we had expected or had been led to believe.

---

nist, himself sympathetic to Reagan, spoke in negative superlatives: "ABC may have set an all-time record for putting its financial interests in trying to be entertaining far above any responsibility to serve the process." "ABC should be forced to put on all its news shows in the future a disclaimer that reads, 'This network is no longer in the news business but only seeks to use the news as a possible source of entertainment.' "[26]

*We do have figures for ABC and NBC (at least for our ten-day comparison sample). All three networks were approximately equal in seriousness.

Chapter 7

Comprehensiveness: "Losing" the Vice-Presidency and the Congress

---

It was a slow newsday in Washington—so slow, that Vice President George Bush made news.

—ROGER MUDD, NBC "NIGHTLY NEWS"

A comprehensive press covers more than presidential elections. There are other political maps besides the electoral college score board. But how comprehensive were the networks and wires in Campaign '80? How broad was their scope? Not surprisingly, coverage of every level of politics other than the presidency was in a very limited supply. In its rush to cover every blunder and event in the Presidential contest, the press virtually lost sight of all the other campaigns.

"Losing" the Vice-Presidency

It has been five decades since John Nance Garner said the vice-presidency wasn't worth a bucket of warm spit. If media coverage is any indicator, today's vice-presidency is worth about half that much. Even Garner might be surprised to see how unnewsworthy vice-presidential politics are in modern presidential campaigns. Although four of the last six vice-presidents have become president, (two in midcourse), the national press consistently ignores the vice-presidential ticket-holders, once they have been selected. On CBS, there was twenty-seven times as much presidential campaign news as vice-presidential in 1980. On UPI, the ratio was even higher, thirty-five to one (figure 7–1).

Even these ratios overstate the amount of attention given the actual vice-presidential nominees. The overwhelming majority of the vice-presidential coverage in 1980 centered on who would be nominated, not the nominees. On UPI during the general campaign (September, October and November), Walter Mondale was the featured candidate in a grand total of one story. George Bush was featured in two. Patrick Lucey, Anderson's running mate, was not featured. On CBS, Lucey and Bush each had one story about them throughout the general campaign. Mondale got shut out.

Recent history and Doris Graber's research tell us that even in 1968 and 1972 (with Spiro Agnew to kick around), vice-presidents were the invisible men of campaign news.[1] In 1972 Thomas Eagleton got more coverage for quitting the vice-presidential race under pressure than Sargent Shriver got for running in it.* We did get something on potential vice-presidents in Campaign '76, but that was a function of the Dole-Mondale debate, a debate acrimonious enough to penetrate the news agendas of the major media. But in 1980, without a vice-presidential debate and with most of the press interest having been expended at the Republican convention over the possibility of a Reagan-Ford ticket, the vice-presidential campaign became a non-event.

Some members of the press used the missing vice-presidential press coverage as a press "issue" on which they, in turn, could peg

---

*According to the Vanderbilt TV News *Index and Abstracts,* Eagleton received 168 references during the general campaign on evening news programs in 1972; Shriver was referenced 165 times.

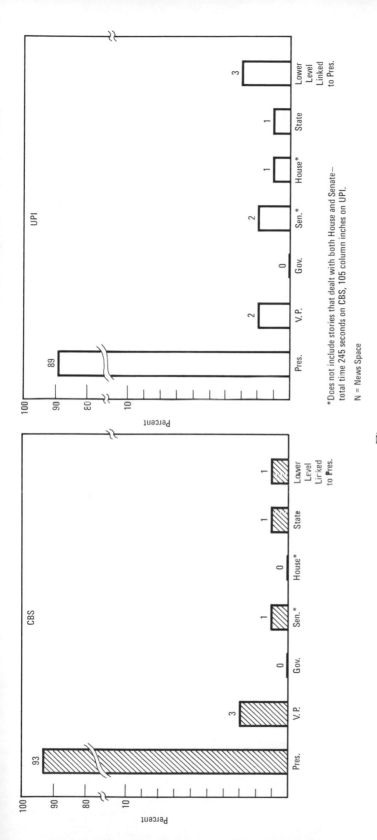

Figure 7–1

Newsspace Devoted to Presidential, Vice-Presidential, Gubernatorial, Senatorial, Congressional, and Local Elections, CBS and UPI

vice-presidential stories. The *Washington Post*'s David Broder, chastising his colleagues for ignoring the vice-presidency, called the Bush entourage and the Mondale entourage two of "the best kept secrets of the campaign."[2] According to Richard Roth, the CBS reporter assigned to Bush, the Bush campaign was known as "Stealth"—invisible to editors and the public.

Whose fault was it that the "blessed realms" of the vice-presidential campaign, as Broder called them, got practically no press? The answer has three parts: one part Republican, one part Democratic, one part journalistic. As for the Republican role, Roth at CBS says that the Republicans wanted very much to keep Bush's visibility in the media as low as they possibly could. Roth told us that Bush's minimal press was "partly a demonstration of the success of the campaign as Bush and his people determined it was going to be run. They were determined not to make news and they didn't." Campaign '80 was one of the very few instances in which a candidate campaigned outside the White House but tried to do nothing newsworthy, the assumption being that press would only want to catch Bush contradicting Reagan or contradicting himself. It was a Republican press strategy to highlight Ronald Reagan and to hide George Bush.

On the Democratic side, things were different. From the beginning of the year, Mondale had been complaining about his inability to make the evening news. (He did not bother to mention the fact that the wires covered him even less.) It was his frustration with the networks' not putting him on television that led to Mondale's remarkable assertion that time on the networks was more important than the veto power.

But Mondale's frustration involved more than ego. As one of Carter's chief campaign aides told us after the election, the strategy in the general campaign was built around Mondale's access to television. Mondale's job was to go out and make Reagan the issue by blasting away at Reagan's record and his unsuitability as commander-in-chief. But Mondale faced, as our data show, something on the order of a news blackout on CBS "Evening News" and the rest of the networks as well.

Based on our interviews about strategy and our findings about news content, the vice-presidential news "blackout" conjures up one of the most novel interpretations yet for the outcome of the campaign, an interpretation suggested by Pat Caddell, Carter's own poll-ster. Bush was, by all accounts, refusing to do anything newsworthy. Meanwhile, the networks were aiding the Republican strategy by not covering Bush at all. Not covering Bush meant not covering Mondale either. "Fairness," plus general lack of interest in vice-presidential campaigns meant that if Bush was not covered, Mondale would also have to be ignored. Under those conditions, only Carter could attack Reagan personally and get the message out on national television. So Carter did what he had to do, serve as his own vice-presidential running mate, his own point man. But Carter's attack on Reagan went too far and, as a consequence, Carter's meanness, not Reagan's unpredictability became the candidate issue of the campaign. In the end, Carter, caught in a media-made trap, undercut the two most important elements of his basic strategy: to appear "presidential," and to have Mondale out on the trail labeling Reagan a warmonger, racist, radical, and so on.

This is the stuff of political science fiction—Marshall McLuhan meets the *Manchurian Candidate*. And, although popular among some of the Carter campaign aides, we have serious doubts about this theory, or at least about its actual electoral impact. What we do not doubt is that all the national media deserve some criticism for ignoring the vice-presidential campaign, not to mention the vice-presidency, in Campaign '80. Richard Roth speaks for most of the reporters who got stuck on the vice-presidential campaign planes:

> We offered it, they (editors) didn't want it. It was a real frustration. I had felt several times during the campaign that CBS News, for purposes of the record, should have run stories they didn't run. But just as in so many other instances, on and off campaigns, there's a time constraint.

In the end, nothing that CBS and UPI did during this campaign struck us as quite so sorry as the news blackout each of them (and all the media) inadvertently imposed on Bush and Mondale. The press knew that if he were elected, Reagan would be seventy in his first year in office, the oldest president-elect in history. Media knew too that Carter had a special relationship with Mondale and that Mondale had been an important force in the White House during Carter's four-year term. Both vice-presidential nominees were newsworthy in their special circumstance in Campaign '80, but neither made the news.

Recent events in the United States indicate that vice-presidents do become president, sometimes very quickly. Vice-President Bush nearly became America's second "quickest" president after the attempt on Reagan's life in March 1981.* Given the amount of fluff that existed in both campaign news agendas, television and print, the news vacuum about the vice-presidential candidates struck us as the year's most lamentable noncampaign story.

State Elections: Where Have All the Governors Gone?

It comes as no surprise to find that national media emphasize national politics. What might be more surprising is how much media "nationalize" the news. "Local" campaigns even at the senatorial level make national news only when these stories can be directly pegged to the presidency; or to curiosity candidates; or to high visibility "politicians" such as Goldwater or McGovern, men who have themselves been defeated for president. The only other conditions rendering local campaigns meaningful to national media involve new national trends in politics. National media work so hard at nationalizing their news copy that CBS and UPI each spent about half as much newsspace on local (city, state, county) elections that were directly "linked" to the presidential race than to all the congressional campaigns, House and Senate combined (figure 7–1).

As for those non-presidential elections which could not somehow be pegged to the presidency, figure 7–1 makes four things clear: first, governor's races have less newsworthiness than rain in Seattle or blue sky in Santa Barbara. In mid-October, Jack Germond and Jules Witcover of the *Washington Star* complained that in Campaign '80, the governors' races were invisible. Germond and Witcover were almost literally accurate in that complaint.[3] All told, gubernatorial campaigns were featured in four stories on CBS and UPI combined, a figure which rounds to 0 percent of the campaign newshole. In the ten months leading up to election day, CBS "Evening News" pre-

*Only John Tyler would have succeeded to the presidency more quickly. Tyler replaced William Harrison within a month after Harrison's inauguration.

sented one gubernatorial campaign story, and it was just under 10 seconds in length.

Second, congressional campaigns are practically invisible too. The House and Senate combined accounted for about 2 percent of the total newstime on CBS. On the wire, which has an alleged tradition of being interested in the Hill, tradition does not seem to hold up very well. Although UPI had twice as much congressional news as did CBS, that still meant less than 4 percent of the column inches in the period from September through November 3.

Third, networks treat the Senate as more newsworthy than the House. On "Evening News," using news seconds as a measure, the Senate campaign attracted more than twice as much newstime as the House campaigns. On the wire, the ratio was less than three to two. As expected, network news has a more senatorial cast, and casting, than print. The Senate, despite recent inroads by the House, still has more appeal for television, although by absolute standards precious little appeal exists for either chamber.

Fourth, the numbers prove that network television has even a greater affinity for "national" politics than does the wire. Adding together the newsspace on CBS given over to the presidential and vice-presidential campaign, the time spent comes close to 97 percent of the total. For the wire, the total for the national ticket is "only" 91 percent. This difference may not appear great, but it actually understates the special affinity for presidential news in network journalism. Added together, the presidency and presidential campaign news consumed twice as much of the total newsspace on CBS as the UPI wire, a phenomenon we examine in much greater detail in chapter 8.

One thing not shown in these figures is the qualitative angle in nationalizing local campaigns. Much of the coverage of the House campaigns focused on the ABSCAM candidates, those members who had been indicted or subsequently convicted for accepting bribe money from FBI agents posing as wealthy Arabs. And in the Senate, the campaign coverage was generally linked to the National Conservative Political Action Committee (NCPAC). Scandals and incipient political trends make congressional elections newsworthy in their own right, in print or on television. The only other things that seemed to help were if the congressional candidate happened to have been a Nazi, a radical, a homosexual, or a member of the Ku Klux Klan.

State Primaries in National Media: Media Federalism

With their compulsion to deal in national presidential politics, national media may not do much for the principle of localism. Cable may change things, but network radio and network television have for fifty years between them, been turning news attention toward Washington. But if governors, senators, congressmen, and mayors have been losing out in the era of national media, the states themselves have been resurrected as a major focus for concern. Primaries and television have produced a new "new federalism" (the politics of states are back) every Tuesday night during the presidential primary campaign.

States completely dominate the news in the first six months of the year. Precisely half the campaign news in 1980 came between the first week in January and the first week in June, and the overwhelming majority of that news was pegged to states. National media cover primaries so heavily that primary coverage has become a "primary" issue.[4] Most of the controversy has until recently centered on coverage of New Hampshire, a state which in 1980 ranked forty-second in population but which has ranked first in news media attention during the primaries for the last thirty years. The case against over-coverage of New Hampshire reads on and on: the state is too small; too unrepresentative; too much controlled by one reactionary publisher;* too personalized; too early. We have offered most of the same complaints ourselves at one point or another.[5]

Intrigued by the entire question of "state supremacy" in press coverage, we looked to see how New Hampshire and the rest of the states had done in attracting media during Campaign '80 and to see whether or not print and television handled the states differently.

NEW HAMPSHIRE PREVAILS

On January 18, Walter Cronkite announced that the Granite State had lost its news preeminence, declaring that "Iowa has replaced New Hampshire as the place we start the elimination process of choosing our next president." But some news values die hard, and when the candidates had finally finished the primary season the first

*William Loeb, publisher of the Manchester *Union-Leader* died in 1981, which will leave, as we look to the future, a vacuum in press power in New Hampshire.

week in June, New Hampshire was still on top, although barely, as the number one media state.

Table 7–1 presents the relative newsspace given the twenty-five most frequently covered states in the period from January through June. And as of 1980, New Hampshire still comes out first, at least in numbers of stories (thirty-one for New Hampshire, nineteen for Iowa). In actuality, Iowa came out ahead in newstime on "Evening News" because CBS went to great lengths explaining the Iowa caucuses to viewers. But in stories New Hampshire still very much dominated. On the wire, the New Hampshire primary received 100 more column inches of newsspace than the Iowa caucuses, and 8 more news stories as well. As usual, the wire moved less quickly than CBS in shifting "historical" news priorities. On UPI, New Hampshire totally dominated Iowa as a news story. CBS, the more volatile news organization, shifted somewhat more quickly in the direction of the caucuses. This is not to demean Iowa as a media success story. In 1972, the Iowa caucuses merited only three items on "Evening News"; in 1976, half a dozen; in 1980, a score. But it was still New Hampshire first for news coverage in Campaign '80. And remarkable as it seems, it was still the New Hampshire returns which "predicted" the two nominees.

Compared with 1976, media did not do less New Hampshire reporting in Campaign '80. They merely did more of everything else, thus expanding the primary newshole. Primary coverage generally expands, rarely contracts. Once a primary or caucus has made its mark in political or media history, it tends to hold on. States like Oregon and California, usually coming too late in the primary campaign to matter in the selection of the nominees, still get covered, although the California stories in Campaign '80 were usually about the declining importance of the later primary states. Despite their own self-doubts about going overboard on primaries, media did as much or more reporting about almost all the caucuses and primaries in 1980 than in 1976. Old primaries never seem to die in the press. They rarely fade away.

Nor did the basic law of primary politics for candidates and media change in 1980. It is still true that those states, and victories, which come first do the best and mean the most. Iowa and New Hampshire on average attracted seventy-four news stories per election on "Evening News" and the day wire combined. The nine states holding their primaries in June averaged fewer than six stories on CBS and

175

TABLE 7–1(a)
PERCENTAGE OF STORIES GIVEN OVER TO STATE PRIMARIES AND CAUCUSES, CBS AND UPI
RELATIVE NEWS ATTENTION GIVEN EACH STATE BY CBS, JANUARY 1 TO JUNE 6

	CBS		
State	News Seconds	Percentage of Total	Number of Stories
1. Iowa	2,940	14	19
2. New Hampshire	2,815	14	31
3. Illinois	2,000	10	20
4. Pennsylvania	1,950	9	18
5. New York	1,515	7	19
6. Massachusetts	1,450	7	15
7. California	1,205	6	9
8. Wisconsin	1,165	6	15
9. Ohio	915	4	8
10. Maine	795	4	7
11. Florida	700	3	7
12. South Carolina	470	2	6
13. Connecticut	395	2	5
14. Texas	345	2	5
15. Oregon	290	1	2
16. Michigan	225	1	4
17. District of Columbia	215	1	2
18. Puerto Rico	175	1	3
19. Minnesota	160	1	2
20. New Jersey	145	1	4
21. Indiana	125	1	3
22. Vermont	105	1	4
23. Alabama	105	1	2
24. Nebraska	95	—	1
25. Louisiana	90	—	2
26. Kentucky	85	—	1
27. New Mexico	65	—	1
28. Arkansas	55	—	2
29. Maryland	50	—	1
30. Alaska	35	—	1
30. Mississippi	35	—	2
30. South Dakota	35	—	1
33. North Dakota	25	—	1
34. Colorado	20	—	1
34. Idaho	20	—	1
36. Georgia	15	—	1
36. Kansas	15	—	1

TABLE 7-1b
RELATIVE NEWS ATTENTION GIVEN EACH STATE BY UPI, JANUARY 1 TO JUNE 6

State	Column Inches	Percentage of Total	Number of of Stories
1. New Hampshire	774	15%	53
2. Iowa	679	13	45
3. Pennsylvania	366	7	25
4. Illinois	349	7	26
5. Michigan	342	7	20
6. New York	307	6	21
7. Wisconsin	271	5	20
8. California	183	4	11
9. South Carolina	172	3	11
10. Massachusetts	160	3	12
11. Maine	136	3	10
12. District of Columbia	125	2	8
13. Connecticut	123	2	7
14. Texas	119	2	7
15. Maryland	108	2	7
16. Ohio	105	2	8
16. Florida	105	2	7
18. Puerto Rico	94	2	7
19. Kansas	67	1	4
20. Oregon	60	1	4
21. Indiana	54	1	4
22. Vermont	53	1	3
23. Kentucky	51	1	4
24. North Carolina	46	1	4
25. Oklahoma	43	1	3
26. Nebraska	30	1	2
26. Arizona	30	1	2
28. Nevada	29	1	2
29. Arkansas	24	—	3
30. Minnesota	19	—	1
31. New Jersey	17	—	1
32. Alabama	16	—	1
32. Delaware	16	—	1
34. Alaska	12	—	1
34. North Dakota	12	—	1
36. Tennessee	11	—	1
37. Democrats Abroad	10	—	1
38. Louisiana	9	—	1
39. Virginia	5	—	1
40. Idaho	4	—	1
41. New Mexico	2	—	1
42. South Dakota	1	—	1
42. Montana	1	—	1

UPI. Iowa caucus voters got sixty times as much news attention per vote as people casting their ballot in the late California primary. Presidential politics and campaign media are *frontloaded* and grow increasingly more so with each passing election.

Frontloading is to election coverage what strategic arms deployment is to national defense. Both are inexorable and understandable, given the reality both of campaigns and of nuclear weapons. What makes the analogy especially powerful is that news people, like policy makers, wish it were not so. Every network and every major newspaper (CBS and UPI included) did a piece about the dubious practice of frontloading. But candidates in Campaign '80 frontloaded too. Reagan had spent about two-thirds of his federally allowed funding for the entire primary period by the end of February. Back in 1976, we saw frontloading as something media did to candidates and to politics.[6] But given what we saw in Campaign '80 in the press and in the campaign, we have changed our minds. Frontloading is something media and politicians do to themselves and to each other.

TELEVISION VS. PRINT

Contrary to expectations, the networks did not have a different set of news standards in handling state politics. For all practical purposes, "Evening News" and the day wire covered the same states and in very much the same way. In only three instances out of a possible fifty state comparison did the difference in newsspace between UPI and CBS go higher than 2 percent. New Hampshire and Iowa, the two most heavily covered states, got almost identical treatment over the wire and on TV (table 7–1). Overall, the wire and the networks constructed very similar "maps" for the primary campaign, covering almost all the states in much the same way.*

STATES AND NEWS SCOPE

Does coverage of the primaries tell us anything about comprehensiveness of news? For one thing, it shows how comprehensive media can be when covering the presidential "horse race." CBS and UPI

---

*We had expected that CBS would spend more time in comparison with UPI on primary states as opposed to caucus or convention states. But despite the fact that the networks had in 1976 gone more heavily with the more democratic procedure (primaries being more directly democratic than caucuses), that was not the case in 1980. As difficult to cover and as elitist as they may be, the Iowa caucuses did as well on network television as on the day wire.

had campaign news stories featuring delegate selection in forty-four states, the District of Columbia, Puerto Rico, the Virgin Islands and Europe.* Only Hawaii, Rhode Island, Utah, Washington, West Virginia, and Wyoming failed to be included.

But comprehensiveness in state coverage does nothing at all for comprehensiveness of news product. CBS and UPI have not adjusted very well to the growth in open party politics. Like the rest of the media, they have merely expanded in scope to include more and more of the primary campaign. In 1980, more polls, more primaries, and more candidates made it all look even worse, or at least more chaotic than in 1976.

What's more, primary news coverage and substantive news are inversely related if not inimical. In January, before the newshole was gorged with primaries, issues got considerable attention: 41 percent of campaign newsspace on CBS. In February, when the real primary season was under way, information about issues fell off dramatically. Issue coverage represented 18 percent of the campaign news time that month on "Evening News." It was not until summer that CBS was able to get back to its January percentages of substantive news.

In 1960, Richard Nixon promised to take his campaign to every state in the Union. He damaged his health and he jeopardized his chances in the process. Just possibly, he cost himself the election by sacrificing his usually sharp political perspective to an ill-conceived state-by-state publicity stunt. Our two sources did much the same thing in 1980, diluting themselves and their quality in the name of forty-four states and a handful of territories. The constant string of primaries and constant string of primary campaign stories worked against excellence in journalism.

There are some positive things to say about primary coverage in Campaign '80. In general, although the press may have overplayed surprise results, in 1980 they usually refrained from declaring losers as winners, and that contrasts with coverage in the late 1960s and early 1970s. Also, as best we can measure, the press covered the caucuses and primaries where the candidates themselves chose to make their most emphatic stand. Using figures from the Federal Election Commission, we found that CBS and UPI gave the greatest attention to states in which candidates spent their legal limit in public funds.[7]

*Ever since the McGovern-Fraser reforms, the Democrats hold a European delegate selection.

But many of the problems with "state supremacy" in press coverage grew worse in 1980. Take for example the problem of frontloading. In November of 1979, Maine and Florida held straw votes for president, none of which were binding and most of which failed to predict in any way Ronald Reagan's real strength among Republicans. Yet those straw polls attracted a dozen stories in November alone on network news. Given that primaries in more than half the states received a total number of stories less than the total afforded those straw votes, one can appreciate how unbalanced campaigns and campaign coverage have become during the earliest phases of the primary campaign.

Considering the way they fight to be first, the states themselves can be blamed for much of this, and the parties and candidates can be blamed as well.[8] But some of the responsibility rests on the shoulders of the media, too. If media can—and do—refuse to let the candidate's own strategy totally dominate the agenda for their day-to-day news reporting, the media can also work harder at refusing to allow the primary calendar to set the agenda for covering the early campaign.

Conclusions: More Serious Than Comprehensive

If, according to conventional wisdom, one types out all the words from an evening news program, the script would not cover the front page of the *New York Times*. But, as CBS critic Jeff Greenfield facetiously points out, if one eliminates all the fluff, the news from the *New York Times* would barely cover the front page of the *New York Times*. Remove the ads, the food sections, the classifieds, and the feature reports about wild-life in Brazil or divorce in California, and one finds that the *New York Times* does have less news than legend would allow.

Obviously, the elite *New York Times* has more news than the less than elite "Evening News." And most everything is treated more comprehensively in prestige print than on television or over the wire. But networks and wires do have lots of news about presidential campaigns and presidents. The presidency, after all, is their stock in trade. Networks and wires treat the presidency and the presidential campaign more seriously than anything else they cover, but both have an obvious problem with depth. They expend tremendous energy covering the national tickets, but, in the process, they practically forget all the rest of the campaigns. Watch "Evening News" for an election year and you will know a good deal about the presidential "horse race" and something about the national issues as well, but practically nothing about the vice-presidential candidates or any candidates for any other office. As far as the national media are concerned, particularly the networks, there is only one office, one "horse race," one level of politics. Having invested so heavily in the presidency, the networks have come to do a fairly serious job in covering the presidential campaign, but only the presidential campaign.

Chapter 8

Covering the "Official" Presidency: "Prime-Time" Minister

The networks took the Rose Garden away from us.

—TOM DONILON, CARTER WHITE HOUSE
STAFF

In 1973, the Twentieth Century Fund concluded that because of public affairs television, "the President enjoys an overwhelming communications advantage over the opposition party and Congress."[1] Not so overwhelming, apparently. Since 1973, the opposition party has removed three incumbents from office, Congress has rallied and become an increasingly important branch in national policy making, and, unlike presidential incumbents, nearly 90 percent of the congressional incumbents who have sought reelection have somehow managed to find it.

The Twentieth Century Fund was right about one thing, however. Even if we ignore all campaign news, neither Congress nor the loyal opposition gets anywhere near the attention of a sitting president, campaign year or no. For all practical purposes, the president, in his official capacity, serves not only as commander-in-chief, but as prime-time minister as well. But what the Fund failed to consider was the *quality* of the coverage and the way in which the media have portrayed our presidents as they carry out their official duties during their tenure of office. This chapter is an attempt to understand the advantages and disadvantages of serving as prime-time minister during the reign of television news.

It would be naive to think that television or the new journalism has stripped the president of all his press advantages. As Sam Donaldson says: "I get used by the White House every time they trot out a story and I put it on the air. . ."[2] At best, television has made press coverage of presidents a media-based, Mexican stand-off. Overall, in fact, our study of Campaign '80 suggests five "realities" about the relationship between presidents and press, three of which imply that the president still holds several trumps in the news process, and two of which suggest very much otherwise. Yet, at base, it does seem clear to us that network news has changed somewhat the balance between press and president. Press coverage of the official presidency no longer ensures a communicational advantage for the president, as it did in the "golden age" of traditional print. Let's look at the realities that apply to press and president in the age of network news.

REALITY 1

Regardless of medium, the major source for "official" news about the president is still the president, or his lieutenants.

People unfamiliar with press often use the recently canceled television show "Lou Grant" as an example of real world journalism. Most of the time that is not the way it is. Perhaps the most unrealistic impression received from programs like "Lou Grant" is that journalists uncover the day's news and that, day after day, press people go out and get the story on their own initiative. Lou Grant's reporters always dig for the news. However, A.J. Liebling comes closer to the mark by describing American journalism as a multibillion dollar cannery, filled with the latest processing equipment, but relying completely on a few tired fishermen out there in leaking boats catching a fish every now and then.[3] More often than not, the media are much better at disseminating news than uncovering it.

Even Robert Woodward and Carl Bernstein, the press heros of Watergate, failed to get to the truth at the bottom of the Watergate scandal. In the end, the *Washington Post* reported, but did not discover, what the FBI, Judge Sirica, and the Nixon White House tapes revealed about Nixon's role in Watergate.[4] In all Washington politics, the press still relies more on the official source for the day's news than on the investigative report. In the *Washington Post* and the *New York Times,* Leon Sigal found that almost half of the Washington news comes directly from the government.[5]

In our study of "official" news about Carter and the White House, we found what Sigal and others have found. Most news about the president in his official capacity comes from him, his press office, or his administration. On CBS and on UPI, White House sources are the basis for most of the news about the president. On UPI, just over 40 percent of the Carter news came directly from Carter, his press office, his staff, or his administration. Fewer than 10 percent came via the investigative route. On CBS, it was the same story, so to speak, only more so. A full two-thirds of the "official" news about Carter came via a Carter-controlled news source. Investigative journalism again accounted for less than 10 percent of the reporting. Even in this relatively small sample of news items,* the balance swings in favor of the president.† Television reporters and print reporters have to depend on official sources for official White House news.

We have no particular quarrel with this reality. No news organization can do investigative pieces day-in and day-out on any political institution. Nor would we want to cope with that aggressive a press corps. In fact, reliance on the president for official news about the president makes sense: reports based on what the White House releases to the press are "objective," are tied directly to a legitimate source, and are easy to process. But regardless of the way one feels about press dependency on the White House, the fact remains that the presidency still serves as the major font of news about itself.

REALITY 2

The "official" president still has considerable clout in determining the day's news agenda, especially in foreign affairs.

We have just discussed the tendency for the White House press to rely on official sources, especially the official presidency for quota-

*This figure includes only official stories that were tangentially linked to the campaign. We did not collect information about the source of the story for items making no reference to the election.

†These percentages make clear that CBS relied even more heavily on the official presidency for its source of White House news, not surprising given the logistics and needs of network newsmaking. In fact, network people not only recognize their particular dependence on the White House press offices, they consider it a special vulnerability.

tions, for information, for cues. Under certain specifiable conditions, White House control of news can go beyond that. In news coverage of U.S. international relations, especially in crisis, the White House and president not only monopolize information, they also have considerable influence over the news agenda. In the long run, modern media can break up the White House news monopoly on hard information, but in the short run, a foreign crisis implies a news agenda set by the president and by his administration. In Campaign '80, we experienced a historic case study in which the White House was able to "control" the media, on and off, for several months. The topic, of course, was Iran, and the issue was the fifty-three American hostages being held there.

Carter and the Hostage Coverage

All told, between January 1 and December 31, CBS and UPI linked President Carter to the hostages in 444 separate news stories. In our study, no news topic approached Iran in terms of coverage. What was true at CBS and UPI was true in all the other media as well. In 1980, the three network evening news programs broadcast 1,031 Iranian news segments on the weekday evening news.[6] The *Washington Post* averaged three Iran stories a day.[7]

As before, the White House and the administration served as the clearinghouse for the bulk of the press reports. Hodding Carter, press secretary at the State Department, became a household word. Day after day, Hodding Carter told the press what was or was not happening in Iran and the press then told the public. At CBS, the White House and the administration were the principal news sources in about two-thirds of the news stories concerning the hostages. At UPI, about half the hostage reports came via the Carter administration.*

More intriguing, however, is the month-by-month distribution of the news about the hostages. According to the evidence in figure 8–1, the presidency does more than serve as newsmaker. The amount of hostage news coming from our media month by month strongly suggests that the president has considerable say as to the very definition of news. By talking up the crisis, by playing it down, or by refusing to talk at all, the government changed the shape of the news day.

In January, February, March, and April, the administration talked

*These figures are based only on the relatively small number of hostage stories tangentially linked to the campaign.

incessantly about the hostages. In May, after the commando raid had failed, the White House decided to de-emphasize the hostages and did so until the Fall when once again it went more public with negotiations and expectations. That was the official agenda, the president's agenda about the hostage crisis.

News about the crisis followed the president's schedule, at least in part. Looking at the peaks and valleys in figure 8–1, it becomes fairly evident that Carter's strategy and press history go very much hand-in-hand, particularly during the first six months of the year. Reality played some part in this to be sure. The enormous increase in hostage news in April came not through Carter's press initiatives, but through his real intiatives: the breaking off in diplomatic relations between the United States and the Islamic Republic, the tightening of sanctions against the Khomeini regime, and the commando raid itself. But reality does not explain the path of press coverage after April.

Following the failure of the commando raid, Carter announced that the crisis had been "substantially alleviated," and made it plain that he did not want his administration to discuss the topic as openly as it had before.* Once the administration stopped talking, the press stopped talking as well. On CBS, according to our figures, the number of stories about the crisis plummeted from forty-seven in April to three in May and then to two in June. On UPI, during the same three-month interlude, the numbers were sixty, sixteen, and three. Without the president or his State Department speaking up on the issue, coverage concerning the hostages fell off a cliff.

Figure 8–1 does not completely test the premise that Carter controlled the news agenda about Iran.† However, William Adams and Phillip Heyl, in a comprehensive study on news coverage of the hostage crisis, have compiled a complete listing of news about Iran for all three networks during late 1979 and all of 1980.[8] Their work makes the same point, that once Carter decided to go silent, the media became quieter, too. All three networks cut the hostage coverage by at least a factor of five between April and June!

There are other interpretations for the silence of May and June.

---

*Carter also referred to the rescue operation as a "limited success" and declared the Iranian problem more manageable.

†There were a few stories that mentioned Iran but did not mention the Carter administration or Carter. We did not include them in our analysis; consequently, we do not have a complete file on hostage coverage, only that very large proportion in which Carter was mentioned.

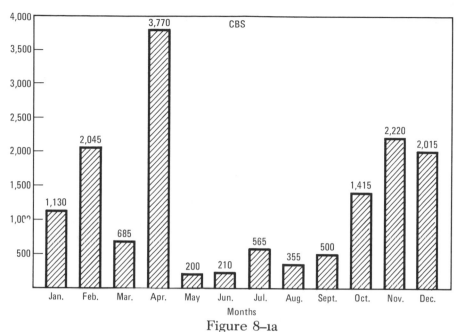

Figure 8–1a

Amount of CBS News Coverage About Iranian Hostages, President Carter
Mentioned (January through December, 1980)

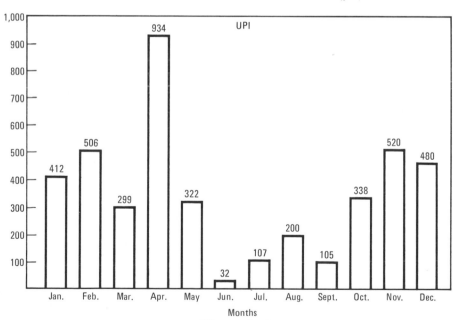

Figure 8–1b

Amount of UPI News Coverage About Iranian Hostages, President Carter
Mentioned (January through December, 1980)

One might argue that the story had really been dying anyway and that April was the exception in an otherwise gradual decline. In this interpretation, boredom becomes the chief factor in explaining the decline in hostage news. Or one could attribute the drop-off in coverage to public frustration so deep that nobody wanted to write or read any more about Iran. But for us, the ebb and flow of the hostage news during the first six months of the year was at least as much a function of presidential news management as it was boredom or withdrawal.

Helen Thomas, who has as good a claim as anyone to the title of dean of the White House press corps, also regarded Carter as a major factor in the dramatic decline of hostage coverage in late spring. When we asked Thomas about the changing tide of news about Iran, Thomas saw Carter and his strategy as a major reason for the change:

> We don't make the news. . . . Our job is to cover the news. . . and if the President is not going to discuss it, we can't exactly run it on the wire with a hot bulletin or an urgent story. . . .
>
> There is no question there is always a certain management of the news. . . . He wanted to get it on the back burner. And to some extent he succeeded in so far as Khomeini would play ball. . . . (The press) couldn't keep it alive, except to say it was still a problem and it wasn't being solved.

We might feel less certain about this interpretation of official news if it did not fit so comfortably with what went on during the remainder of the year in the campaign news. Campaign news reinforces the notion that the rules of objectivity allow media to be "captured" by what the newsmakers want to discuss. We do not, of course, believe that politicians capture the news agenda all the time, or anything close to it. But just as President Carter influenced the newshole concerning Iran, the candidates, as a group, shaped the newshole concerning the issues of the campaign. In fact, we can start with the most vivid example, the hostage "issue" as it was covered in the campaign news per se.

Despite the fact that no ongoing event in the history of television news produced more coverage, the hostage "issue" did not top the list of issues covered in the full-fledged campaign news. In fact, the hostage issue did not even come close to matching the economy as the "most covered" policy issue. The reason is simple: neither Reagan, Carter, nor Anderson wanted very much to discuss the hostages. Each had his own reasons. Reagan was leading in almost every poll and did not need or want to touch so sensitive a nerve as patriotism.

Anderson had seen what the liberal position on the hostage issue had done to Kennedy in the first two months of the campaign. After April Carter had no reason to raise the hostage issue unless it was to announce a safe return. With nobody willing to discuss it, the hostage issue was not covered much in the hard campaign news. During the entire campaign, the hostage issue came up a total of eight times on CBS.

Media do not always discuss what candidates want discussed. The debate-debate got more coverage than candidate "discussion" would have indicated. But the fact that the hostage crisis dominated all phases of news except campaign news shows that candidates do influence greatly what issues the media will or will not address during the campaign. So, for example, none of the candidates chose to speak about the major issue of crime and none of the media did either. On CBS, there were zero campaign stories about crime! When media do cover policy issues, the candidates still tend to set the agenda.

Differences in Print and Television

In their coverage of Iran, both UPI and CBS followed the president's lead, but, as usual, the relationship of press to White House was not exactly the same across the two media. First, CBS was measurably more interested in the Iranian crisis than was UPI. The hostage crisis alone counted for 19 percent of the noncampaign news stories on "Evening News." On the wire, it was barely 10 percent, about half as much. Conventional wisdom apparently holds true here: Iran was a television issue more than a print issue. And compared to ABC, CBS was at best a fairly close second among networks. ABC "World News Tonight" presented 5 percent more hostage coverage than "Evening News," and 25 percent more than NBC "Nightly News."[9]

Size of coverage was not the only difference between the wires and the networks. Although "Evening News" covered Iran much more zealously than the wire, CBS "dropped" the issue more quickly after Carter had "dropped" it on April 30. For every foot of newsspace the wire had given the crisis in April, the wire gave 3 inches in May, only about one-fourth as much. But on CBS, the drop was much more extreme. For every minute in April there were 3 seconds in May. In ratio, CBS hostage coverage declined at a rate six times faster than wire coverage.

This fits almost too perfectly with the organizational theory of network news, news determined by bureaucratic imperatives.[10]

Under this interpretation, the networks behave differently from print because networks have different "needs," chief among them, celebrities as newsmakers and newsfilm for every occasion. Theoretically, CBS dropped Iran more quickly than the wire because CBS was more vulnerable to Carter's news schedule. In removing himself from the story, Carter had a greater effect on television's newshole than on the newshole of UPI.

That interpretation holds only for a while, however. During the fall campaign, CBS crept back to its original level of interest in Iran. By October it was, once again, the wire that was less interested in the hostages. In a sense, CBS seems to have come to terms with its own vulnerability during the months after the raid and before the election. Cameras and film may shape network news, but they do not tyrannize. If Carter had enjoyed any extra leverage in shaping the network news agenda right after the raid, he lost the advantage eventually, as the networks began to look ahead to the first anniversary of the hostage crisis.

At the outset, Carter played a unique role in hyping the hostage story by telling the public that he could neither sleep nor campaign in his usual fashion so long as the fifty-three Americans remained captive in Tehran. Carter's own statements about his personal, emotional involvement in the crisis were a dramatic cue to the media, and they took the cue very seriously. In May, he exercised informal presidential prerogative once again by backing off the story and closing off the flow of information to the press. But by October, presidential control had all but evaporated. By the first week in November, Carter had lost control of the press, the negotiations, and the election. Like a modern day sorcerer's apprentice, Carter had, in part, initiated a flow of information that had turned into a flood.

Historically, presidents have possessed a first-strike capability, the right during a crisis to serve as national spokesman through the national news media. The hostage crisis proved that presidents can still set press in motion when national security and honor are at stake. But media themselves can only be held presidential hostage for so long. And for Jimmy Carter, media could not be held hostage long enough.

REALITY 3

All Media are created presidential, but electronic media are created more presidential than others.

Covering the "Official" Presidency

So far, we have mostly emphasized the similarities in media coverage of the official president. But as expected, there are important differences between traditional print and network news coverage of the incumbent president. The first involves the scope of coverage.

Television news loves the presidency. It may not like the incumbent; it may not like any incumbent, but the office of the president has become the *sine qua non* of network journalism. Network correspondents themselves grouse about the near obsessive emphasis the news divisions place on the White House. Ed Bradley, having done one too many Amy Carter stories for CBS, finally complained about reporting on her tree house at the White House: "This is the sort of thing that eats up our time. Photo opportunities, briefings, releases, more photo opportunities. Most of it doesn't mean a damn thing. But the White House grinds it out and we eat it up. The networks want everything we can give them on the 'President.'"[11] ABC's Sam Donaldson, the most famous of network White House correspondents, says the same thing: "I mean I have to argue *not* to be on 'World News Tonight' some nights, because I don't think I have a story. Whereas many of my colleagues [not covering the President] at ABC are desperately trying to get on."[12]

All news media (print, radio, television) are, of course, presidentially oriented. Mel Elfin, senior editor at *Newsweek,* makes the point by concluding that for a White House correspondent, "the worst thing in the world that could happen to you is for the President of the United States to choke on a piece of meat, and for you not to be there."[13] But some media take the presidency more seriously than others. Television takes the presidency most seriously of all.

Traditionally, the wires have been the news organization in charge of the "body watch"[14]—the moment-by-moment monitoring of every presidential movement. And in terms of protocol, AP and UPI still rank slightly higher than the networks in their relationship to the president. The wire people, for example, still get to ask the first question at a presidential news conference. But as a function of newshole, the wires do not even come close to matching the networks. The evening news has replaced the wires on the body-watch. In every category, CBS showed a greater affinity for White House politics than did UPI. In percentage terms, CBS devoted more news space to official White House coverage; more newsspace to stories linking Carter to the campaign; much more newsspace to the campaign per se (see table 8–1). Almost one-third of all the news on CBS touched on the presidency or the campaign. Just under one-sixth of all the wire reports did that. In proportion, the "Evening News" turns out to be twice as presidential in news scope as the wire.

Part of this is a function of comparing a relatively short newscast with a comparatively long wire printout. But the qualitative evidence leads to the same conclusion. The wire has no lead story, but the "Evening News" does. And the lead story on television almost always involves the president in some way, shape, or form. We included 255 week news days in our news year, and CBS led with a story containing a reference to the presidency or the presidential campaign 151 times during that period! In six cases out of ten, the day's top story somehow involved presidential politics or the president. Whether one compares networks to wires, to *Time* magazine, to the *New York Times,* the result is always the same: "The President represents the single most important story that the networks follow on a continuing basis."[15] On occasion, CBS has bragged about its unique tie to the presidency. In one of its news ads, CBS pictured three presidential correspondents from "Evening News" on the White House grounds and concluded "the President doesn't make a move without them"—hyperbole, perhaps, but a nice indication of how much the presidency means to "Evening News."

We were prepared to find network television more presidential than newspapers. We were not prepared to find a presidential focus on CBS almost twice as great as in the wires. Quantitatively speaking, presidents not only appear as prime-time minister, they also serve as television's communicator-in-chief.

TABLE 8–1

PERCENTAGE OF ALL NEWS STORIES (A) DEALING WITH CARTER AS PRESIDENT, (B) OFFICIAL STORIES LINKING CARTER TO THE CAMPAIGN, (C) DISCUSSING THE CAMPAIGN

	CBS	UPI
White House "Official" Stories	9.7%	6.6%
Official Stories Linked to Campaign	4.6	2.4
Presidential Campaign Stories	15.9	7.4
	30.2%	16.4%
	(N=5204)	(N=20,033)

REALITY 4

Compared with the wires, networks treat the incumbent more critically and spend more newsspace covering "presidential problems."

At this point, it would appear that the official presidency might wish to work only with and through networks. In 1980, CBS covered President Carter "as president" twice a day on the average, followed his news priorities in Iran and relied on the White House as its principal source of information about the president. What's more, CBS delivered almost twenty million viewers per night.

Were we to stop at this point, the networks might well appear to have, as the Twentieth Century Fund claimed, an enormous political advantage over the opposition, the Congress, practically anything or anyone. But news coverage of the official presidency is not always the proverbial bed of roses, let alone a metaphorical Rose Garden.

For the last ten years, in contradiction to the thesis that networks help incumbents, a new theory has evolved. Starting with Daniel Patrick Moynihan,[16] and continuing on through David Paletz and Robert Entman,[17] the more contemporary thinking is that network news has become, at best, a double-edged sword and that the national electronic media have, in Walter Mondale's colorful phrase, helped to turn the presidency into the nation's "fire hydrant."[18]

Not everyone believes that the national press has weakened the presidency. Michael Grossman and Joyce Kumar still regard the media, television or other, as a presidential plus.[19] But our research makes us wonder. We found that the wires may still serve as a communicative advantage, qualitatively and quantitatively. But on network news the picture is very blurry. President Carter got constant attention from evening news, but, in the vernacular of contemporary social work, he got very little "quality time."

Explicit Criticism

We have already seen that CBS treated presidential candidates more critically than UPI and that frontrunners had an especially hard time with network journalism. Apparently, the same phenomenon spills over into the press coverage of the official presidency as well. Candidates, frontrunners, and incumbents all received more explicit criticism on the "Evening News" than on the day wire.

Just as with the campaign news, we scored each item about the official presidency for explicit criticism or explicit support. And as before, we used the same standards—if the reporter made critical comments in a ratio of three to one, or more, we considered the story "critical." Conversely, if the ratio went three to one positive, we labeled the story "supportive."

As before, when examining the campaign news, both CBS and UPI generally behaved objectivistically when covering President Carter. On the day wire, no less than 98 percent of the "official" news mentioning Carter came up "neutral," that is, contained no explicit evaluation whatever of Carter or his administration. On "Evening News," the figure was lower but still notable. In ninety-two cases out of one hundred, the journalist took no explicit position on Carter's competence, integrity, decency, consistency, or any other personal qualities.

As usual, CBS behaved more "explicitly" than the wire. And, as usual, CBS reported more critically. In these few instances in which there was any evaluation, the now traditional pattern prevailed. The wire produced almost perfect equality between positive, negative, and ambiguous reports. CBS, however, presented directional news in a ratio that was decidedly negative; eight to one negative, in fact. So the usual trilogy of findings holds here as it has so often before: overwhelming neutrality in covering the newsmaker; slightly less reticence in television than in print; considerably more criticism on television than through print.

Presidential Problems

With so much "neutral" coverage, it might still seem that President Carter was winning the battle for press in 1980. Neutral press ought not to hurt an incumbent, especially if he serves as major spokesperson about himself. But it was not quite so simple as that for Carter, or for the incumbency.

First, we have not made any provisions here for innuendo or "fairness." These figures on neutrality only deal in explicit criticism. In reality, there was considerable implicit criticism in much of the "official" press coverage—criticism we neglected to calculate.* Second, quality of coverage goes beyond criticism. It also includes topic.

Assume, for an instance, that CBS had, every day for a year, reported objectively and neutrally on Hamilton Jordan and his legal

*For these "official" stories, we have no measures of good press or bad press. We used that classification only for campaign or campaign-related stories.

problems related to drugs. Assume also that UPI covered none of that but reported instead Carter's day-by-day diplomatic relationship with Anwar Sadat and the People's Republic of China. This would produce two very separate press images of the Carter administration and one would not need to be Jody Powell to figure out which was a better news deal.

Needless to say, conditions were not so black and white between CBS and UPI. But CBS did spend more newsspace and energy on topics that made the president look bad. In fact, "Evening News" did twice as much "problem" journalism as UPI.

Problem journalism is not necessarily exposé; nor is it always investigative reporting. Problem journalism includes coverage of the major and minor embarrassments tied directly or indirectly to the president, or to his administration. Problem journalism is to "official" White House news what candidate issues are to campaign news, the less than pleasant side of the newsmaker's "personal" life. Coverage of Hamilton Jordan's legal battle concerning his alleged use of cocaine is a classic instance of "problem journalism."

Other than the president, almost nobody in government ever faces problem journalism. Unless the problem involves the government official directly, the press rarely spends any time with it. Even Ted Kennedy, whose personal life has always been a major press focus, rarely has to contend with problem journalism. Just after the election, for example, Kennedy aide Rick Burke claimed that somebody was trying to kill him—that some mysterious person had attempted to break down his door and tried to stab him. The national press barely covered this string of bizarre incidents, even after Burke acknowledged that he had invented the whole story. Had Kennedy been president at the time, Burke's personal problems, whatever their outcome, would have been one of Kennedy's larger press problems, at least until the issue had been settled or the mystery solved.

But Kennedy was not president in 1980. Carter was. And President Carter had lots of press problems: Billy Carter, Tim Kraft, Hamilton Jordan, Benjamin Civiletti, and so on. All of these problems were real, of course. Responsible press does not invent problems; but responsible press does have to decide how to handle them. CBS and UPI followed separate strategies in covering problems. Both media handled Carter's problems objectively, but CBS handled them much more frequently and much more fully.

Whether one considers the numbers of stories or the amount of newsspace, "Evening News" spent just under twice as much time on Carter's tribulations. We identified a dozen basic Carter problems in 1980* ranging from things as personal as the final phases of the Bert Lance affair through topics as political as the open convention controversy. On CBS, Carter's problems accounted for 17 percent of his newsspace; on UPI, the figure was slightly less than 10 percent of Carter's total newsspace. Moreover, on UPI, "Billy" stories were about the same length as the rest of the "official" news reports about Carter, just under 10 percent longer. On CBS, "Billy" stories were dramatically longer than that; 40 percent longer than the news items not about Billy. The same holds for almost all of Carter's problems. In proportion, there were more stories, more newsspace, more concentration on problems in network television than in traditional print.

What makes this particularly intriguing is that technology does not seem to be a factor here. The usual bromides about networks letting visuals determine the news agenda do not hold. Neither Hamilton Jordan nor Billy Carter provided much in the way of exciting film or video per se. We can imagine several reasons for the closer tie between television and presidential problems, but video is not a major one. Whatever the reasons, the fact remains: CBS treated President Carter more critically and less respectfully than did the wires. Even in their noncampaign news coverage, presidents pay for their time on television, and at a higher rate than in traditional print.

REALITY 5

Wires cover incumbents as incumbents; networks cover incumbents as politicians.

October 3, 1980, President Carter not only left the Rose Garden, he left the White House compound completely. Carter was on his way to Sterling, Virginia, a Washington suburb, where he planned to sign into law a fifty-billion-dollar reauthorization plan for federal aid to higher education, the largest education bill in history.

The short trip to Sterling took place not because the White House was short on pens. The trip was designed to ensure network news

*The problems are: Bert Lance, Hamilton Jordan, William Miller, the UN blunder, Ramsey Clark, Billy Carter, the Stealth bomber, Carter's racism slur, Carter's warmongering charge against Reagan, Carter's divisiveness charge against Reagan, the hostages as a campaign issue, the open convention controversy, and Tim Kraft (covered as a separate story only on UPI).

coverage of "the president" as opposed to Jimmy Carter. "It was a moving Rose Garden," said one Carter aide, "an offer the evening news couldn't refuse." But they did refuse: neither ABC, CBS, nor NBC bothered to cover the trip or the legislation.

The wires, of course, did cover the trip to Sterling. The wires tend to cover everything the president, as president, does. But, despite the usual network obsession with the presidency, on "Evening News" the trip to Sterling, Virginia, never happened.

One Rose Garden story omitted does not a thesis prove. But we found considerable evidence, both hard and soft, to suggest that networks have grown much tougher about covering "the president" and were much freer about covering "the Carter campaign." The wires treated Carter "officially," the networks treated him politically.

The Rose Garden campaign rests on the basic premise that voters are more impressed with an incumbent acting as an official president than they are with an incumbent who acts like all the rest of the candidates. But in this instance media play the pivotal role. If the press refuses to cover the official presidency and insists on doing campaign reporting instead, the Rose Garden strategy withers away.

Every reporter with a White House assignment recognizes that the press secretary wants to keep the press working away at "official" news. But some media work harder at politicizing the official news stories. As a news medium, the networks probably work harder at covering the politics of presidential news than any of the rest. When compared with the wires, the networks covered President Carter almost as if he were just another candidate, not the official president.

Figure 8-2 presents a month-by-month description of Carter's news "status"; his ratio of "official" press to campaign press between January and October. UPI and CBS awarded Carter a very different news status: the wires emphasizing the president and the networks emphasizing the candidate. In January, both media started out concentrating on the president, not the candidate. The election was ten months off and Carter was not campaigning. Gradually, both media shifted their attention from the Carter administration toward the Carter campaign. By October, neither source was reporting much official news about Carter.

However, the two media spent the year defining Carter differently. CBS invariably covered Carter less officially than the wire. Excluding "problem coverage," just under two-thirds (62 percent) of Carter's newstime on CBS was campaign coverage; on UPI, the

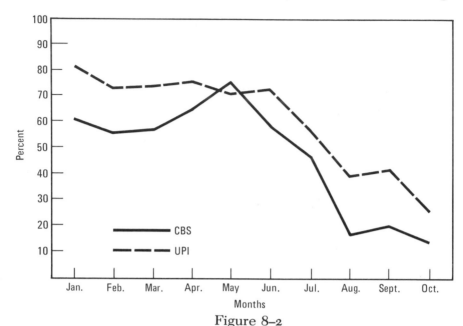

Figure 8–2

Percentage of Carter's Total Press Coverage Devoted to His Official Role on CBS and UPI (January through October, 1980)

figure was just over one-third. There was a twenty-seven point difference between the two news sources in their willingness to define Carter as "the President."

In August, September, and October, during the general election, CBS was more than twice as likely to cover Carter as campaigner. Whatever the reason, these month-by-month figures make it perfectly clear that Carter's news image on network television was consistently more "political" than it was on the wire. On a case-by-case basis the conclusion is much the same.

We have already considered the trip to Sterling, Virginia, an official visit that the networks neglected to carry, but that the wires dutifully covered in full. There are, of course, other sterling examples. Perhaps the most instructive involves wire and network coverage of the United States-China grain accords announced by the White House on October 22, 1980, just two weeks before the actual balloting. The Chinese grain deal, several months in preparation, was considered by the White House a major international event, a boon to American agriculture and one more step toward cementing relations with the People's Republic.

The wire, apparently, also saw the Chinese grain deal as a coup, an economic coup. On the day it was announced, UPI devoted two and one half stories to the grain sale. And, although the UPI reporters mentioned the political ramifications, the wire treated the story as an "official" story, a news item about President Carter, not campaigner Carter. Raymond Wilkinson, in fact, filed his October 22 report from Peking, underscoring the notion that this was an international news story, not simply a piece for "Campaign '80." Wilkinson explained the international and political impact of the grain sale:

"China Signs Bonanza Grain Deal with U.S."
Peking (UPI)—China and the United States signed one of the largest grain deals in history today, providing a financial bonanza to American farmers and an expected political windfall for President Carter.

Under the four-year agreement starting January 1, the Chinese will buy between six million and nine million tons of wheat and corn to cover shortfalls in its own crop, and imports from other producers, helping meet the rising demands of the world's largest population.

The deal, one of the largest ever concluded and similar to the Soviet American grain accord, will net American farm producers an estimated $2 billion annually. . . .

President Carter is expected to reap political advantage from the deal, which will partially offset curtailed grain sales to the Soviet Union following the invasion of Afghanistan.

CBS, however, had no such story on "Evening News." As it turned out, it devoted just one comment to the grain deal. It came as the last paragraph of a Campaign '80 piece, a story summarizing Carter's political stops that day in Beaumont and Waco, Texas. The paragraph CBS did devote to the grain sale was *not* a summary; it was more an afterthought. In fact, Jed Duvall wrote the story in such a way that the grain announcement came up sounding distinctly like a liability, not an asset for Carter. Duvall implied that the timing of the announcement had itself become a mini-campaign issue, not a windfall:

Here in Waco, a grain growing area, the President announced an agreement to sell China enormous amounts of grain—White House aides say the agreement has been in the works for a year and they deny the timing is mere campaign wizardry.*

*"Evening News," 22 October 1980.

What the wire had explicitly labeled economic "bonanza," CBS News implicitly labeled political bunk.

Jed Duvall was not the only CBS reporter who turned Carter's official behavior into campaign news. Lesley Stahl, on more than one occasion, closed her "official" stories about Carter with this less-than-official-sounding sign-off: "Lesley Stahl, with the Carter campaign at the White House." Consistently and incessantly, the network people chose to treat White House news, and news about Carter, more politically than did the staff at UPI.

Granted, the networks never promised him a rose garden. But the question still remains: why did the network journalists cover the official presidency so much more politically than the reporters and editors at the wire?

In chapter 10, we will answer that question in a much grander perspective. We will offer four broad-gauged theories to explain why network news differs from traditional print in almost every variety of political reporting. But there are narrower explanations for this particular variation of the network's insistence on covering the White House as campaign headquarters. As usual, reality plays a part. Particularly where the networks are involved, the White House does behave more politically in an election year and "deserves" less "official" coverage. Even though he felt the bite more than anyone in 1980, Jody Powell agreed that there is a need for covering presidential politics a bit more cynically during the course of the campaign. "A pretty good idea," Powell called it. Powell also offered another explanation for the less "official" and more cynical reporting coming over the networks. Pointing back to the Duvall piece, in which the Chinese grain sale was practically dismissed as an example of "campaign wizardry," Powell emphasized Duvall's unfamiliarity with the long-term negotiations in Peking and with U.S. agricultural policies in general:

> This is not to be critical of Jed [but] whoever wrote the China grain deal story [for UPI] knew what the hell they were talking about and they knew it had been going on a long time. . . that it was significant. . . that it was not one of these campaign gimmicks.
>
> If you don't know, the inclination is to view any announcement in that way. If you do know about it, it's different.

Powell's point was a good one: the less the reporter knows about the president's official action, the more likely he is to use the political angle and to discount the official story. Networks have fewer reporters in Peking covering Chinese agriculture.

Another Carter campaign official saw the differences less a function of manpower than of newsspace. Tom Donilon, who served as Carter's principal floor leader at the convention, felt that the network news shows could not find the time for both "official" news and campaign news and that campaign news always has higher priority. According to Donilon, "the networks wanted to run the political story instead. . . it was format. The papers could cover three or four stories on the President; the networks could do just one."

Perhaps the best explanation for Reality 5 comes from a deeper appreciation of the realities which preceded it. Almost everything we have seen to this point suggests that the networks feel a greater vulnerability to presidential exploitation than most other news media. Compared with UPI, CBS proved to be much more dependent on government sources in its coverage of the president. Compared with UPI, CBS proved somewhat more "responsive" to the president's decision not to go public any longer with the hostage negotiations. Compared with all other media, CBS, NBC, and ABC proved most likely to make the president the day's lead story.

But the networks sense more than simple reliance. They sense exploitation from the other side as well. In fact, the presidency has become more concerned with its network news image than any other image, especially during the general campaign. One Carter political aide put it bluntly, "We [the campaign staff] met every morning of the general campaign at 8:00 A.M. in Hamilton Jordan's conference room. The meeting consisted virtually of nothing else than deciding what we were going to do that day to get on the evening news."

Reporters realize that the White House prefers television coverage to anything else. So the result has been that the television reporters do what they can to compensate. Network correspondents do not discuss this topic very freely, but Powell, working from the other side of the podium, felt that network reporters do live with their own special anxiety:

> They recognize their vulnerability to manipulation and compensate like hell for it—in many cases, overcompensate for it. TV more, I think because they know. . . that they're being manipulated and so forth. And they're sensitive to criticism from other journalists. . . to protect themselves from that allegation.

This is not new to 1980. Network journalism has been trying to compensate for news management at the White House at least since the days of Richard Nixon. But it is very possible that President Carter made the networks more sensitive than usual, first by insisting he was not behaving politically and second, by doing what he did with the news media on the morning of the Wisconsin primary.

On April 1 at 7:18 A.M., President Carter invited the networks *and* the wires into the Oval Office to announce an imminent breakthrough in the hostage crisis. The wires covered the meeting and the announcement as highest priority news. The networks covered Carter's remarks live from the White House. Carter literally made the morning news with his talk of a breakthrough. By evening, however, the breakthrough had broken down, but Carter was, by then, well on his way to winning a lopsided victory in the Wisconsin primary, a primary he needed badly in order to dilute the effect of Kennedy's surprising success the week before in New York and Connecticut.

This was the highest form of Rose Gardening—the Oval Office campaign. And although the Carter people still adamantly insist that they believed the hostage negotiations had been settled, the media, especially the networks, never accepted that premise. The network people still feel that they were used. Jeff Greenfield refers to Carter's behavior on April 1 as having crossed "the line between a skillful use of incumbency and outright manipulation."[20]

It was just after the Wisconsin primary that CBS did its longest, toughest, most investigative report on Carter's manipulation of the incumbency. It was not a coincidence. Lesley Stahl, who did the April report on the Carter Rose Garden campaign, singles out the press conference as the precipitating event in the CBS decision to do its investigation:

> That piece was inspired by the Wisconsin primary when President Carter called us into the Oval Office and made the announcement about the hostages.
>
> We really decided to do an objective job and go back and look at the calendar. We didn't know what we'd find. . . we had no idea what we'd come up with. . . . We found striking patterns [of manipulation].

What is most interesting perhaps is that Helen Thomas, who covered that same press conference for UPI, did not feel used. She did not take Carter's behavior as a sign that she should dig any harder in reporting from the White House. Comparing her own feelings with those of the network reporters who covered the press conference, Thomas concluded that she "didn't have that same feeling of being had."

Conclusion

The most comprehensive study ever done concerning White House news concludes that the modern relationship between president and press "is still favorable for the Presidency." So say Michael Grossman and Martha Kumar.[21] We come closer to David Paletz and Robert Entman as to the nature of White House press. In *Media Power Politics*, Paletz and Entman view the relationship as at best a double-edged sword for incumbent presidents.

> So a president faces the press with an ambiguous mixture of strengths and weaknesses. He employs secrecy but is beset by leaks. He controls the release of information, but not for too long. He can badger, berate, and bully the press, but at the risk of resentful reporting. He offers up good news; the bad is sure to follow.[22]

Interestingly enough, Paletz and Entman seem to regard all this as a function of network news, not print.[23]

We see "official" press coverage as a possible advantage, one which accrues to those presidents who actually do well in office. Given the modern media and their method of newsmaking, incumbents should regard the press as neither inherently advantageous nor inherently destructive.

At one time, White House press was a near inherent benefit to the incumbent. We agree with Grossman and Kumar that the "golden age of partnership between the White House and news media" came during the Eisenhower administration.[24] But the good old days are over. Helen Thomas agrees, speaking about the official White House press corps:

> We're still herded; we're still behind ropes; we're still treated like cattle. . . . But there is a little difference in the climate, in the atmosphere that says. . . basically you think at bottom line sometimes you *are* a human being.[25]

The "rules" of official White House news still provide some advantages over some circumstances. President Carter was able to influence the news agenda during the first few months of the Iranian crisis. And President Carter could always get the media to cover him on his own terms, when he predicted or even implied that the hostages might be coming home. When Carter spoke as president, he made news. When he spoke as president, the media, including the networks, quoted some of what he actually said. As for the president's special resources in dealing with reporters, Robert Pierpoint admits that when he covered presidential press conferences for CBS it was so important to get to ask a question—personally and professionally important—he wore his loudest clothing. Pierpoint was hoping to have a better chance at catching the president's eye as the chief executive moved from questioner to questioner.[26]

But the media have their own resources. So, even if the president manages the news flow, reporters can raise that as an issue or quote others who will raise the issue on their own. And Pierpoint, once called upon, usually did ask tough questions. In an age of network journalism, the president may determine, more than ever, what the newshole is. But presidents do not do nearly so well at determining news quality. The networks have made it very hard to control tone.

Grossman and Kumar do not believe that the media have made much headway in coping with presidential press advantage. But even Grossman and Kumar agree that network journalism has made a difference:

> In particular, television has been a major arena for the expression of ... conflict. . . . Television reporters have not chosen to confront the White House directly. . . What has occurred is that reporters now present news about the White House along with an item that casts doubt on the credibility of what [the White House] said. . . . They indicate to their viewers that a cynical approach is a realistic approach when analyzing the motives of the President. . . .[27]

We are still uncertain as to whether all the media coverage, when taken together, comes up as a plus or minus for the president. But we do know that, in comparison with traditional print, network treatment of the official presidency makes the life of the president and of his press secretary solitary, poor, nasty, brutish, and short. Networks have covered the Rose Garden on occasion, but more and more often they focus on the thorns, not the roses.

PART III

Conclusions and Implications

Chapter 9

Old News, New Media: Hard-Core Comparisons

Print is gray and abstract, TV looks and sounds like
spontaneous life.

—WILLIAM HENRY III, *TIME* MAGAZINE

FOR the last several chapters, we have been dealing
with the differences between traditional print and network journalism, and looking at the entire array of stories in each. But that technique has to this point combined hard news, soft news, features,
exposés, and commentary. In order to reach a clear set of conclusions
concerning print and television we now reduce wires and networks
to their very least common denominator: sentences and words in
hard news reporting.

Getting down to the "hard-core" campaign news proves again
three important similarities between traditional print and network
TV: (1) that the wires and networks usually stay inside the limits of
"Objective Reporting"; (2) that the wires and networks confine
themselves to the "horse race" metaphor in well over half the stories;
(3) that the wires and networks stay inside the boundaries of balance
and fairness. If anything, hard-core reporting is, when compared

with the rest of the news coverage, more objective; more "horse racist"; and more balanced in tenor and scope.

Hard-Core Similarities

Ninety-nine percent of the CBS hard-core pieces took no explicit position on candidate competence; neither did 99 percent of the hard-core wire stories. Ninety-nine percent of the hard-core pieces on "Evening News" said nothing explicit about candidate integrity, nor did the wire. Even on the consistency criterion, where the bulk of explicitness occurs in campaign news, both sources behaved the same way, with a general reluctance to make an explicit case.

As expected, "horse race" evaluations accounted for almost all the explicit conclusions drawn from either source: 41 percent of the hard-core stories on CBS said something explicit about the electoral successfulness of the principal candidate; 32 percent of the wire stories did that. And again, as expected, CBS and UPI in their hard-core news expressed nearly equal amounts of interest in the "horse race." "Horse race" was the major theme in three-quarters of the hard-core reporting on CBS, and the same was true for the wire. Not surprisingly, "horse racism" is particularly prominent in the day-to-day campaign reporting, where the "horse race" provides the "events" for the day's hard news.

Fairness and balance are trickier concepts. Still, as usual, CBS and UPI divided space equally among "equal" candidates, and both gave big shares of newsspace to anybody doing better than expected. Nobody but "losers" and minor parties was denied space in the hard-core reporting. As for "fairness," in either medium less than 20 percent of the hard-core stories could be classified as "good press" or "bad press." And as for nonpartisanship, in a world in which virtually all national journalists appear to vote Democratic, Reagan had better "press" than Carter on both the "Evening News" and on the day wire. Hard-core reporting was generally balanced and generally fair.

208

Hard-Core Differences

Despite their similarities, CBS and UPI reported hard news differently in at least six important ways. Hard political coverage on CBS was more personal; more mediating; more analytical; more "political"; more critical, and more thematic. It would be hyperbole to claim that in their hard-core coverage CBS and UPI presented two wholly different campaigns to their respective audiences. But in at least half a dozen respects, the two media did present a different message and a measurably separate reality.

MORE PERSONAL

In the most literal sense of the word, neither medium is "personal." In the hard-core, only 5 percent of the newsspace on CBS dealt with candidate qualifications, background, style, and so forth; on the wire, only 3 percent. Personality journalism exists in *People* magazine, not in network news and certainly not in wire copy. But extend the sphere to include news about candidate behavior, and all the national media become more "personal," especially the networks. Hard-core coverage of blunders, gaffes, scandals, and candidate issues consumed almost twice as much of the "Evening News" as the day wire.

Symbolizing the more personal quality of network news is the relative attention given the debate about the debates; first, the Reagan-Anderson debate in Baltimore and then the Carter-Reagan debate in Cleveland. The wire did not ignore the debate-debate issue; but it ranked fourth among all "issues" on UPI. But on CBS it ranked first, at least in hard news coverage. On "Evening News," there was more hard campaign news about the debate-debate than about the hostage "issue" or the economy.

MORE MEDIATING

We do not mean that the networks are more conciliatory. We mean instead that television works harder to tell us what the candidate is up to, not what the candidate did. All media "mediate," that is decide what to include and what to ignore in the day's real world events. But some media are more mediating than others. And, in the hard news about candidates the wires usually transcribe; the networks usually translate.

We "followed" President Carter for the month of September through three separate realities. We followed him first in the *Weekly Compilation of Presidential Documents*, the complete transcription of every word the President utters in public during the course of his time in office. Second, we followed him over the wire as he appeared on UPI; third, we followed his coverage on "Evening News." We counted the number of times each medium quoted the president or paraphrased his remarks. We tried, in essence, to establish how much of Carter's own rhetoric made it past the reporters and editors and came through as hard news at CBS and UPI.

During September (Carter's most public month of campaigning), UPI quoted Carter in ninety-nine separate statements. CBS quoted him eighty-four times. This was not simply a statistical gimmick. The stories we analyzed were very nearly equal in length. And in fact the difference is very much understated, because the Monday edition of the day wire had so little Carter news from which to quote (the wire is written on Sunday evening, a time during which there is almost never any breaking White House news).

Qualitatively, the differences in level of mediation become even more obvious. UPI was much more willing to lead with what Carter said, to start the story with "Carter on Carter." CBS preferred to lead with what Carter was experiencing, or with what Carter was thinking or doing. Nothing makes the point clearer than the way each medium covered Carter's press conference on September 18, in which he declared the press to be "obsessed" with his meanness toward Reagan.

CBS led "Evening News" with the press conference, but it did not begin with Carter—"Carter on Carter" came later, in the fourth paragraph of the story.

WALTER CRONKITE: Good evening. President Carter, at a White House news conference today, found himself questioned repeatedly about the level of his election campaign; specifically about his charge that hate and racism have been injected into the race. Lesley Stahl reports.

LESLEY STAHL: Just in case he didn't get any questions about his accomplishments in office, the Democratic nominee for President had a five-minute opening statement on the subject, in which he claimed that new signs on the economy are "encouraging," that inflation has been "dampened down" and that the energy picture is "excellent."

But then the questions came, the very first one about his charge that Ronald Reagan was stirring up hatred and racism in the campaign.

Then came President Carter, 120 words into the report.

On the wire, Helen Thomas put Carter in the lead and chose to quote him:

Carter Says He's Prepared to Use Atomic Weapons: Washington (UPI)— President Carter says, if necessary, he would use atomic weapons to defend the security of the United States and Western Europe. He warned potential aggressors "their attacks would be futile."

Emphasizing as it did Carter's plans for nuclear weapons, the UPI headline indicates that all journalism has its mediating elements. This was not a press conference remembered for its news about possible nuclear war. Nonetheless, CBS did much more mediating of message than UPI. The wire played the conference as a straight news piece, not an analysis of Carter's political standing and strategy. In fact, Thomas did not even mention the meanness issue until the thirteenth paragraph of her story. UPI let Carter get his own message out, CBS went immediately into its role as mediator.

MORE ANALYTICAL

For quite some time there was a naive assumption that network news was not analytical, but in the last few years that assumption has come unstuck. In 1979, Lou Cannon, national reporter for the *Washington Post*, expressed what he considered a professional heresy— the notion that network journalism has grown more analytical than print.[1] Thomas Patterson tested that notion and his findings turn Cannon's heresy into reality. Not only were the networks more interpretative than day-to-day press, they were, in their coverage of the 1976 presidential campaign, slightly more interpretative than even *Time* or *Newsweek*.[2]

What Patterson found for 1976, we found in 1980. In its hard news reporting, CBS turns out almost three times as analytical as the wire. Networks are not interested in theory, but they are forcefully analytical. Even in the hard news, where analysis is less appropriate, network campaign reporting was one-third explanation, and two-thirds description, an unheard of ratio in the world of traditional print. On UPI, interpretation accounts for just slightly more than one-ninth of the hard news column inches.

MORE POLITICAL

Hard-core television journalism politicizes news much more than the wires. It is not so much the tangential references to the campaign in stories that are not campaign stories per se—both media did that. We are talking for the most part about the ratio of "official" news coverage to campaign press coverage, the extent to which media choose to portray leaders as leaders, or as politicians. During the course of the year CBS presented "leaders" in a campaign role two-thirds of the time. On UPI, the ratio was barely one-half.* Regardless of how one gauges, networks treat news and officials more politically than the wires, a point driven home by the way in which Stahl and Thomas each handled the Carter press conference quoted above.

MORE CRITICAL

Hard news does not offer as many chances for criticism as soft news or features, but that does not alter the basic pattern. On "Evening News," the ratio of bad press to good press for principal candidates was two-and-a-half to one—71 percent of the directional press being negative. On the wire, the ratio was on the order of two to three, with 39 percent of the directional newsspace turning up as bad press. Again, the majority of hard news was ambiguous or nondirectional. But no matter how we measured, television came up as more than twice as critical, more than twice as negative.

Admittedly, this is one of the few findings that directly contradicts past research. Almost all of the major studies of campaign news coverage during the last dozen years argue that media are not critical and that network television is less critical than print. Doris Graber, who has done more of this sort of thing than anybody else, concludes that "the tenor of discussion on television was substantially more positive than in the press. For 1972 . . . 52 percent of television commentary on qualifications of candidates was positive, compared to 36 percent of press commentary."[3]

We think part of the problem is procedural. Most of the other research does two things we chose not to do. It includes information about winning or losing in the measure of good press/bad press and

*These figures represent the ratio of official coverage to political coverage in all news stories, not simply hard news items. We collected the evidence in a way that precluded measuring the precise amount of "official" coverage that was hard news.

also includes comments by partisans. We excluded both types of information.

As for partisans, the issue seems clear. As we noted in chapter 5, if Carter's campaign manager said Carter has a fine record, we did not consider that legitimate grounds for classifying a report good press. Or if Bill Brock, Republican National Chairman, accused Carter of ruining the economy, we also considered that irrelevant in scoring a news story one way or another. Hence, the exclusion of almost all partisan comments from our measure.

More important, news about winning or losing seriously confounds a candidate's real press score. According to Richard Hofstetter, who included comments about successfulness in his measure of good press, all three networks covered Richard Nixon favorably in 1972 and in a ratio of three to one, good press to bad.[4] However, that does not fit our reading of media history in 1972. But because Nixon was clobbering McGovern in the polls and in the campaign, Nixon looked like a winner and was labeled so by the press.

Yet we do not consider objective reports about winning to be a good measure of "good press." In Campaign '80 it became clear that news about winning was not good press—and for two reasons. First, as each candidate discerned, the more you looked like a winner, the tougher your press became. And second, winning in the primaries in Campaign '80 hurt politically, at least on the Democratic side. Whenever Carter appeared a certainty to win the nomination, primary voters shifted toward Kennedy, and they continued to do so until the primaries ended in June.[5]

If one considers news about winning as innately good press, then given the way the media work, frontrunners will almost always have good press. National media do not hide or wildly misrepresent the polls or the returns—they emphasize them. In fact, if we add in all the CBS references to Carter winning, or being ahead in the race, Carter would have had a positive press score on "Evening News"! But nobody believes that Carter had good press in Campaign '80, because candidates and voters all recognize that winning is not the essence of a good image. In some instances it is the reverse. For us there is no question as to negativity. Outside the boundaries of news about winning, the overwhelming majority of the directional news, hard core and soft, was critical, but only on television, not over the wire.

MORE THEMATIC

To this point, we have ignored what some media scholars see as the basic difference between print and television, the thematic nature of television as contrasted with the discursive nature of print. Paul Weaver practically built a reputation as a press analyst on his discovery that the two worlds of press differ most fundamentally in their use of theme.[6] "Whereas," writes Weaver, "newspapers focus on a diverse mass of specific events, television depicts something more directly thematic and melodramatic—the spectacle adorning the national dramas of the whole and the parts of conflict and consensus, war and peace, danger and mastery, triumph and defeat and so on."[7] In light of our findings, Weaver's conclusion goes too far. Most of the reporting on "Evening News" was more straightforward than Weaver's words imply. But Weaver is right on the mark with the basic point. Compared with traditional print, network journalism does emphasize storytelling and deemphasizes description.

We have saved this difference for last, not because we reject the premise, but because, despite its potential importance, we found almost no sure way to quantify news items as to their thematic nature. But examples prove the point that networks are more thematic, if not more melodramatic, than print. One particularly clear collection of instances took place on Labor Day, the traditional kick-off for the general election campaign. On Labor Day, CBS chose to tie eight uninterrupted minutes of campaign news about Carter, Reagan, and Anderson into one theme—one long story with one central message. On Labor Day, campaign reporting on CBS read like a trilogy— Carter, Reagan, and Anderson and how they each tried to pander to a particularly important constituency.

Charles Kuralt gave the three hard reports a preface which cued viewers as to the day's political theme—campaigning in search of the most needed voting bloc.

KURALT: Campaigns in this country traditionally start on Labor Day. So President Carter went home to the South today, John Anderson went home to Illinois, and Ronald Reagan went to a place where he could make a speech with the Statue of Liberty over his shoulder—each of them trying to appeal to a constituency he will need to win the presidency.

Then came Lesley Stahl and the same theme:

LESLEY STAHL: President Carter chose the heart of George Wallace country for today's traditional campaign kick-off; he chose Alabama because he's concerned that the Wallace vote among Southerners and blue collar workers may be slipping to Ronald Reagan

Then back to Kuralt:

KURALT: To win, Ronald Reagan will have to make inroads in the big industrial states. So he started out today in a tough one—New Jersey. Jerry Bowen has that story.

BOWEN: Ronald Reagan seems to have pulled out all the stops as he brought his campaign to heavily Democratic New Jersey for a rally set against the New York skyline and the Statue of Liberty.

Kuralt again:

KURALT: Independent John Anderson also bore down heavily on economic issues as he campaigned in Illinois. Bernard Goldberg has our report.

And finally Goldberg:

GOLDBERG: It almost rained on John Anderson's parade today, but after a few minutes under the umbrella the sun came out and Anderson began walking the suburbs of Chicago, trying to win some support in Calumet City, where workers wear blue collars and normally vote Democratic.

Not every day was Labor Day on CBS, and few editions of "Evening News" were as well-scripted in theme as this one. But hard campaign news on CBS, if longer than a minute and a half, often had a theme, if not a message, about politics and politicians—much more often than the hard copy on the wire.

UPI has no narrator, no anchorman, no interlocutor such as Charles Kuralt. What wires have in hard news reporting is the traditional inverted pyramid, stories heavy on who, what, where, when, and distinctly lacking in theme. Here are the opening lines from Carter, Reagan, and Anderson stories on the wire covering the same Labor Day campaign stops:

WESLEY PIPPERT: President Carter, saying he is looking to the campaign with relish, headed homeward into the South to begin his re-election bid built on twin themes of a secure peace and economic strength.

DONALD LAMBRO: Republican challenger Ronald Reagan picked a Democratic stronghold in the New Jersey-New York area to formally kick off his campaign for the White House.

PETER BROWN: Independent John Anderson went home to Illinois to begin his fall campaign and immediately went after President Carter and Ronald Reagan on the issue of nuclear arms policy.

Even in the hard-core news, CBS was presenting messages and themes; UPI was filing items and reports. And in every instance the theme on "Evening News" was more political than the action coming over the wire.

Summary

In hard news and soft, the networks practice a new form of campaign reporting, a combination of criticism and analysis that has eaten away at the inverted pyramid of traditional print. So, while the wires still provide information (who, what, where, when), the networks increasingly offer instruction (why and how). And above all, the networks treat all aspects of politics more negatively and critically. In the last analysis we have two measurably different genres of political reporting, old and new, traditional and contemporary. In traditional journalism, the news is evidential, detailed and generally respectful. But in network journalism, the news about politics and politicians is more inferential and hostile. Traditional print continually spits out fact-laden news. Much more often network journalism presents a short story, complete with moral. Print works to be informative, while network news shades markedly toward the didactic.

Chapter 10

Explaining the
Differences: Four
Theories of
Press Behavior

It's a crime to be critical on the wires. . . . I mean, Jesus,
everytime somebody over at the wire develops that kind of
talent, a newspaper grabs him.

—CBS, ANONYMOUS

Commentary? Everything the networks do is commentary.

—UPI, ANONYMOUS

HAVING compiled a list of observed differences between traditional print and network journalism, we asked people
who reported and edited those stories whether they felt our findings
were valid. Almost everybody at UPI and CBS said yes. In fact many
reporters expressed some surprise we would spend so much time
proving what they thought to be obvious, that the wires inevitably
report fact and the networks inherently convey messages. But about
the inevitability, the inherency, and the obviousness of all this, we
disagree.

As for the inevitability, it is worth recalling that it was not always the case that networks were the more colorful national news medium. Before David Brinkley's smirk there was the dead-pan of John Cameron Swayze. In the 1950s, network news was actually *less* colorful, less critical, and less analytical than traditional print.* If there was a Golden Age of television journalism back in the 1950s—and we have serious doubts—it was in documentary, not news programming.

Erik Barnouw, America's most heralded television historian, reflects on the peculiarly uninvolving reporting of early 1950s television:

> Television news. . . was an unpromising phenomenon. . . . The main substance of the programs continued to be newsfilm items threaded by an anchorman. . . . *Analysis, a staple of radio news in its finest days, was being shunted aside as non-visual.* [Italics ours.][1]

As for incisiveness, Barnouw suggested that television news, in its early years, had none. To Barnouw, television was a medium uniquely susceptible to reliance on formal news sources and generally unsuited for making judgments or offering criticism.[2]

But Barnouw's history pales in contrast with the assessment of television journalism made a generation ago by Richard Nixon, a man no longer remembered as a defender of electronic media. Having lost his race for governor of California in 1962, Nixon held his now infamous "last press conference," the one made legend by his statement to reporters that "you won't have Nixon to kick around anymore." At that same press conference came Nixon's stunning comparison between print and television. "I think," said Nixon, "that it's time our great newspapers have at least the same objectivity, the same fullness of coverage, that television has. And," he concluded, "I can only thank God for television and radio for keeping the newspapers a little more honest!"[3]

Television of the 1950s was neither analytical nor critical, let alone didactic. It was early television that Richard Nixon found so estimable in 1962. By 1964 Nixon and the Republican party had changed their minds. Just two years after Nixon's "last press conference" in which he praised television, literally to God, the GOP issued "Stamp-

---

*Two years after Edward R. Murrow began "See It Now" (television's replacement for "Hear It Now") he was accused directly of settling into what Erik Barnouw called "comfortable affluence." Murrow responded, "you may be right," (Erik Barnouw, *Tube of Plenty: The Evolution of American Television* [London: Oxford University Press, 1975], p. 172.

Out Huntley-Brinkley" buttons at its national nominating convention held in San Francisco. President Eisenhower in his formal address to the delegates openly attacked "sensation-seeking" newsmen who he charged were trying to destroy Barry Goldwater and the Republican party. And while Ike expressed his antagonism from the rostrum, the delegates on the floor shook their fists at the network anchormen perched above the convention floor.

What caused the change? In part it was the hyperbole of Richard Nixon and then the added hyperbole of the Goldwater-dominated GOP. But a real change in network journalism had taken place between Campaign '60 and Campaign '64. It was a period in which the networks doubled the length of their evening news programming and forced the wire services to join with them in their electronic pool coverage of the 1964 presidential campaign.* By 1964, network journalism had begun to mature and had already developed much of its contemporary style.

What forces pushed, and continue to push, ABC, CBS, and NBC from what they were to what they are? What now causes the networks to behave differently from the wires and from traditional print? How did we come to develop the genre of journalism that is network news, so different from its origins in the 1950s and early 1960s? Although the issue is still undecided, four theories dominate all others: the first emphasizes markets; the second stresses manpower; the third involves "mission"; and the last deals in morphology.

Markets: Ratings as a First Cause

Nobody we spoke with at CBS News ever once mentioned the ratings. The silence was deafening. Although we consider them slightly overplayed as a news force, ratings are almost always used to explain anything in television—journalism included.[4] Ratings represent the ultimate in market forces, a day-by-day monitoring of pro-

*Until 1964, the print press and the wires tried to maintain their independence from the networks by using their own facilities to report election returns. But in 1964, recognizing reality, the wires pooled their resources with the networks for reporting election returns. The new organization was called the News Election Service (NES) and symbolized, on behalf of print, the notion that if you can't beat them, join them.

gram popularity in a free market. And because the size of one's ratings determines advertising rates, losing in the Nielsen ratings means losing at the bank. A one point loss in the ratings of evening news programs can cost a network ten million dollars profit over the course of a single year.

We could trot out dozens of critics to document the theory of news influenced by ratings and markets. But it seems more useful to have the network people themselves make the case for ratings as a force in television. Although none of our respondents mentioned them, the CBS anchormen have gone on record, candidly and publicly about the Nielsens. Dan Rather, in his autobiography, written before he became full-time anchorman for CBS, admitted that there is "no dodging the fact that ratings *are* a hard reality."[5] He continues:

> I don't want to kid anyone, including myself. The day I return to the office after anchoring the Saturday Evening News my opening remarks are: How'd we do in the numbers last week. I am elated if we did well, deflated it we did not. I have to believe the same holds true at NBC and ABC. I'm sure Tom Brokaw and [the others] walk into their offices and ask "How'd we do in the numbers last week?"[6]

Rather is not alone among anchors in his assessment of ratings and markets in television news. Rather's predecessor, Walter Cronkite, has expressed remarkably similar sentiments about ratings.* With uncharacteristic harshness, Cronkite not only has acknowledged the importance of ratings, he has defended them publicly:

> Let me say right here, that I am not one who decries ratings. Those among us in the news end of the broadcasting business who do are simply naive. *Of course* ratings are important, and no one—newsmen, program managers, salesmen or general managers—need hang his head in shame because that is the fact. We've been cowed into that position by a bunch of newspaper critics who conveniently forget their own history. . . .[7]

To appreciate the dynamics of market forces in network news and wires one must understand that there are really two market theories, micro and macro. Micro looks toward market pressures on each edi-

*Cronkite should have an unusually keen sense of the market factor in television news. In 1964, he was, because of ratings, unceremoniously relieved of his anchormanship at that year's Democratic National Convention in Atlantic City. CBS Chairman of the Board William Paley himself made the decision to drop Cronkite as convention anchor and replace him with Roger Mudd and Bob Trout. CBS and Cronkite admitted that it was the poor ratings during the Republican convention that led more than anything to the switch. Then in 1982 CBS dropped Cronkite's *Universe* series, again because of poor ratings.

tor, producer, and especially on each reporter; macro involves ratings pressures on the news organization.

MICRO LEVEL

The theory here is straightforward. With so many people eager to replace them in their jobs, network reporters and news producers behave more aggressively, and more controversially, in order to survive, and to advance.

Jane O'Reilly spent two weeks with a dozen network correspondents as they covered the 1972 presidential conventions. O'Reilly came to the less-than-flattering conclusion that competition among reporters was the most important factor determining their behavior. O'Reilly, in fact, tied personal competition directly to network news content referring to that competition to explain why it is network reporters do not work as a team and why network reporting differs so fundamentally from traditional print journalism:

> . . . the name of the game is competition: not just NBC against CBS, but (Douglas) Kiker against (Cassie) Mackin. A magazine writer can flip the page on an author and the magazine is still there. But when a network correspondent is on the air, he *is* the network. The idea is to get on the air, and it might be unwise to share information which would get the other person on the air. . . Television reporters can't take the words home and make sense of them later. Their job is to keep moving, find a story or a piece of the story, get it on the air and find another. . .[8]

O'Reilly makes the tie between content and personal competition explicit. But she is not alone. Gary Gates makes a similar argument in his book *Air Time: The Inside Story of CBS News.*[9] To Gates, as with O'Reilly, network journalism magnifies the competitiveness of being a reporter and produces a style of reporting which reflects that unusually intense competition.

MACRO LEVEL

Most analysts choose not to emphasize the reporters and to avoid the micro level interpretation of network news. In part, this is because it is safer to attack the system than the people who work within it. Most critics prefer the macro level theory of ratings to explain the network news genre—a theory that emphasizes the corporate angle. Fred Friendly, former CBS producer and contemporary critic of network journalism, explicitly blames the *system* for the special qualities of television news. Friendly considers most reporters and producers to be the victims, not the perpetrators, of network journalism.[10]

Nightly news broadcasts make money. News departments, on the other hand, make much less. In fact, like the football team at a large university, the evening news show carries the rest of the department on its back. But evening news, like all commercial television, makes money only if the ratings hold. Low ratings means decreasing revenues. What's worse, at least from the perspective of the networks, is that a low-rated news program feeds a smaller audience into the prime-time programming, magnifying the losses in viewers and profits throughout the evening.[11]

Macro theory holds that the network news organization will adopt a news format that audiences will appreciate, or at least tolerate. Network news, as a genre, is reduced to being the byproduct of a set of decisions based on ratings, advertising rates, and corporate profits. In theory, ratings demand that network news programs be dramatic and thematic, stylized and contentious, and, above all, entertaining.

Reuven Frank, president of NBC News, came close to admitting this in a memo he sent to his staff in 1963 in which he outlined what a news story should look like when written for the evening news:

> Every news story should, without any sacrifice of probity or responsibility, display the attributes of fiction, of drama. It should have structure and conflict, problem and denouement, rising action and falling action, a beginning, a middle and an end.[12]

This directive not only contrasts with the traditional print notion of news writing (the inverted pyramid), it also suggests that networks really do have a unique definition of news, one which comes very close to our own findings concerning content. The most immediate explanation for this definition of news is the criterion of entertainment. And behind every memo arguing for entertainment in news programming is the invisible hand of the free marketplace, the A. C. Nielsen Company and the ten-million-dollar ratings point.

The pressure of the ratings and markets have allowed one critic after another to treat television news itself as entertainment. Audience and ratings have, in fact, played a major role in news decisions as trivial as that of CBS changing the set for "Evening News" after

Cronkite's retirement. Cronkite's best color was beige. Rather's best was blue, so the set changed in 1981 from beige to blue.

More relevant to us, ratings can be used to explain why traditional print, as a news system, does not act as aggressively or as critically as network news. Ron Cohen, Washington news editor at UPI, told us that the special force of the ratings makes the networks and their staff covering campaigns behave more aggressively and more hostilely than the people at UPI:

> You're talking about millions of dollars. You're not talking about whether a person's ego is satisfied or not. And if somebody ain't making it, then somebody else is going to take his place.
>
> If [our reporter] gets beat on a story, we're not going to yank him off and put him in the Agriculture Department. Because. . . the way we rate ourselves against AP is not as scientific as the way the networks rate themselves against each other.

But do ratings adequately explain all the differences in content? We think not. We tend to see ratings as extremely powerful in local television news but something less in network journalism. Powerful as they are, market theory and ratings fail to explain at least some of what we discovered about network news.

First, unless one wishes to wallow in tautology, market theory almost precludes substance. There is no mass market for substance. Yet we found at least as much "substance" on CBS as on the wires and at least as much, if not more, than in historic print. Network news has, in fact, become more substantial, even in the face of greater ratings competition.

Second, ratings could easily be used to predict news reporting that would be much less critical than print, not more critical. Just as member newspapers and their readers helped to force the wires into their role of being nonpartisan, market forces might well predict that network affiliates and their viewers would also force networks to play it straight. In the early days, networks were straighter in news format for just that reason: fear of offending viewers, sponsors, or affiliated stations. For a generation, ratings were used to explain why television was not critical, not analytical, not investigative. Even in television, the market can only explain so much. News people and news organizations work within a market system, not under it. So, for CBS and UPI we need a little something extra besides Nielsen to understand the process.

Manpower: Network News and the Star System

For nearly two hundred years press critics have pointed to personnel to explain the presumed shortcomings of American journalism. De Tocqueville offered manpower to explain the pedestrian state of the early American press to his contemporary French readers:

> The characteristics of the American journalist consist in an open and coarse appeal to the passions of his readers: he abandons principles to assail the character of individuals, to track them into private life and disclose all their weaknesses and vices.[13]

De Tocqueville was neither first nor last to blame reporters for the quality of American news content. In the style that made him legendary, Mencken too, invoked manpower as the principal reason for what he considered the "disreputable," "feeble," and "vulgar" state of American print. "There are reporters by the thousands," wrote Mencken, "who could not pass the entrance examination for Harvard, Tuskegee or even Yale."[14] And it was Walter Lippmann, not Mencken, who finally concluded that journalism is the last refuge of the vaguely talented.

In the modern era of mass media and mass sociology, critics still explain content by focusing on personnel. But now the emphasis is on comparing print reporters with broadcast reporters, young reporters with old reporters, and so on. And there are several contemporary press critics who consider personnel to be the principal factor in the special character of television news. In fact, there are at least three current theories that explain network news as a function of its unique personnel.

DEMOGRAPHICS AND THE SOCIOLOGY OF JOURNALISM

Fifty years ago, Leo Rosten began what has become a growth industry: interviewing journalists. In the last ten years alone there have been no less than three comprehensive studies concerning the sociology of American journalism.[15] Most comprehensive of the lot was a study done by three sociologists working through the University of Illinois at Chicago Circle. Having interviewed over thirteen hundred journalists nationwide, John Johnstone, Edward Slawski, and William Bowman uncovered two basic types of reporters—"neutrals" and "participants." Neutrals see the press as an impartial and straightforward dispenser of political information. To them, "news is viewed as emerging naturally from events and occurrences in the real world."[16]

Participants, on the other hand, regard the news media as having a more challenging role: "The (participant) journalist must play a more active, and to some extent, more creative, role in the development of the newsworthy." "Here," says Johnstone and his colleagues, "the newsman has personal responsibility for the information he seeks to transmit. . . sources provide leads but the reporter must sift through them for the real story."[17] Reading over the definitions of "neutral" news and "participant" news, one comes away with an almost too perfect distinction between wire news and network journalism.

What makes this especially important for us is that neutrals and participants have two distinctly different demographic profiles, and that almost all the demographic characteristics associated with a participant view of journalism fit the profile of the network press corps. Journalists with higher levels of income, higher levels of education, and higher levels of status are more likely to be "participant." Younger journalists too are more likely to think as participants than as neutrals.[18]

All four of those characteristics, with the possible exception of age, distinguish network from wire personnel. We have no figures on industry-wide salaries, but we do not need formal documentation to argue that network people make more money than the people working at the wires. Barbara Walters' 1976 contract with ABC for one million dollars a year shocked the industry. But her contract salary has been dwarfed by Dan Rather's. Anchors are exceptional, but network personnel clearly operate in a different tax bracket from wire people.

What is more surprising is that network people have more education than wire reporters, at least those operating inside Washington. Stephen Hess found that in 1977, 63 percent of the network reporters he interviewed had done graduate work or held graduate degrees. Only 25 percent of the wire people had that much formal education.[19] Not only did the network staffs have more formal schooling, they also had slightly more prestigious academic credentials. Compared with wire reporters, a higher percentage of network correspondents attended highly selective universities, and a much higher percentage majored in the sciences and the arts. Over 40 percent of the wire people in Hess's survey had majored in journalism, a non-prestige curriculum, while only a quarter of the network people had majored in that field.[20]

As for professional status, it is hard to make that case one way or another. While wires generally receive higher rankings than networks in terms of professional "prominence,"[21] the overwhelming majority of the news corps would prefer working for network news rather than the wires. According to Hess's survey, 65 percent of the Washington wire reporters would be willing to work for a network; but only 10 percent of the network people would be willing to work for a wire.[22] Professional status, certainly professional visibility, seems to be more generally associated with national television than with the wires.

As for age, the network reporters are slightly younger, but the real difference is that wire reporters in Washington are very young or very senior. The networks have many more reporters in Washington who began their career during the 1960s, when participant journalism was most fashionable.[23] In this, and almost every respect, the network people have just the "right" sociology to be "participant" journalists; the wire people on the other hand, size up as "neutrals," at least in terms of their demographic profile.*

*Although demography is not our favorite theory for explaining differences between network news and traditional print, demographics do seem to explain some of them. Demographics might even help explain apparent differences between individual correspondents as well as between media. Consider, for example, the demographics for Rather and Cronkite. Rather is comparatively "young" and college-educated; Cronkite is in his sixties and never finished his degree. Cronkite made a name for himself covering the war in Europe; Rather and his generation grew famous covering Vietnam and Watergate. Given these differences in background, Rather "should" be more participant in his reporting, Cronkite more neutral. And, in fact, both men behave as their sociology would predict. During the general campaign, 84 percent of Cronkite's pieces turned out to be principally descriptive. For Rather, the figure was 43 percent. Direct comparisons are always tricky; Cronkite did dozens of campaign stories between September and November, Rather did fewer than ten. Cronkite sat in the anchor position most of the time; Rather generally held the microphone of a field correspondent. But despite those differences, the fact that Rather's campaign reporting came out twice as interpretative as Cronkite's suggests an important point about the last two generations of anchormen in network television and about the importance of background in reportorial style. Cronkite, who learned his craft in the age of objectivity, thinks and writes more as a "neutral." Rather, product of postwar sociology and journalism, writes more in the vernacular of network television. One final fact on the case histories of these two men: Rather trained for the most part as a cub reporter in local radio and television, while Cronkite got most of his experience in journalism working for UPI. The Cronkite and Rather cases suggest demography does count—that wire trained reporters reflect one demographic background but that television reporters reflect quite another.

226

PSYCHOLOGY OF JOURNALISM

Stephen Hess, who has just completed the most systematic study ever done of the Washington press corps, asserts that "there is a personality type in journalism, or at least traits common to many reporters."[24] Hess concludes that "the relationship between personality and journalism may be the most promising field of study for explaining why news is as it is."[25] Hess never deals directly with "comparative" personality in journalism, but in the last ten years several media analysts have argued that network news people have, as a class, a different personality from people in print and that the network news personality produces a news content distinct from print.

William Henry of *Time* magazine and former television critic at the *Boston Globe* argues that network reporters do have a predictable form of personality, or at least a predictable style. Henry describes the stereotypical television news person as "ostentatious," "self-important," and "arrogant."[26] Timothy Crouse, author of *The Boys on the Bus*, found that the general supposition among print reporters is that network news personalities are little more than dilettantes, glamour boys, know nothings.[27]

Jane O'Reilly is one of the few writers who goes all out in linking the television personality to television journalism by tying the network ego to network news content. Having followed NBC reporters around the floor at the Democratic convention in 1972, O'Reilly writes, "if television is telling me its people are humble about their larger role, they never struck me as being humble about themselves. They are like actors. Exactly. These. . . people are the ingenues in a star system."[28] O'Reilly believes that the audio-visual media attract more narcissistic, more aggressive, more theatrical people—either as reporters or as management—and that the most narcissistic, aggressive, theatrical people prevail. The network news personality wants to present news that is more theatrical, more stylized, more dramatic, more conflictual, more thematic.

Until recently, most of this theory was, at best, speculation, and, at worst, envy. But within the last five years, two social scientists have moved some of this theory past the point of possible and on toward the level of plausible. Stanley Rothman and Robert Lichter have actually been administering psychological tests to prominent journalists and to business leaders and checking both sets of elites for "narcissism," "power motive," "need achievement," and so forth, technical labels for qualities such as self-centeredness and ambition.

Rothman and Lichter persuaded 225 reporters and news officials from the major networks, the major news weeklies, the *Washington Post*, the *New York Times*, and the *Wall Street Journal* (but not the wires) to participate in a novel experiment. They asked each subject not only to answer a battery of political questions, but also to interpret a series of ink sketches depicting fictional characters in various social circumstances. Although the Rothman-Lichter study has not yet been completed, the preliminary indications are that, when compared with business leaders, news people from the Eastern Establishment exhibit unique personalities, which measure high in "narcissism" and "power-motive," low in "need achievement."[29] Compared with leaders in the business community, prominent news people were more in keeping with the contemporary stereotype of the news personality.

Rothman and Lichter do not find differences between people who work for the prestige print press and those who work in network journalism. Interestingly enough, people at the *New York Times*, the *Washington Post*, and the networks reacted almost identically in their interpretations of the ink sketches, scoring almost equally on all the personality measures. These findings lend credence to the notion that network news is very much a part of the Eastern Establishment press in temperament and outlook.

Unfortunately, but significantly, Rothman and Lichter chose not to include the wires in their sample of the national news elite; they decided, in essence, that wire people were not in the same league with the national dailies, the national weeklies, and the three networks. But the fact that network news staffs and the staffs of the prestige press test out with similar personalities allows us to believe something just as important: that the elite media (networks and prestige print) are of a "type," not just a demographic type, but possibly a psychological "type" as well. It might well be that network news differs from traditional print because network news is part of a separate news psychology—the news psychology of the prestige press. Although Rothman and Lichter never say so directly, their evidence suggests that networks behave differently from wires because network people think and act like the prestige press, while wire people do not.

In chapter 12, we return to this same notion that networks and the prestige press comprise a news type, psychological or otherwise. But, despite all the assertions and even the new evidence concerning personality per se, it seems to us that this tie between the elite press and network news is not so much a matter of psychology as sociology, not so much temperament as training, not nearly so much personality as professional role.

SEXUAL JOURNALISM

To this point, we have explained press behavior by considering either demography or psychology. But Campaign '80 produced a new theory of network news behavior, one that emphasized sexuality.

William Safire of the *New York Times* was perhaps the first to express publicly what is undoubtedly the most controversial interpretation of national campaign journalism. Writing in early October of 1980, Safire adapted the manpower thesis by attributing the special character of network journalism to the female correspondents who covered the campaign. Network campaign reporting, wrote Safire, is explained by "the rise of the female television reporter."

> In campaigns past, when most television reporters following the candidates were men, the standard practice was to show a film clip, running a minute or so, of the candidate making that day's pitch. . . .
>
> Along came the explosion of hiring women to report the news on television. . . .
>
> Thereupon, early this year, the talented phalanx of female ferrets transformed itself into a set of svelte stand-up savants. . . . No more Ms. Nice Guy. Politicians were no longer subjects to be listened to and reported upon, but targets whose deceits and unsupported assertions had to be interpreted on the spot.[30]

Safire also went on to blame female TV reporters directly for growing public disgust with all candidates.

Not surprisingly, the women who report for the networks responded to the theory as just another form of sexism. Barbara Walters complained that when Mike Wallace conducts a tough interview he's considered authoritative, but when she conducts a similar interview, she's considered "a bitch" or "a witch."[31] But, do female correspondents really behave differently, more critically in this case? Looking at those reporters who did more than five campaign stories on CBS and excluding all those stories in which winning or losing was at issue, there is practically no relationship between the correspondent's sex and the correspondent's penchant for criticism (figure 10–1). Roger Mudd turned up as the most critical correspondent (a finding supported in the qualitative evidence as well); Bob McNamara came in second; Lesley Stahl and Phil Jones tied for third. Grouping the statistics for all the women and for all the men at CBS, female reporters proved to be 2 percent more critical of the candidates than their male colleagues. As for Safire's contention that female reporters do more interpretation and less reporting than men, that premise too falls flat. On "Evening News," 32 percent of the campaign stories coming from the men emphasized interpretation (as opposed to description); for the women, the figure was 35 percent.

The differences between the sexes do not begin to approach the differences in content between the wire and CBS. Lesley Stahl was tough, but not quite so tough as Roger Mudd before he left for NBC, and certainly no tougher than Sam Donaldson at ABC. Sexual journalism does not explain much about network news. Anatomy was not destiny in covering Campaign '80.

Mission: How Journalists Define their Work

Almost nobody stresses differences in "mission" as a motive force in traditional print and network journalism. Nobody, that is, but the reporters themselves. Mission means nothing more than role—how journalists and editors define their professional responsibilities. Yet our interviews convince us that news people spend considerable time thinking about what their job entails, or ought to entail, and that these attitudes about their work really do make a major difference in how they behave.

Hypothetically, mission and role should matter to us if we can demonstrate that network correspondents and wire reporters define their work differently from one another. They do. We found that wire reporters and network correspondents not only have different notions as to their professional mission, those notions split precisely along the dimensions of content where CBS and UPI went their separate ways.

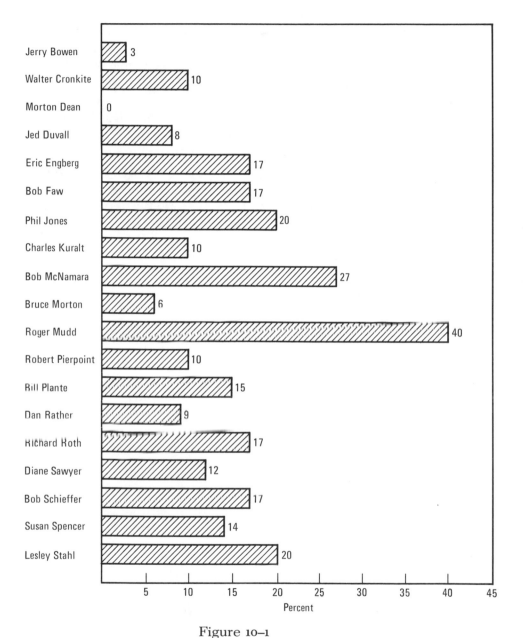

Figure 10–1

CBS News Reporter's "Bad Press" Score, January 1–November 3, 1980, Only Those Stories In Which Winning or Losing Was Not At Issue, Principal Candidate Only, Reporters Filing At Least Five Presidential Campaign-Level Stories

We asked each person we interviewed at CBS and UPI about our findings. We should start by saying that most reporters agreed with most findings. There were some exceptions. Wire people tended not to believe that they had done less issue coverage than CBS, although most did agree that wires present considerably less interpretation or analysis. Network people also took some exception to our findings, but generally they disagreed more with our labeling than our conclusions. Richard Roth, for example, said that he was fairly certain that networks behaved more "critically," not that they behaved more "negatively." We were, however, surprised by the general level of agreement, even in areas where reporters might be expected not to admit a finding. But what surprised us more was the frequent invocation of mission to explain the messages we had been receiving in 1980.

In some instances this *was* expected: reporters, for example, consistently invoked their professional commitment to objectivity to explain why it was that we found no value judgments about issues from either source. But when responding to less obvious questions, mission was just as much a part of the answer. When asked why the wires and networks behaved as distinctively as they had, these reporters and editors almost always emphasized mission.

Here, for instance, are two responses—one from CBS, one from UPI—as to why the wire was so heavily descriptive:

BILL PLANTE, CBS: The wire services operate under a. . . mandate which requires that they record exactly what's been seen, exactly what happened, what was said. . . . The wires have to operate very much on that. . . .

HELEN THOMAS, UPI: We are supposed to keep our copy as straight as possible, in the sense of reporting what the [candidate] said and not assume too much. . . when you write for a wire service, you are supposed to attribute almost everything. . .

Mission not only explains the "straightness" of the wire, but it also was used to explain the greater subjectivity of television. Again, the reporters agreed as to the importance of mission, they disagreed only as to its soundness.

MARTY PLISSNER, CBS: We would prefer that our stories do more than (say what happened)—do convey some kind of meaning. For a story to be worth doing at all it needs to have a point.

WESLEY PIPPERT, UPI: The [network] correspondents often are a little bit more, or considerably more, subjective in what they say. Sam Donaldson —and I don't mean to single him out—he's always talking about that kicker, that lead-in sentence and that final sentence—the closer.

DIANE CURTIS, UPI: The networks are allowed to [be more analytical]. . . . I think in their news stories they are just allowed a little more leeway. I am not sure that's so bad; the issues are complicated and it's necessary to do that. . . . They can be more critical; we are not, we're the record.

The networks see themselves as having one mission; the wires see themselves having very much another. The wires consider it their job to write for the record. The networks, on the other hand, consider film of the candidate's words as record enough, and their job to analyze and to criticize what the candidate's words really mean. Networks espouse one form of journalism and traditional print believes in another. That is the essence of mission theory. In Campaign '80, both the networks and the wires apparently practiced what they tended to preach.

Morphology: The "Organizational" Theory of News

Morphology is the study of structure and form. And, for the last two decades, social scientists have been working late to publish research about the influence of form and structure on news content. What we call morphology, most analysts call the "organizational" theory of news. It really started with Bernard Cohen in the 1950s, following the publication of his classic, *The Press and Foreign Policy*. [32] Since then, each decade has brought forth one major organization-and-news theorist in the social sciences. Edward Jay Epstein came forward in the 1960s, [33] Leon Sigal in the 1970s, [34] David Altheide in the 1980s. [35]

Edward Epstein is most relevant to us, because his thesis involves network news organizations directly, not the organizations involved in local television or national print. Epstein's theory of network journalism holds that the "pictures of society that are shown on television as national news are largely—though not entirely—performed and shaped by organizational considerations." [36] Epstein never says, but he definitely implies, that the organization—the shape and form of the news organization—defines the reality of the day's news, that reality itself is secondary. Hence, the catchy title of his book, *News from Nowhere.*

But what are organizational considerations? To Epstein that meant (1) legal considerations (the FCC guidelines, licensing regulations); (2) economic considerations (affiliates, ratings, budget, audience flow); (3) technological considerations (camera crews, necessity of film, and so forth). Unfortunately, to regard all these as organizational considerations is to simply repeat much of what we've said so far, especially our remarks about ratings and audience. So, in order to make Epstein's theory more useful, we have narrowed it down to those organizational factors which are not economic (market factors), but pertain instead to morphology, or the shape of network news.

We see two specific dimensions relevant to morphology of network news: (1) FCC policy and (2) the necessity for sound and video. Distilling even further, we think that the two most important factors in the morphology of network news are quite simply the Fairness Doctrine and the necessity for video.

The Fairness Doctrine requires that broadcasters (licensees in the parlance of the FCC) give reasonable opportunity for all points of view in news or in public affairs programming.[37] (Print reporters are not bound by the Fairness Doctrine, or any other federal policy pertaining to television or radio.) Fairness is an especially likely place to find explanations for the difference between television and print.

If news is determined by legal (structural) considerations, as Epstein contends, the Fairness Doctrine should be a good explanation for the uniqueness of television news content. Given that the Fairness Doctrine mandates "fairness" in news programming, one test of its impact might involve balance in the news. But did CBS produce more balanced reports than the wire? We have our own measure here: the percentage of stories classified as "ambiguous" or stories with both positive and negative information about the candidate. Ambiguous stories are literally in balance. And ambiguous stories, as a proportion of that total newshole, give some hint as to the special power of the Fairness Doctrine to influence network news. Excluding "horse race" assessments, which are not relevant to "fairness," 27 percent of the CBS news items came up ambiguous as to principal candidate. On the wire, the figure was also 27 percent. Ambiguity in reporting is not the only test, or even a great test, of the influence of the Fairness Doctrine on network news coverage in 1980. But combined with the fact that both CBS and UPI took virtually no observable position on any issue, the case for "fairness" as a major force in news making on network television is weak. Compared with the concepts of "mission" and "market forces," the Fairness Doctrine pretty much pales in contrast as an explanation of network news style.

Video represents the second clear-cut morphological (structural) difference between print and broadcast journalism. The wires have no pictures other than photographs. But, since its inception, network journalism has lived with an obligation to be visual, and lived as well with the criticism that its news is virtually determined by pictures— is pictures. William Henry makes the point best by suggesting that the basic difference between print and television news is that "TV reporters carry a 2,000 pound pencil."[38] But Henry may have better insight when he argues that the joke is old, that the cameras have grown smaller, crews more mobile, and networks more flexible. There is no more 2,000 pound pencil. What we conclude, after a year's viewing, is that video and sound per se do not explain all that much of network news.

Argument for this heretical idea comes from Tom Shales, television critic of the *Washington Post*. Shales has criticized virtually every phase of network campaign reporting, but one thing Shales does admit is that the networks have broken the tyranny of film. "As for TV news," says Shales, "it has become persistently less visual during recent years even though there have been leaps and strides in the technology of getting pictures on the air." Concludes Shales, "television is not a visual medium."[39] Shales wishes that it were.

Nor is Shales the only critic to recognize that whatever the essence of evening news, video is not it. Reuven Frank, NBC News president, makes exactly the same point:

There's no such thing as photo journalism on television now. . . . You have a guy standing outside a building telling you what is going on inside . . . . It used to be in covering news for TV that writing was the last act. . . . Now the standard way of doing it is that the words are written and spoken and then the pictures, such as they are, are hung on the words.[40]

In noncampaign news, video seems to account for more. At times the hostage coverage practically lived on film, but only at times, and mostly at the beginning of the crisis or when the militants were shipping film. Eventually the networks ran out of pictures, but then they switched to less-than-visual interviews. Just like newspapers, the networks interviewed the State Department, the hostage families, any talking head that seemed legitimate. And in the autumn the networks brought the hostage story back, without new pictures, relying, as all networks can, on their very extensive film libraries. Whatever the reason for Cronkite's decision to count up the days of the hostage crisis—one by one—it was not in the interest of video. Apparently, the time has passed when networks are tyrannized completely or even frequently by their own need for video. And this goes double in campaign news where so much of the tape is pedestrian, or the same old stuff.

As for John Anderson and the CBS "connection," Anderson *was* different, but he was not especially telegenic. Straight and wooden, Anderson made for lousy video but, as odd man out, he also made for good copy. Whatever the reason CBS covered Anderson so much more fully in the early campaign, audio-visuals were not the major factor. And when it had direct access to audiotape of Barry Commoner's radio advertisement using the word "bullshit," CBS decided not to do a story.

There are instances of news through video. The wire did not cover the wild turkey at the White House. Only CBS, with its tape of the turkey, gave that story any play. And videotape also meant slightly more campaign news stories about candidate consistency. But pictures did not set the news agenda as much as legend would imply. The stories about the Stealth bomber, the UN vote against Israel, even the debate-debate were not visual stories, but they all got big play on "Evening News." The fact is most of the candidate issues covered heavily by CBS were not good video stories. Flood lights, cameras, and sound equipment may irritate print reporters and may also symbolize vividly the crucial importance of television in the campaign strategies of every presidential candidate, but video did not seem to dictate all that much of the day's news in Campaign '80.

As for all organizational (morphological) factors taken together, it would be folly to dismiss them as irrelevant to news, print or broadcast media. One of the most important differences between CBS and UPI, the relative attention each gives the presidency, is in small part a function of organization. With a larger share of its news organization in Washington, CBS has a larger affinity for the White House news story. But even in this case, "organization" seems like the intervening factor. CBS invests a larger percentage of its news structure in Washington reporting in the first place because of ratings and its own self-assigned mission.

Summarizing the Theories

That network news is different from old-fashioned print is certain. Why it differs still remains subject to debate. We are convinced, however, that all four interpretations have at least some merit. Networks practice a more highly charged variety of campaign journalism: in part because of heavy ratings competition (market forces); in part because of its unique personnel (manpower); in part because of its self-defined role (mission); and in part because of its special laws and technology (morphology).

What remains unanswered, if not unanswerable, is the relative importance of each factor. But we have, among the four, our favorite factors and our not-so-favorite factors. Least compelling is the manpower thesis. The theory of sexual journalism simply does not hold. And although the theory that network news people have their own psychology, hence their own reportorial style, is fascinating, in the end it still remains just that—theory. The only really persuasive aspect of manpower theory involves the sociological differences between network people and wire people (higher status, higher income, and so forth) with the network people consistently possessing those demographic characteristics associated with a more wide-open style of news. But even this, the sociological side of manpower theory, falls a little short, for reasons soon to be explained.

The second factor from the bottom is the organizational/morphological interpretation of network news. The idea that camera crews, video or FCC guidelines produce much of the special quality in network news content is subtle, and it fits nicely with all the organizational theory that social science has been using for decades to explain the behavior of political institutions. But subtlety is not always validity. We find it hard to pin-point precisely what the organizational theory of news is, even though so many analysts adopt it as their own. But if organizational theorists of news intend to say that

237

the need for video and regulations from the FCC represent the major forces in network news content, then we disagree.

Given that network news so rarely bumps up against its legal boundaries, it seems difficult to use the Fairness Doctrine as a major explanatory factor in television journalism. In fact, given that we found television more obstreperous than print, the whole idea of broadcast news as straightjacketed by the FCC seems illogical. As for the special influence of video, while it is certain that network news emanates from where the video crews happen to be stationed, camera crews now go where they once feared to tread. And networks *do* report nonvisual stories, especially in campaign journalism.

Even in international news, video loses out to plot. In 1982, when the networks covered the Falklands war between Britain and Agentina, the coverage was intense and heavy, but the visuals were mostly limp and sporadic. Held completely away from the actual battles by the British and Argentines, the networks still kept up their verbal reports day and night. Network news incorporates video; video does not incorporate network news. And in the end, as to the importance of organization generally, we side with Herbert Gans. Having studied CBS, NBC, *Newsweek,* and *Time,* Gans concluded that "in the last analysis, the news determines the news organization more than the organization determines the news."[41]

What Gans saw as more important in the news process was what we refer to as mission, the role these people in the media adopt for themselves when reporting, editing, and producing news. We see mission as one of the most underrated theories in explaining differences in news people and differences in news content. Wire people know what wire news should be and they work hard at producing a product that fits their mission. In Diane Curtis's words, their job is to serve as "the record." Network people see their job differently. The networks see themselves as the medium of explanation, or as Sam Donaldson put it, the part of the press which should "tell the American people what the President *means* when he says thus and so."[42] Curtis and Donaldson report the news in keeping with their own respective job descriptions.

What makes mission theory even more persuasive is that network journalism is filled with the types of people more likely to accept the mission that Donaldson, among others, espouses. We have seen that network news people have precisely the kind of sociology that produces the professional attitude which calls for analysis, criticism, explanation, and so on, or what we referred to earlier as the *participant* orientation toward newswork. In part because of their background and training, not their psyches, network people ascribe to themselves a more participant role, while wire people think of their mission as more neutral in every way. Demographic and sociological factors explain press behavior, but mostly when incorporated into the notion of role.

As convinced as we are that role and mission have been underplayed as factors in news, we still regard ratings as the weightiest factor among the four, especially if one wishes to understand the thematic (story-telling) nature of television journalism. Because ratings are so constant, so competitive, and so costly, it would be, in Cronkite's word, "naive" to see them as anything but important. The ratings point is still the dominant factor in explaining network news, and in understanding who makes it in network reporting.

Some dimensions of network news are not best explained by ratings. But the insistence upon stories with a point and the more analytical nature of the reportage follow primarily from the heavy obligation of television to hold viewers. In the last analysis, network news differs from traditional journalism mostly because ratings always impend, but also because the networks have created a newsperson with a unique mission—a mission much more in keeping with prestige print than with traditional journalism.

Chapter 11

Implications for Candidates and the Press: Coping with Each Other

---

Those who live by the media, die by the media.

—MODERN WASHINGTON PROVERB

SO far, our primary mission has been academic, not practical. But before turning to the major theoretical question of what all this means to the public, we feel a need to say something about what it all means to prospective candidates. Given all these "truths" about campaign press, what ought a politician do about the national press in campaigning for president? With Campaign '80 as model, we have half a dozen suggestions about coping with press, networks particularly, when conducting a national campaign or even running a national administration.

Consistency First

Film may not tyrannize network correspondents as much as it once did, but video can still tyrannize candidates who change their mind. Network news does monitor consistency somewhat more closely than traditional print. Video libraries make it simpler and more entertaining to cover contradictions, so consistency counts more than ever in presidential campaigns.

CBS correspondent Richard Roth agrees that networks do more consistency checking than most print sources but he sees this as less a consequence of videotape than news beats. Roth stresses the fact that CBS and the networks assign a particular correspondent to cover a particular candidate. Wires tend to rotate reporters more and to rely more on regional reporters and local stringers. Stringers do fewer pieces on inconsistency because stringers are not generally around for the candidate's original statement. The network correspondent, on the campaign bus from the beginning, knows what the candidate said before. Compared with the wire reporters, network correspondents not only have the video and film, they also have the perspective of a year-long campaign.

But all reporters believe in "consistency checking," not just television correspondents. Consistency represents the most "objective" kind of evaluation available. can the candidate at least be consistent with himself? For candidates, the moral is an old one, but more important than ever—consistency in policy, consistency in comment, consistency in every conceivable dimension.

In 1960, Richard Neustadt suggested that in large measure, presidential influence, even in office, was a function of consistency. In *Presidential Power*, he argued that one's professional reputation as president was established by staking out a position and speaking coherently and consistently to it.[1] But Neustadt made that point before the age of television, before videotape, before new journalism had come into being. His thesis also predated the age of the coast-to-coast primary election campaign. Given all these changes, consistency has, perhaps, become the most important public relations skill —other than style—in conducting a presidency or a presidential campaign.

How does the Prince, or prospective Prince, keep faith with press if he *must* change course? Nothing makes inconsistency easy in coping with campaign reporters, but the simplest strategy calls for having a campaign lieutenant or staff member present the inconsistency. For a while at least, networks will only have a videotape of the candidate and his aide in contradiction—a much less appealing news story than the "candidate against himself."

The second strategy involves plausibility. In 1981, as president, Reagan changed his mind about a "clean" tax bill. Reagan had insisted on no major adjustments to Kemp-Roth, just a straight across-the-board cut. But recognizing that the opposition in Congress was offering so many tax "sweeteners" to those Democrats thinking of voting for Kemp-Roth, Reagan had to change his mind or jeopardize his bill. He wound up offering sweeteners to groups as visible as the oil industry and as invisible as peanut growers. Reagan then had his chief aide, James Baker, admit the inconsistency and, cleverly enough, explain it by invoking politics. Baker told the press it was worth changing their position on a peanut program to get the $750 billion tax program the administration wanted. Press people can even enjoy an answer like that—politics is their business too.

President Carter, on the other hand, showed us how *not* to be inconsistent. Following the failure of the rescue mission in April, Carter said he would violate his pledge not to campaign until the hostages returned, because, he told his audience, the situation in Iran had been "made more manageable," calling the commando raid a "limited success." Carter knew that the press would come down heavily on his reneging from the original pledge; but he should also have realized that offering a highly implausible explanation which sounded wholly self-serving would only exacerbate a bad press situation, not improve it. Even in contradiction, the Prince keeps faith better by using a plausible explanation for changing his mind, especially if the explanation is candid about the politics involved. As a rule, the press will make less of an inconsistency that is tied to an honest remark about political reality than a transparent excuse tied to principle.*

*During the campaign, Arnold Sawislak, in a commentary labeled "Consistency and Vipers," advised Carter, Reagan, and all politicians on how one copes with inconsistency. Sawislak recommended admitting the inconsistency and letting it go at that. Only amateurs, according to Sawislak, tried to pretend there was no inconsistency or that principle forced the switch. "The real veterans, men like Everett Dirksen and Emanual Celler, accepted it as a hazard of the workplace." (UPI, 15 August 1980).

IMPLICATIONS FOR CANDIDATES AND THE PRESS

"We're Number 2"

For more than a dozen years, presidential candidates have tried to avoid the label frontrunner, especially during the primaries. The first reason for poor-mouthing involves one's own campaign staff. Candidates assume, probably correctly, that the field hands slough off if their man is perceived as running ahead of the competition. But there is a second factor involved—media. And carrying the label frontrunner is a distinct disadvantage in terms of press. The problem is not so much a double standard as to winning or losing: in 1980, CBS and UPI did not declare winners as losers, at least not very often. In almost all instances, CBS and UPI called it reasonably straight: winners were labeled winners; losers were losers.

But being treated as a frontrunner, especially the long-term frontrunner, has become a new liability in press relations. The networks not only cover frontrunners much more often, they cover them much more critically. Networks also save most of their investigative work for the frontrunner, and most of the innuendo as well. Doing well in the primaries means more coverage, but it also means more real scrutiny. Given real-world limitations in time, energy, and patience, media always focus their investigative skills and critical faculties on the candidate who has the best chance of becoming president.

We have no quarrel here; it makes sense. We chose to investigate CBS, in large part because CBS represents a frontrunner among media, hence, a more legitimate and interesting concern. But candidates who are frontrunners, or who become frontrunners, need to adapt to a higher degree of scrutiny. Poor-mouthing oneself is the best available technique. Candidates should declare themselves "number two" until it becomes impossible to maintain that position, or at least until poor-mouthing by the frontrunner threatens to become a feature story in its own right.

Reagan handled this problem about as well as he possibly could have, playing down his victories and playing up his challengers. He kept insisting throughout Campaign '80 that he was "cautiously optimistic" about his chances of winning. George Bush handled his near-frontrunner status least effectively by declaring himself "number one" and literally telling the press in February that if he were to win in New Hampshire, there would be no stopping him in his quest for the nomination. Bush declared himself the "Big Mo" candidate—the

243

candidate with momentum. But, if we assume that Bush ever really expected to win the nomination, the "Big Mo" strategy may have been among the worst ever adopted. Declaring oneself the momentum candidate not only sounds superficial, it also sensitizes the press to any and all shifts in momentum. Worse yet, the "Big Mo" strategy sensitizes the press to its own problems in covering campaigns.[2] Momentum, after all, is a process born of press. Momentum implies that a candidate has somehow used media events to political advantage and somehow exploited the news media for his own personal gain. All things considered, to declare oneself the frontrunner is, in most circumstances, to be illiterate about the news media.*

Anderson's Dark Horse Lessons

John Anderson blazed a trail for the modern-day independent candidate. But to nobody's surprise, Anderson's own trail eventually led nowhere. After the election, Anderson became a college professor and TV commentator, not president of the United States. But Anderson, at least for a while, made some good decisions about press. The early Anderson campaign provides a set of lessons about media coverage for the dark horse presidential candidates of the future.

ANDERSON LESSON ONE: START IN A PARTY

If one is thinking about running as an independent, one should think again. Prospective independents should, as Anderson did, run inside their own party and for as long as is legally or politically possible to do so. Independent candidates have even less press legitimacy than minor party candidates. As far as the media are concerned, only Democrats and Republicans deserve national attention.

Running inside the party does more than confer major party status; it also provides a platform, both literally and figuratively. It was the GOP which gave Anderson his platform in Iowa, New Hampshire,

*If Bush had never expected to win the nomination but assumed that Reagan would, Bush's strategy actually made sense. By stressing "Big Mo," and deemphasizing his personal and political differences with Reagan, Bush offended neither conservatives nor Reagan very much. "Big Mo" may have hurt Bush with the press but may have helped him with an audience that mattered more, Ronald Reagan, the man who could make Bush VP.

and Illinois, a platform from which he could debate the other Republicans as if he were their equal. Independents do not get the chance to debate anybody but other independents. In the eye of the media, debates by independents are no debates at all.*

ANDERSON LESSON TWO: BE ODD-MAN OUT

Anderson's performance in the Republican debates also teaches a second lesson: being odd-man out pays, at least in terms of press. The correspondents we interviewed acknowledged that Anderson's contrast with the other Republicans made for good television, not visually but thematically. Anderson was the only one in a field of half a dozen Republicans who supported Carter's grain embargo; who publicly favored gun control; who wanted to raise taxes. There was an "Anderson Difference," and it not only appealed to the press corps politically, it also appealed to them professionally. The Anderson Difference meant news, especially as the networks define news.

If it pays to be different when coping with press, it costs to be different when coping with the rank-and-file, particularly the Republican rank-and-file. The more they knew of John Anderson, the less the Republicans liked him. After his performance in the televised Iowa debate, 1 percent of the Iowa Republicans preferred Anderson.[3] Anderson lost support among Republican identifiers after his appearance in the Illinois debate. After his one on one debate with Reagan in September, Anderson lost more support among conservatives than any other political group.[4]

John Anderson's decision to be odd-man out was a good one but only for an independent candidate who has not yet come out of the closet to deny the basic tenets of his own party. Being odd-man out will only help in the long run if one eventually intends to run as an independent.

ANDERSON LESSON THREE: STAY AS YOU WERE

Anderson's general campaign proves that candidates who choose to speak the vocabulary of the new "new politics" ought not to identify themselves with the old "new politics." By choosing David Garth as his campaign manager and media consultant, Anderson

*Ironically, now that he has a legal claim to public funds in 1984 and practical claim to press attention as well, Anderson is the one independent who need not worry about pretending to be a Democrat or Republican.

violated the consistency rule of media campaigns; combining, as it did, the straightlaced Anderson and the unlaced David Garth.

Garth was not Anderson's only inconsistency. Although his original campaign was predicated on the "romance of ideas," by late spring, Anderson had agreed to serve as commentator for NBC during the Republican National Convention, a decision which made Anderson look anything but romantic and made him, in fact, look like a self-serving politician. In late July, he met with Ted Kennedy to discuss their mutual, if less than romantic, interest in the upcoming Democratic convention, another move that was tailor-made to make Anderson look cynical. Even before the conventions, Anderson had begun to undermine his own campaign theme, to engage in the most egregious sort of inconsistency. He traveled to the Middle East and, in a period of less than twenty-four hours, directly or indirectly contradicted himself as to his formal position on the fate of Jerusalem, expressing the Israeli position while in Israel, the Arab position while in Egypt.

The impact of all this, especially on the networks, was devastating. Bob McNamara, who covered Anderson for CBS and who covered him so positively at the beginning, told us how much Garth and the inconsistency hurt Anderson:

> Anderson changed. In the beginning. . . he was a different sort of person. By the time of the Mideast trip, he was a box of Post Toasties. It was managed by a guy named Garth, and the trip was nothing more than a publicity stunt. For a guy who supposedly had cornered the market on courage in Vermont, he was running around the Middle East telling everybody there what they wanted to hear.

It is hard to win as an independent—nobody ever has. Had Anderson kept up his low-key confrontational campaign, he almost certainly would have lost. If a candidate insists on defining himself as outside the political mainstream, eventually the mainstream will reject him. If a candidate honestly feels he'd rather be right than president, he may be right, but he won't be president. Had Anderson really become a viable candidate, he would have faced even greater press scrutiny than he did in late spring and summer, especially given the feeling in the media that Anderson was partly their own creation. Like George Bush, John Anderson always had to worry that the press might turn on him for having made him the challenger he had become. But Anderson would probably have done better at the polls, and almost certainly better on the "Evening News," had he not turned against himself and contradicted his original campaign.

Using the Wires and the "Locals"

Every major candidate got better press in the wires than on television. Candidate Reagan actually did fairly well on the wires, getting more good press than bad, as we have defined those terms, and Carter too did better on the wires. Wires almost never treat candidates as harshly as the networks, and in the hard news reporting the differences seemed even more pronounced. Wires do not flack, they simply cling to a more demanding definition of objectivity. They rely less on political storytelling, so they have fewer opportunities to be critical. And wires prefer to report events rather than to interpret motives.

The lesson here is simple: all candidates should try to communicate as often as possible through the wires. But like the public, candidates too often neglect or forget about the wires, concentrating, for obvious reasons, on television. Yet traditional print provides the best conduit for communicating what the candidate wants communicated—his own point of view.

The same basic lesson applies to almost all the local press. Local reporting of presidential politics and campaigns, like wire reporting, takes far fewer liberties and shows much more respect for all political leadership. In fact, presidents can take special advantage of local press and traditional print. On September 3, Lesley Stahl spent a good part of one story talking about Carter's media strategy, pointing to one of the last loopholes in American campaign reporting, the local loophole, through which the media-savvy candidate can still slide.

In a filmed conversation with Stahl, local newsman Wendall Anschutz admitted that he would give Carter's exclusive interview with KCMO-TV, Kansas City, big play. And with Carter having agreed to an "exclusive," Anschutz also suggested that the president would have an easy time of it, that Carter would be pleased with the result:

I suppose we'll give this more than usual because, let's face it, a local station doesn't get a one-on-one interview with the President very often and we aren't going to look a gift horse in the mouth. We're going to use that story and play it for all it's worth.

Given the realities of local and traditional press, the major candidates would seem to profit most from playing the wires and the local press. Majors are, after all, the ones the networks criticize most and are also the ones least in need of name recognition. But major candidates seem to pay less and less attention to the "advantages" of wire reporting and local print (seduced, we suppose, by the nearly sixty million people who, on the average weekday evening, in a campaign year, watch at least some part of the nightly news).

Despite their advantages, local press and national wires all have obvious limitations, the most crippling of which is having a limited audience. Wires and local press offer a smoother ride for presidential candidates, but a much slower ride as well.

The Rose Garden—A Tough Row to Hoe

There has always been an incumbency strategy, but the "Rose Garden campaign" as we know it, began in 1976 when President Ford opted to use the Rose Garden quite literally as a ceremonial background for his presidential "photo opportunities."

We have already pointed out that by 1980 the Rose Garden campaign did not fit all that well with the campaign news agenda the networks had in mind. But how well did the Rose Garden strategy work in 1976 when it was presumably new? As far as the press was concerned, the Rose Garden campaign came a cropper even in its first real outing. Bob Schieffer, who covered much of the '76 campaign for CBS, directly denied that President Ford succeeded in his Rose Garden campaign. Said Schieffer, "We pointed out what they were doing every story. I don't think Ford got anything out of it."[5] Given that Ford fought back from a thirty point deficit in the polls in 1976, Schieffer probably overstated the case, but clearly the networks have been sensitive to Rose Garden campaigns for as long as they have existed.

Under the conditions which prevailed in January 1980, with the hostages in Tehran and the Russians in Kabul, the Rose Garden strategy worked perfectly well. The public rallies to the defense of the president when it considers the nation's security in jeopardy. Even the press feels less adversarial during international crises, but by early February, CBS and Roger Mudd had apparently concluded it was too late in the crisis and too early in the campaign for Carter to adopt the Rose Garden ploy. On February 12, at the end of a sarcastic feature concerning Carter's decision not to campaign actively, Mudd showed his audience an aerial view of the fabled Rose Garden and asked what he called "the big question":

> So the big question hanging over the Carter White House is this: Do Americans really not want their President campaigning and debating during a foreign crisis? Or do they simply think that Jimmy Carter is hiding, in the Rose Garden?

For reasons peculiar to 1980, Carter started rose gardening in midwinter. But under normal circumstances, working the Rose Garden in mid-winter is as much a political as a botanical blunder. Given the way the press, networks especially, behaves, the Rose Garden has become a tough row to hoe and is getting tougher all the time.

There are incumbents who would do better campaigning when nobody is around. Ford had a tendency to forget what state he was in whenever he left the Rose Garden. Carter, too, made his campaign advisors very anxious: the first time out in public after the attempt to rescue the hostages, Carter unexpectedly slurred his own former secretary of state, Cyrus Vance. But even if the incumbent president does have liabilities as a campaigner, rose gardening should be a strategy of last, or near last, resort. For almost any incumbent who seeks reelection, the Rose Garden ought to be tended very late in the campaign.

Playing Down Media

All media strategies have built-in liabilities. Presidents who have used modern media to govern or the Rose Garden campaign to get reelected have not done well at all. Since 1964, in fact, using reelection or tenure of office as the criterion, nobody has done well at being president.

The same problem seems to apply to campaigns per se. There has been an increasing emphasis on using the news media, and fewer and fewer well-regarded campaigns. Jimmy Carter's first campaign represents the one case in which a candidate built a successful presidential bid almost solely around media, but Carter lost a thirty-point lead in the polls between September and November of Campaign '76. And even if Jimmy Carter exploited the national media to become president, the strategies he used did not serve him well in office or with his reelection campaign. He wound up carrying three fewer electoral votes in 1980 than had Goldwater in 1964.

Given the circumstances prevailing on November 4 and given the scope of his defeat, Carter might well have lost to Reagan had campaign news come via smoke signal, let alone network television. But Carter's press relations and press image did not help. Yet it was not for lack of trying. Carter met 600 times with press people during his four years in office, on average three times per week.[6] Carter's case suggests that he tried too hard—not so much to cultivate the news media but to manipulate them. The White House press and national campaign reporters have a particular sensitivity about being used. Presidents and candidates who use the news media less often or who play media down will probably do better with press in the long run.

We are not recommending abstinence. No president and certainly no presidential candidate succeeds by stonewalling the news media. We recommend only that presidents who lack any real appreciation for news reporting or for news people (Carter, for example) not pretend about their feelings, not go overboard trying to relate to the Washington press corps. Even those presidents who honestly like reporters and enjoy dealing with press will do better underexposing themselves. Since the Eisenhower years, there has been a correlation between press initiatives by the White House and support in the public opinion polls, but the correlation is negative, not positive. Eisenhower, who spent less time manipulating press than any of the modern presidents, did best at maintaining his public support. Nixon and Carter, who worked hardest at manipulating the press, did least well.

But what about the obligatory, day-to-day interaction between presidential politics and the press? Overall, the comparison between the Carter White House and the Reagan White House seems to reconfirm the theory that playing down media helps with the media, if only a little. Reagan has met less with the press, formally and informally. Reagan has relied less on his press office than his predecessor. And unlike Carter, Reagan has chosen his media advisors from a pool of people whom he had not known well before his election. If nothing else, comparing the Reagan press operation with Jimmy Carter's does suggest that deemphasizing press relationships has some advantages for incumbents. Attempting to govern by media borders on the suicidal. Neither candidates nor presidents can live by the media forever, or, in the age of network journalism, even for very long.

Reform

What might the media themselves do to cope better with campaigns and campaign reporting? With as little taste as we have for advocacy and with a keen sense of the implausibility of reform, we have six suggestions for the press, with particular emphasis on broadcast journalism.

LESS POLLING

All three networks got into polling trouble in 1980. The CBS poll never picked up on Reagan's relative popularity in late autumn and actually put Carter ahead in its last publicly announced preelection poll. ABC triggered a rush of professional criticism by secretly planning with Louis Harris a post-debate phone-in poll that had a built-in bias favoring Reagan. NBC also provoked a hail of criticism by predicting a massive Reagan victory several hours before the polls closed in the West. NBC was not alone but it was first to declare a Republican landslide, and, as always, the early predictions led to claims that the networks had unwittingly played a role in decreasing turnout and defeating Congressional candidates.

We share much of the conventional wisdom on these issues. We hope never to witness again a surprise pay-as-you-phone-in survey the likes of which ABC offered up immediately following the Carter-Reagan debate. We also regret the obsession to be first on predictions and the traditional pattern of calling elections while the nation still votes. But, in fact, these problems fall somewhere outside our major concern—nightly news programming. We prefer to concentrate our recommendations on the polling the media do as an ongoing campaign news story.

The main problem with polling, even good polling, is that it is so "objective" and so "newsworthy" (at least for the moment) that it drives out all other forms of news. Polls have a higher priority in the newscast than most other forms of campaign reporting. And, of course, polls tend to be among the least substantive kinds of political journalism. Worst of all is the new "state poll" strategy in which networks tell us how the race is going in Ohio, Texas, Pennsylvania, and so on. State polls cost a good deal and tell us little. If we believe anything about reform it is that polling, especially state polls, has gone too far in network news.

LESS COMPENSATION FOR INCUMBENCY

Part of Jimmy Carter's press problems involved reality—he was not among our greatest presidents. Part of his news problem involved style. He obviously failed to charm the press corps. But we also feel that Carter paid a price simply for his status as incumbent. Network correspondents seemed to work overtime at being critical in order to compensate for the assumed public relations advantages of incumbency.

Having sat in the White House Press Room with the press corps, having watched modern-day news management by the press office, we can appreciate the media's jaundiced perspective. Nonetheless, the press, particularly the networks, ought to realize that despite all the news management, Lyndon Johnson, Richard Nixon, Gerald Ford, and Jimmy Carter all left office ahead of time, either through declination for renomination, resignation, or defeat. All the TV-era presidents have gone home earlier than expected. But Mudd, Rather, Chancellor, and Donaldson have all kept their jobs. It goes too far to argue that network journalism has denied the incumbency, but the fact is that anchorman is a much safer career than incumbent president.

The public probably heard a little more about Carter's meanness and manipulation than the case allowed. In part that excess stemmed from the fact that the contemporary news media feel compelled to treat incumbents worse than anybody else. As of 1980, incumbency per se has become something of a public relations non-advantage. As of 1984, the media ought to let reality about the incumbent speak for itself.

CONTINUED SELF-CRITICISM

In the last few years the media have grown slightly more self-conscious. ABC has a regular series, "Viewpoint," which deals in the foibles and failures of network journalism, and "60 Minutes" has even done an investigative report on itself. And in Campaign '80, the press presented more press criticism than ever before. But the press still needs to do more. Fewer than 1 percent of CBS campaign news dealt with media! And most of that coverage was about media advertising, not about news. The press is not everything in campaign politics, but press clearly represents more than 1 percent of the story.

For obvious reasons press people choose not to emphasize the notion that media are a major political factor. On more than one occasion, Walter Cronkite conspicuously played down or even ignored the importance of the press in the early campaign. In March, for example, he did a full-length feature concerning the recent decline in American political parties. Cronkite dutifully mentioned every factor usually associated with party decline, with but one exception—the growth in modern media. Cronkite's failure to mention television news as a contributing factor was part of a general pattern on television, playing down the issue of the press, while playing up almost any other factor in analyzing political change.

But press has itself become one of the major campaign issues, and, as with any campaign issue, it deserves attention, more attention than the press has given it. The media need not take sides on the "press" issue, but they ought to cover some aspects of press besides the controversies over NCPAC ads or debate-debates. In the future, the news media ought to cover the news media, and not pretend that press is not an issue.

CUTTING DOWN ON CLOSERS

Networks love closers—the kicker, the last line that sums up. But in hard news, closers often impose a message that is either trivial or subjective, or both. The usual kicker merely implies a cynical motivation for candidate behavior.

We can imagine half a dozen reasons for closers in network journalism, but we think that they debase the quality of the reporting. Judy Woodruff, White House correspondent for NBC, made the same point in her report on a week in the life of a network correspondent. "I sometimes chafe at the need to think up some clever line to close the piece with. Sometimes I believe they are superfluous and it is better to end simply with another line of information, or an interesting quote. It is true, though, that the audiences expect each piece to be a self-contained story with a beginning, a middle and an end."[7]

We know of no research that confirms the theory that audiences expect a beginning, a middle, or an end, but we agree with Woodruff's first premise. Closers are more appropriate for books and documentaries than for hard campaign news or hard political reporting. Most days on the campaign do not produce a unifying theme. At best, day-to-day campaign activities produce a lead, not a conclusion. Reality provides fewer closers than network news.

PLAYING DOWN THE PRESIDENCY

Just as recent incumbents have become too reliant on media, the press has become too interested in the presidency. "Evening News" devoted almost a third of its newstime to the Office of the President or to the presidential campaign. Grossman and Kumar found that even in print, coverage of the presidency increased by more than 50 percent between mid 1950 and mid 1970.[8] Press is as often seduced by the presidency as the president is seduced by notions of governing via the media.

It is not easy to decide which topics are more important than the presidency or the presidential campaign. But by investing as much time, equipment, and planning in covering presidential politics as they do, the media, particularly television, wind up overcovering almost every aspect of nonessential presidential life; personal disputes among White House staff, less than relevant details about the First Family, nonevents, and uninspired human interest reports.

We do not necessarily think that more coverage of congressional campaigns is the way to go, but clearly vice-presidential campaigns deserve more attention than they now receive. Whatever other priorities the media might establish for themselves, we think that by limiting, or at least freezing, the level of presidential news coverage, journalism would improve. With less coverage of the presidency, the press would have time and incentive to do more serious reporting, especially in its foreign news coverage, where sensationalism is most likely to occur.

Every reporter expressing his or her opinion to us about the topic of news priorities felt that the presidency does get too much news attention. Why should we disagree? The momentum in favor of more presidential press seems inexorable. But an expanded and inflated presidential newshole implies, at the very minimum, wasted space in journalism.

BEEFING-UP ON SUBSTANCE

And finally, as to substance, especially on television: we did not find the networks worse than other news media or worse than they themselves have previously been in covering the issues. American media have been downplaying issues and substance for as long as we have had issues and substance. The increasing number of candidates plus the increasing number of primaries make it almost impossible to shift radically away from spectacle. But even though CBS and the other networks apparently tried harder this time around, substance still failed to compete on anywhere near equal ground with events, "horse race," and human interest.

Given the reality of commercialism and mass politics, demanding an end to superficiality and sensationalism seems almost worse than naive. We make no demands. Perhaps the only sensible recommendation is that the media look one last time at our findings concerning the Nashua coverage, or the Billy Carter coverage, or Reagan's Polish joke coverage. With the debate-debate getting more hard news coverage than the economy, the evidence speaks for itself. There is no need for a closer on reform.

Chapter 12

Implications
for Us All:
Are We What We Eat?

All I know is just what I read in the newspapers.

—WILL ROGERS

JUST after Ronald Reagan became president, part of the Media Analysis Project went to Europe. The plan entailed experiencing American politics without access to American media—no wires, no networks, no Eastern Establishment press. Our only American news outlet, day-to-day, was the *International Herald Tribune.*

The *International Herald* is a dozen page daily, owned in part by the *New York Times* and the *Washington Post.* Although the *Times* and *Post* contribute articles, the *Herald* has its own staff and is printed in Europe. Despite the fact that its readership is primarily American, the *Herald* is *not* an American newspaper: the focus is decidedly international. During the time of our stay in Europe a mind-numbing 73 percent of the front-page stories in the *Herald* had nothing directly to do with the United States! Compared to the *Herald,* the *New York Times* comes out hopelessly provincial.

256

In a matter of days the *Herald* began to have a marked effect on our perceptions. President Reagan no longer dominated the news or our thoughts. Reagan had become a political figure, not a mandarin. Congress lost its personalities, its committee system, its leaders. The Hill became an undifferentiated legislative entity, either passing bills in final form or rejecting them at the last. The Supreme Court had neither concurring nor dissenting opinions—just opinions, cold and formal. In two weeks time, the *International Herald* had begun to subvert our sense of America as center of the political universe. By changing the venue of news, the *Herald* had altered our perceptions of political reality.

Admittedly, arguing by analogy is like eating soup with a fork. But our experience in Europe leads us to believe that "we are what we eat" and that just as an international newspaper makes us more sensitive to international politics, a network news system also changes our political frame of mind. Having changed the lenses, the networks have changed the images of national leaders and national politics. Using content as a guide, we regard network news as having played a role in changing the political tenor—having moved politics from the temperament of the wires and traditional print to something more in keeping with the disposition of network journalism.

The Wires and the Age of Objectivity

In order to appreciate how network journalism does this, it may be useful to consider the more fundamental press revolution from partisan local print to nonpartisan wire copy—the last of the cataclysmic revolutions in press content. For just as the networks replaced the wires in the late twentieth century, the wires replaced the local press of the late nineteenth.

Although the exact timing is disputed, at some point during the last quarter of the nineteenth century American campaign reporting moved into the age of objectivity, leaving behind the era of partisan press.[1] Before this revolution, content was notoriously subjective and partisan. After this revolution, content was increasingly objective and impartial, at least in coverage of national political campaigns.*

In a classic study of 147 midwestern newspapers covering presidential campaigns, Donald Shaw discovered a dramatic collapse, during the 1880s, in the percentage of news stories considered "biased" for or against either major party presidential candidate. Shaw found that 42 percent of the campaign news in 1880 had an observable partisan slant. But by 1884, the percentage of biased campaign stories had plummeted to three![2] After 1884, bias in campaign news never approached the level of the 1880 election, at least not in the upper midwest. The percentage of biased campaign items between 1884 and 1916 was only one-fifth of what it had been between 1852 and 1880.

Shaw's explanation for this cataclysmic change is as relevant to us as it is straightforward. The wires did it. Shaw points out that at precisely the same period that the wires replaced local reporting of campaigns, the revolution of objective campaign news began. Between 1880 and 1884, when the percentage of bias was cut by 40 percent, the percentage of campaign news coming over the wire doubled, jumping from 47 percent to 86 percent in that four-year period. To us, and to Shaw, the conclusion seems almost unavoidable: the "drop in news bias appears to have been directly related to an enormous increase in politically impartial use of relatively unbiased wire news."[3]

Despite a brief interlude with yellow journalism in the 1890s, by 1920 American campaign news and political reporting had passed through a revolution the likes of which had not come before and has not come again.[4] The objective and nonpartisan nature of daily journalism, which the wires helped to bring about at the turn of the century, still serves as the major standard of national news reporting.† Even the interlude with muckraking journalism at the turn of

---

*The age of objectivity was interrupted markedly in the 1890s by the yellow journalism of William Hearst and Joseph Pulitzer. But for the most part yellow journalism was confined to the day-to-day press of New York City.

†Of course, other factors helped to establish objectivity in press. For one thing, the public was becoming increasingly educated, hence, more interested in factual reporting. Michael Schudson makes that argument in his *Discovering the News: A Social History of American Newspapers* (Basic Books: New York, 1978). And newspaper people were themselves shocked by the role William Randolph Hearst's journalism had played in stimulating Leon Czolgosz to shoot and kill President McKinley. Hearst's *Evening Journal*, in an editorial attacking McKinley, declared on April 10, 1901, "if bad institutions and bad men can be got rid of only by killing, then the killing

the century failed to staunch the flow toward objectivity (muckraking was more a part of the periodical than the daily press, and muckraking was not very much concerned with national campaigns). By 1920, daily press coverage of national political campaigns came to look very much like what one reads today in almost any average American daily.

Precisely how the wire journalism of the early 1900s changed politics has become a matter of debate, with disagreement ranging from one end of the political spectrum to the other. Dan Schiller sees the original adoption of Objective Reporting as an impediment for the progressive elements in American society during the age of industrialization. With journalists and editors coming more and more to depend on "legitimate" sources for news, there was no place for radicals in the news or inside the press.[5] In that light, objectivity worked against the left and in favor of the capitalist establishment or, at the very least, the reporters themselves.[6]

One could, of course, make the opposite case: that had the publishers of the major big city newspapers (almost all capitalist Republicans) been able to compel editors and reporters to be subjective during the industrialization of America, the news reporting would have soon enough been pro-Republican, not pro-reform. Even in 1932, the overwhelming majority of the newspaper owners endorsed Hoover.[7] Given the nature of the big industrial press after the turn of the century, had there been no honest commitment to Objective Reporting behind which the working press could "hide," there might never have been a sustained progressive movement.

Whatever the specific consequences for the left or right, moving from a localized partisan press toward objective wire copy did have general consequences for the electoral process. What the wire wrought at the turn of this century made a difference in the political environment and especially in political campaigns. Campaigns became more a matter of public relations and less a war between two opposing camps.[8] In the generation which separated Theodore Roosevelt from cousin Franklin, the wires and the objective press which flowed from them made news management a major political

---

must be done." A copy of Hearst's attack was found on Czolgosz immediately after he fired the fatal shot at McKinley, enraging the nation and striking at the heart of yellow press. See Frank Luther Mott, *American Journalism: A History of Newspapers in the United States* (Macmillian: New York, 1950), pp. 540–541.

preoccupation of incumbents and challengers. National daily news became a neutral party, an institution which lent support to those who could master its routines, not to those who owned the newspapers.

It also seems likely that the era of objectivity helped to bring on the decline of party politics. By the midpoint of the wire era (the 1920s), the parties had begun to weaken, in part, we suspect, because a nonpartisan press and nonpartisan radio had already begun to make party less relevant. By 1928, in what we may wrongly assume to have been a totally party-based political environment, almost 20 percent of the national congressional districts split their vote for president and their party vote for the House of Representatives.[9]

Stephen Hess argues that "despite the tremendous changes in communications technology in the twentieth century, there has been no neo-Orwellian revolution in the presidential selection process. The modern presidential campaign was invented in 1896 by William Jennings Bryan and Marcus Alonzo Hanna."[10]* In fact, 1896 was almost precisely the time at which most of the American press was switching over from nineteenth-century partisanship to twentieth-century wire copy. Hess does not specifically cite the wires, but he does point out how Mark Hanna adopted a strategy of using media to hype McKinley's personal strengths, something which could be done over the wires but not done so easily through the party press.

It is almost impossible now to sort out what the revolution in objectivity did to political campaigns, or to the broader process. Objective journalism very much predates objective social science. But the wires and the mode of news which they engendered did change national politics, electoral and otherwise. The wires and Objective Reporting changed the tone and tenor and calculus of national political life. So too with network news.

As a news form, network journalism has just possibly meant less to our political communications system than the wires and the age of objectivity, but it seems almost impossible to believe that network news, as a genre, has meant nothing at all.

---

*Hanna, the major architect of Republican party strategy and politics at the turn of the century, was among the first to institute the modern campaign. By raising four million dollars in 1896 for his public relations effort, Hanna, McKinley's campaign manager, was able to overwhelm Bryan and the Democrats.

The Politics of Videonews: A Media-Based Theory of Political Change

Half a dozen years ago George Watson at ABC News made what appears to have been an off-hand remark: "I think the networks are a verbal and visual wire service."[11] Watson may have been expressing conventional wisdom or simply his own opinion, but in either case, obviously, we are convinced that Watson's premise is wrong. If this book has proven anything, it has proven that network journalism is different from wire copy.

The differences are not galactic. But when combined with what we already know about the enormity of the network audience and the credibility of television news, the shift from traditional print to network journalism represents a real change not just in news but in the relationship between the national government and the public it serves.

We will not attempt to cover what the very existence of television has meant for campaigns and campaigning. The mere fact that Ronald Reagan began his campaign standing before the Statue of Liberty; that Jimmy Carter put together a motorcade to drive himself into Virginia to sign a bill into law; that John Anderson took his campaign for the American presidency to the Wailing Wall in Jerusalem; and that all of them did these things in time for inclusion on the evening news, proves that the presence of television and cameras has reshaped the calculus of campaigns.

Obviously, too, network journalism has increased the importance of "appearances," literally and figuratively. Once asked by a CBS producer what had changed most in politics between his first years in Congress and the final days of his presidency, Lyndon Johnson snapped, "You guys in the media." Thinking about visuals, Johnson went on: "All politics has changed because of you. You've broken all the machines and ties between us in Congress and the city machines. You've given us a new kind of people. Teddy, Tunney. They're your creatures, your puppets. No machine could ever create a Teddy Kennedy. Only you guys."[12] There is an entire literature grown up about the coming of faces and film in politics.[13] But pictures in television are like speed in electronic communication—something we all already appreciate and something not much related to our principal mission here, a consideration of the changes wrought by network news content.

If we ignore the most obvious differences between network television and traditional print, those of lights, camera, action, we come away with at least as important a finding: that the stories have changed as well as the scenery. Network journalism does more than show faces in rapid succession; it also tells a different kind of story. And we think that the electorate has come more and more to see politics in America the way the networks present it, not the way it once appeared and still appears in traditional print. We think that as a function of its content and its style, network journalism has played a part in changing the tenor of American mass politics. It has made us all more presidential, more political, more volatile, and more cynical than we were in the era of traditional print, or even traditional radio. The new American electorate is, in part, a consequence of the new American media system.

Evidence of Network News Influence: Relevant Research

Inventing media-based theory is human; proving media-based theory is divine. Proving beyond all reasonable doubt that network journalism has made us over somewhat in its own image is near impossible. But circumstantial evidence suggests that network news has moved politics in the direction of its own image, made its own form of storytelling the political vernacular of our time. Evidence comes in two forms, analogical and historical.

ANALOGICAL RESEARCH

For the last ten years, political scientists and communications scholars have been testing our thesis, at least indirectly. Their work involves agenda-setting (the idea that the news media determine public priorities and what issues the public takes most seriously, least seriously, and so on). The proponents of agenda-setting argue that the public reflects the issue concerns of the media. Not everybody accepts this thesis, but most of the recent evidence shows that the media do set much of the public's agenda.

As a concept, agenda-setting goes back at least to the 1920s, back to Walter Lippmann.[14] As terminology, agenda-setting goes back to the 1970s, back to Teddy White.[15] In contemporary social sciences, however, the phrasing and the theory practically belong to Maxwell McCombs and Donald Shaw.* It was McCombs and Shaw who worked earliest on the scientific evidence to prove that media do set the public's priorities. Together they found that the public agenda in their original research community (Chapel Hill, North Carolina) was virtually identical to the news agenda in the local press.[16] Later on, in a second study, McCombs and Shaw found that when the press changed its agenda about the issues of the day, the public followed suit. And in all their work the press influenced the voters much more than the voters influenced the press. Their conclusion is that "the priorities of the media are transferred largely intact onto the public agenda."[17]

Most of the newer evidence inspired by Shaw and McCombs goes in favor of agenda-setting. Two political scientists at Yale, for example, found that by doctoring a series of network news programs and showing those programs to a group of paid subjects, they could influence the political priorities of their subjects and move them in the direction of the doctored programs. People who viewed news programs laced with environmental news became more environmentally concerned. And so too with news about national defense. Watching programs with news about defense problems edited into the broadcast made subjects more sensitive to the defense issue.[18]

The most recent and most comprehensive study done on agenda-setting finds that in Campaign '76 media concerns in three urban markets produced public concerns. Media issues became public issues. In Syracuse, New York, in Evanston, Illinois, and in Lebanon, New Hampshire, the themes of the 1976 campaign, as reported by newspapers and television in those three communities, became the themes in the minds of the locals. The agenda-setting influence of the media applied to issues, to candidates, even to interest in the campaign.[19]

---

*Bernard Cohen was the first modern political scientist to speak about the power of the press to influence public perception as to what was important or unimportant. But Cohen did not use the term agenda setting, per se.

If the public accepts the media's implicit "line" on what the issues are, then the public should also accept the media themes as to how much criticism is appropriate; how much candidate personality should count; how much the presidency matters; how important politics really are. If the media become more critical, more analytical, more personal, more political, then the public should, as a matter of course, become those things as well.

In fact, several scholars find that to be much the case: media, as opposed to simple reality, not only help determine the issue agenda but also influence the political temperament of the public at large. Arthur Miller, Edie Goldenberg, and Lutz Erbring, working at the University of Michigan, have found that media set mood as well as agenda, set tone as well as priorities. Conducting what may be the most comprehensive analysis ever done concerning the impact of the news media on political culture, Miller and his associates set out to find what effect press has on attitudes toward government, not just issues or candidates.

Using the 1974 congressional elections as their focus, Miller and his team interviewed 1,000 respondents in thirty-eight states; found out which newspapers those respondents actually had read during the campaign; then analyzed 9,000 news stories from those very same papers. In essence, the Michigan study tied voters directly to their own local newsprint. Miller and his associates found that critical newspapers produce cynical readers, and uncritical newspapers produce less cynical readers:

> [M]edia style. . . had an effect on the degree of popular dissatisfaction found in America in 1974. Readers of papers containing a higher degree of negative criticism directed at politicians and political institutions were more distrustful of government and also somewhat more likely to believe that the government was unresponsive.[20]

Has anybody found that television affects tone, disposition, or mood? Has anybody shown that watching network television produces any sort of observable effect? The answer again is a qualified yes. And again the answer comes from Miller and company at Michigan. In the same study that demonstrated a strong link between newspaper criticism and public criticism, Miller, Goldenberg, and Erbring found that exposure to television was, in and of itself, a predictor of political cynicism.

Although they play down the effect of TV news, one of their conclusions about the 1974 elections was in perfect keeping with our argument: "Among the measures of exposure to the news media, only television exposure is consistently, if weakly, related with cynicism; those who watched television news more frequently were the more cynical."[21]

Analogically then, our theory holds: the media agenda becomes the public agenda; the tenor of the media influences the tenor of the times; exposure to television fosters a political response in keeping with its own style and substance. But we remain unsatisfied. None of these studies dealt in networks and wires and none considered changes through time. We need something more "historical" to make our case.

HISTORICAL EVIDENCE

If the shift from wire-based news to network journalism has made any difference in mass politics, then there should be signs of change marked in the riverbed of public opinion. If our special variety of agenda setting "works," then the public should be absorbing the new messages and behaving accordingly. In most respects the public has been behaving accordingly, proving that, in some measure, "we are what we eat." We can begin with the most visible difference between traditional print and network news, the predilection for the presidency.

Presidential Politics: Network News and Presidential Orientation

Television news was practically born covering the presidency. NBC televised Franklin Roosevelt's formal opening of the New York World's Fair in 1939. And since FDR, the networks have grown increasingly concerned with White House politics. By 1980, we found CBS news twice as "interested" in the presidency as was UPI. Nothing is quite so presidential as an edition of the evening news.

But have our politics become more presidential since the early 1960s and has there been any indication that the heavier media concentration on the White House has meant more public concern about the presidency? Using almost any indicator the public has become more presidential.

One of the most peculiar indicators of presidential mystique has been the rise of criminal attacks on the president. Assassination attempts in the United States have become much more common in the modern news era, but only at the presidential level. Before the nationalizing influence of radio and television, criminal assaults were focused on state political leaders. Since the advent of radio and television news, that focus has changed dramatically. Three-fourths of the assassination attempts against governors came before the age of network radio (1800–1930). But less than half of the presidential attacks came during that period.[22] Since the age of television (1963), presidential assassination attempts have come at a yearly rate six times faster than in the nineteenth century; for governors, however, the ratio goes in the opposite direction.

Obviously, there are other factors involved here. One could attribute this shift in assassinations to transportation as well as communication. It is, after all, easier to travel to the presidency in the modern era. But network television has made the president more central, more personal, more important. Even though security has increased markedly since the Kennedy assassination, threats and moves against the president have continued to multiply.

Beyond this admittedly macabre indicator of concern lie the more traditional measures of interest. Perhaps the best indicator of growing public interest in the president has been mail flow. Public letters to the president have been counted systematically at the White House only since Eisenhower, but even this abbreviated history proves the point: growing presidentialism. Eisenhower averaged just over eight hundred thousand letters per year during his term of office. Carter averaged over three and a quarter million. Reagan, in his first year, received over five million letters.

Letters to the government are a particularly good indicator of increasing interest in the presidency, because Congress also receives letters and has, since 1960, kept a relatively systematic accounting of those letters. By comparing increases in "real" mail to the Congress and to the president, we can see just how much more presidential we have become since 1960. Junk mail aside, we find that letter writing to Congress has, between 1960 and 1980, gone up by 250 percent, from just under twelve million first-class letters in 1960 to twenty-nine and one-half million letters in 1980 (House of Representatives only).* But back at the White House, the increase between 1960 and

---

*This figure indicates first-class letters and comes as close as possible in eliminating the effects of mass-generated mail. The much higher figure on mail increase coming from the postmaster at the Capitol includes all congressional mail: interoffice, intera-

1980 was over 500 percent. And in Reagan's first year, the increase was almost 770 percent (see figure 12–1).

As with the increase in criminal assaults against the presidents, growing mail flow to the White House may reflect any number of things besides news orientations: growing population, social mobility, increasing levels of education. It would be foolish to think that the media account for all that growth in our presidential state-of-mind; but it would also be foolish to think that changes in the media have caused none of it.

"Political" Politics

Networks not only prefer the presidency, they also prefer the political aspects of the job. In covering the incumbent, in covering the national scene, in covering anything, the networks treat the news

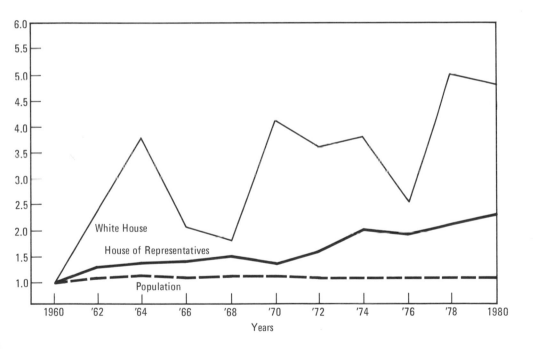

Figure 12–1
Rates of Increase in Population and Mail Flow to the House of Representatives and the White House, 1960–1980

Source: *Committee Reports,* House of Representatives.

more "politically" than traditional print. It was "President" Carter on the wires, "candidate" Carter on "Evening News." But again, has the content made us more "political" as we have moved from one news form to another? Have we been "politicized" by the content or by the new electronic media in any measurable way?

Political science is at odds with itself over this. If one uses voting in presidential or congressional elections as the standard, we are less political in the age of television. In every presidential and mid-term election since 1960, a smaller percentage of those eligible to vote has seen fit to bother.[23] Nobody disputes the fact that "turn-out" has been coasting downhill since the age of television.* Ronald Reagan won a "landslide" in 1980 with only 28 percent of the eligible vote.

But nonvoting may be a misleading indicator of political involvement, political thinking, or even politicization. Part of the problem is definitional: is nonvoting a political act? Or is it a nonpolitical act? But the larger problem is empirical: voting is down but almost everything else is up. Virtually every other indicator of political activism besides turnout has gone up since the early 1960s or, at a minimum, stayed pretty much the same. Interest in national politics has gone up; so has the amount of public discussion. The percentage of the electorate sending in campaign money has gone up and so has the percentage of activists.[24]

Mail-call in Washington proves not just that the public has grown presidential but also that the public has become much more politically active—politically aware. Ronald Reagan gets four times as much mail as Franklin Roosevelt, despite FDR's 3-cent stamp. Part of this is single-issue mail generated by groups who have learned how to pressure government through participation. But single-issue groups may themselves be a function of network news bringing politically stimulating information to a previously unstimulated populace. Single-issue groups have always come to Washington, through the mail or in person. But since the age of network journalism we have had at least six distinct generations of single-issue movements in just twenty years: the civil rights movement, the antiwar movement, the environmental movement, the women's movement, the right-to-life movement, and the nuclear freeze movement. It is al-

*The 1982 Congressional elections marked the first time in two decades that turnout did not decline. According to Everett C. Ladd, turnout in 1982 was approximately the same as in 1978, the preceding midterm election.

most certain that the federal government has never experienced as many different waves of participation in so short a time. Whether one counts letters or phone calls, the move on Washington has been dramatic in the age of network news.

Consider, for example, the number of rallies and events held in Washington during the last several years. The National Park Service, which has jurisdiction over permits for these events, has records that extend back only to the early 1970s. Since 1973 the number of permits has more than tripled, catapulting from a low of 316 in that year to an all-time high of 1055 in 1981. These rallies were not organized by party or by parties. This activism has been self-starting. And this recent activism cannot be chalked up to greater mobility or improving transportation.

As far as Washington political leadership is concerned, voting is a misleading indicator of involvement or politicization. Along the Potomac, the idea that political participation has been in decline in the age of television is regarded as naive.

Media are not the only factor here to be sure, nor is content the only factor in media. But the content we watched, as opposed to the content we read, did have a more politicizing message.* In fact, David Weaver and his colleagues have recently corroborated the point by establishing that in the 1976 campaign a diet of network news, as opposed to local print, produced greater political interest. Much to their own surprise, Weaver and his team found that "the media, especially television, had an important influence on. . . interest. . . . In line with the agenda setting theory, frequent use of television to follow politics during the primaries played a significant role in stimulating subsequent voter interest."[25]

Personalization

We did not find anything approaching personality journalism in print or television. But CBS did spend much more energy on style, candidate behavior, and what we have loosely labeled "candidate

*Modern media can also be used to explain the paradox of participation—that while activism is up, turnout is down. Traditional print for the last one hundred years has provided descriptive information—quotations from candidates and officials. Traditional print, by being so objective, so nonpartisan and uncritical, presented news that neither encouraged real activism nor discouraged ritualistic voting. With the wires serving as the link between national government and national electorate, ritualistic turnout was higher, but real activism was lower. Hypothetically, network news, by relying on analysis and criticism does something approaching the opposite: it discourages ritualistic voting but encourages political activism.

issues." In that sense, network news has been more personal in its approach to national politics.

As before, content fits history. Network news has come into its own at the same time in which image has become a more important factor in presidential voting and presidential support. Using national survey research, Samuel Kirkpatrick, William Lyons, and Michael Fitzgerald have come up with a conclusion tailor-made to our theory. Since 1952, "candidate images. . . have nearly doubled in their explanatory power."[26] Scott Keeter took a historical look at the impact of "televisual" qualities, such as references to smile, speaking ability, sincerity, and so forth, on voting preferences for president since 1952. His statistics show a marked increase in the impact of those televisual qualities over the last thirty years. Between 1952 and 1976 the statistical effect of "televisual" qualities had increased by a factor of three.[27]

One can easily overstate the extent to which electronic journalism has made "image" an important component of vote. Since Washington's unanimous election in 1788, candidate image has always been important in American presidential politics. Eisenhower, last of the radio and print presidents, was not elected because of his stands on the issues or his Republican credentials but, in the main, because of his style and personality.[28] But in the 1950s, party was generally a bigger factor in the vote than image. It was in the 1960s, in statistical terms, that image drew even with party. And in the 1970s, image actually pulled ahead.[29]

This follows from news content, but only in part. Compared with the wire, CBS did spend more of its content on personality, personal problems, and campaign issues; in proportion about twice as much. But personalization represents an instance in which content is a secondary factor in political change. Compared with print, network news is somewhat more personal in content, but it is much more personal in *form*. Some changes do not require subtlety of explanation. Video and audio themselves could account for most of the increasing weight of candidacy and image.

Criticism and Cynicism

But some changes are mostly a consequence of content. Growing cynicism may be one such case. No difference in message between old news and new media came across more vividly than the difference in criticism. In the end, every major candidate in Campaign '80 got a more critical press on CBS than on UPI, explicitly or implicitly. We suspect that all three networks have been outcriticizing print since the Johnson-Goldwater campaign.[30]

It seems reasonable to assume that with the networks accentuating the negative year after year, and with the public moving from traditional print to the networks for their information about candidates, voters would take the hint. They have. The circumstantial evidence is overwhelming. Public affection for candidates has been falling since the coming of television and has fallen most precipitously with the coming of the network news era.

Since 1952, in every election but one, the nation has consistently expressed less enthusiasm in its final two choices for president. The one exception to this trend was 1976 when candidates Ford and Carter, together, received a higher approval score than Nixon and McGovern in 1972. But, of course, Nixon-McGovern was a very easy act to follow. By 1980, things were back to "normal." The Reagan-Carter choice represented a first in the history of national survey research. For the first time ever, both candidates elicited more unfavorable comments than favorable (figure 12–2).

Looking at specific candidacies since 1952, the pattern holds. In the three elections prior to 1964, no major party nominee had a negative image in the public's collective eye. Since 1964, there have been six candidates with opinion scores below zero. This might be regarded as nothing other than a question of reality, but that presupposes that candidates really have grown worse—a hard case to make, if one uses Eisenhower as best man during the last thirty years.

Richard Nixon's peculiar case renders a strict "reality" interpretation especially hard to defend. Nixon is the only candidate who ran in two separate "eras"—in 1960, under a news system dominated by print and again in 1968, well within the modern era of network journalism. Early and late, Nixon's political history denies the premise that reality was the major reason for the public's changing heart toward political leadership.

In Campaign '60, Richard Nixon not only had a positive personal image, he had an image that dwarfed his opponent, John Kennedy. Seventy-one percent of all the comments made about Nixon as a candidate in 1960 were favorable; for Kennedy the percentage was 60.[31] More astounding is the fact that on comments specifically involving character, Nixon beat Kennedy by twenty-one points. In

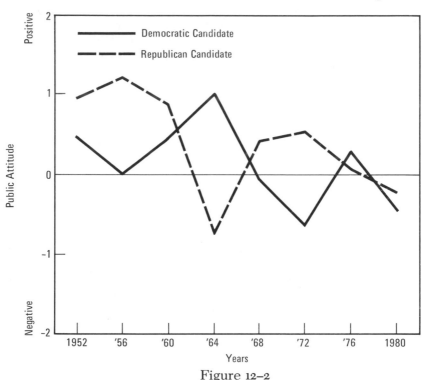

Figure 12–2

Index of Public Attitudes Toward Democratic and Republican Nominees for President, 1952–1980

SOURCE: Arthur H. Miller and Martin H. Wattenberg, "Policy and Performance Voting in the 1980 Election," paper presented to American Political Science Association, New York, 2 September 1981.

1960, three-quarters of the comments about Nixon's character and background were positive![32]

Richard Nixon had, as of Campaign '60, done little to deserve his very positive image. But Nixon had had the fortune to serve in an era of good feeling in the national (wire-based) press, a golden age of White House and press relations. In the 1950s, Nixon had communicated to his public through a traditional print system that had not by any measure made criticism its stock-in-trade. In 1968, the "new Nixon" returned to presidential politics. His overall image had, by then, fallen fourteen points from 1960. It is conceivable that his eight-year hiatus had produced enough "reality" to merit the decline. It is also conceivable that public cynicism toward all public officials had, by 1968, simply rubbed off on Richard Nixon. But, just as conceivable is the premise that Nixon left Washington in 1960 under a print system not given much to criticism, and that he returned to face a new kind of information system, modern networks instead of traditional wires. By 1968, Nixon, like all other presidential candidates, was communicating to the nation through national television, not through local print.

Additions, Corrections: Other Factors Besides News

Were we lawyers, this would be the time to rest our case, having marshalled as much circumstantial evidence as possible in our own defense. But this is not an exercise in advocacy, and there are several pieces of evidence that do not fit perfectly in what has become a theory of videopolitics—evolutionary political change through network journalism. From least to most important, here are eight "problems" with the theory.

WHAT ABOUT AUDIO-VISUAL?

In what must seem sacrilegious to students of McLuhan, we have consistently avoided reference to sound, film, graphics, video. But one need not be a McLuhanite to recognize that print comes in only two colors—motionless black and background white. Network journalism, on the other hand, dances in colors, lights, and sound. Yet we have ignored all of that audio-visual message, concentrating only on the words themselves.

For a few years, political scientists toyed with the idea that the messages on television had less effect on public opinion than print messages, that the agenda-setting power of print was greater than television.[33] That premise has begun to founder. The most recent research finds that television winds up more effective than print in translating a public agenda to a general audience.[34] But nobody argues that television loses effectiveness because it has voice and motion and visuals. In fact, those are the very things which make the content more credible and more memorable, if not necessarily more persuasive.[35]

Working with the common denominator of sentence and word and ignoring the audio-visual dimension was, admittedly, a sacrifice of reality to methodology. But the sacrifice meant only that we were stripping away some of television's most powerful communicational advantages. Factor in sound and sight and the case for videopolitics grows stronger, not weaker.*

NEWSPAPERS VS. WIRES

It is altogether possible that wires do not reasonably represent newspapers in the coverage of politics, especially now in the modern era. Do actual newspapers differ, have actual newspapers from the past differed in content from network news? Apparently so.

In a massive study of half a dozen American newspapers, starting back in 1885 and extending to 1975, Richard Rubin and Douglas Rivers found that print does have a distinctly different focus and scope than networks in covering national politics.[36] Using the CBS "Evening News" as their "representative" network, Rubin and Rivers compared "Evening News" with a relatively prestigious group of newspapers: the *Chicago Tribune,* the *Milwaukee Journal,* the *New York Daily News,* the *New York Times,* and the *St. Louis Post-Dispatch.* Starting their print and television comparisons from 1960, they discover much the same dual reality that we found in 1980. Selecting at random fifteen front-page news stories for each news source from each year, Rubin and Rivers found network news more national, more political, more volatile in its news focus than print. In what may be the most intriguing comparison with our own results, they found CBS three times as likely as print to cover political news; and the biggest split in political focus came in the early 1960s, the turning point between the age of print and the age of network news. By the 1970s, the "Evening News" had a newshole four times more "political" than the better-than-average newspapers Rubin and Rivers chose to study.

Most remarkable is their assessment of the historic change in news-

*There is one aspect of visuals that might be troublesome, however, not so much in reference to effects as to the objectivity of news. It is, of course, possible that the video portion of the news could be unobjectively edited, even unfair. But, we found almost nothing to support that premise. Visuals were about as "objective" as the text: visuals reinforced text. We also found few instances in which reporters rolled their eyes, raised their eyebrows, or used voice inflection to imply anything beyond what was in the actual copy. On fewer than five occasions did body language or voice seem to add anything approaching a hidden meaning to the verbal report.

papers since the 1880s. Newspapers have, since the age of objectivity, remained consistently local and "largely unpoliticized." During these ninety years between 1885 and 1975 "the unpoliticized nature of press has remained remarkably constant."[37] As for fundamental differences between CBS and the modern newspapers of the 1960s and 1970s, Rubin and Rivers conclude: "the evidence indicates that not only the volume and the intensity of news differ between the two media but that television plays a much greater role in politicizing news."[38]

Part of the reason for this is that most newspapers still get most of their campaign news from the national wires. Although there has been a decrease in wire dependency, we find that even in Campaign '80, at least a decade and a half into the era of "new journalism," 54 percent of the hard campaign news we analyzed in the *Boston Globe*, the *Columbus Dispatch,* and the *Seattle Times* came via the wire services. Had it not been for the *Globe,* the one major newspaper among the three, the percentage of wire-based campaign copy would have been only nominally smaller in 1980 than it had been in 1940 and 1960. The wires may no longer be the backbone of local press coverage, but they have yet to be relegated to tailbone.

WHY NOT RADIO? WHY NOT *TIME* MAGAZINE?

If network television could inadvertently alter the political milieu, why not network radio during its salad days, the 1930s and 1940s? Radio news had an enormous audience, a national focus, celebrity newscasters. Radio news even had a tight ratings competition. And by 1939, over 40 percent of a national sample preferred radio to print for following national and international news.[39] But radio never fully replaced newspapers as a source of campaign information for the national electorate. In 1952, radio's swan song in presidential politics, newspapers still prevailed as the major source of news by about 10 percent.[40] Yet it is almost impossible to deny that radio per se changed the relationship between leaders and their publics. Radio, as a medium, made a difference in presidential politics. When Herbert Hoover was president, he refused to use the radio for communicating to the nation. The Hoover White House received on average forty letters per day. Roosevelt invented the radio fireside chat and the number of daily letters addressed to the White House swelled to four thousand.[41]

But what about radio news? Is there any independent effect there? Yes, but probably not the type we have experienced in the age of television. And the reason would be content. In 1938, Paul Lazarsfeld systematically compared radio news and print news in Cincinnati, Ohio; what he found then was that radio was, overall, less political than newspapers,[42] not by much but in marked contrast to today's television.

Radio failed to do what television has done because radio developed under a different set of rules about content and under a very different set of conditions as well. As for the rules, the FCC had, after 1940, put radio journalism in a straightjacket, promulgating in 1941 the now almost quaint "Mayflower doctrine," which held that "a truly free radio cannot be used to advocate the causes of the licensee." "A license," wrote the FCC, "cannot be used to support the candidacy of. . . friends. It cannot be devoted to the support of principles. . . . In brief, the broadcaster cannot be an advocate."[43]

As for the conditions, the radio industry had, from the very outset, put reporters and commentators on notice that radio news would not jeopardize radio advertising by going too far afield. H.V. Kaltenborn, among the toughest of early radio commentators, was dismissed from his original series on WEAF in New York for saying what radio believed he ought not to say.[44] There were famous radio voices in the early 1930s who were profoundly political. Father Coughlin was the most legendary. But they, like Coughlin, were generally not reporters. Not until the late 1930s did radio develop a distinctly analytical news format.[45]

Inordinate fear of advertising and advertisers represented only one type of condition that was different in the halcyon days of radio. Radio news came of age just in time for World War II. Radio came into its own during a period in which press saw itself as an ally against a real international peril—facism. Television, on the contrary, came into its own during an historic epoch in which the enemy was not nearly as clear or as threatening. World War II and the war in Vietnam taught very different lessons to the swelling ranks of young journalists sent off to cover those very different wars. Reporters came back from Europe in 1945 convinced our effort was noble. Few returned that way from Vietnam. In its heyday, radio news content worked to defend American political interests, not to discredit its political leadership. As such, it is at least possible that radio in the 1930s and 1940s did to national politics what network news has been doing in reverse since the 1960s, with radio moving content and opinion in *support* of national political leaders.

If radio journalism failed to make so fundamental a change as television news because of content, *Time* magazine failed for a host of different reasons. *Time* magazine was a major change in twentieth-century journalism. Unlike traditional print, *Time* was (and is) a national news organ. David Halberstam concludes that Henry Luce and his weekly were among the "first true *national* propagandists."[46] And unlike traditional print, *Time* magazine was almost shamefully partisan.* *Time* also differed from traditional print in its penchant for the analytical. Analytical reporting has been a way of life at *Time* magazine for the last five decades. According to Thomas Patterson, *Time,* in 1976, was just as analytical as network news reporting.[47]

Given all this, *Time* should have produced political change. Henry Luce probably did reshape American political history, not so much perhaps in the arena of political culture as in the convention halls of the GOP. But despite his best efforts in either forum, Luce had three things working against him. First, *Time* never had the audience, not the mass audience anyway. By 1932, radio had an audience of fifty million listeners. *Time* had "only" 500,000 subscribers (one one-hundredth of today's network evening news audience). *Time* was always more an upper-middle-class medium than a mass medium.

Second, *Time* lacked credibility. Unlike radio and television, *Time* squandered its believability in pursuit of its own partisan mission, promoting Luce's "American century." At no time since the 1950s has more than one-tenth of the public regarded news magazines as highly credible, and *Time* magazine bears responsibility for at least some of that lack of credibility.

And finally, *Time* magazine failed to do what network journalism has done because *Time* never went much beyond preaching to the converted. Unlike network news, which attracts almost everybody, *Time* reached an audience disproportionately Republican and conservative. *Time,* as novel as it was, produced a content more likely to reinforce the partisan opinion of its readership than produce subtle shifts in the nation's political culture. Whatever effect it had on national politics during its golden years, *Time* magazine could not

*After the 1952 presidential election, in which *Time* had brutalized Stevenson and lionized Eisenhower, Luce was called on to defend his obvious partisan treatment of the campaign. Luce responded by saying that "it was *Time*'s duty to explain why the country needed Ike. Any other form of journalism would have been unfair and uninvolved."

have been as consequential a force in mass politics as network news has been.

CONTENT OR AUDIENCE?

Time magazine may not have been a major watershed in political journalism, but *Time* has, for the first time, forced us to flirt openly with the idea of audience. Until now we have given audience much less credit than it deserves. Readers and viewers are a major factor in any discussion of media-based political change. Had the audience stuck with print, by definition, there could not have been a video evolution in politics. But the importance of audience transcends mere definition. Because the network news audience is unique in size and in shape, audience has to be a factor in understanding the cultural effects of political television.

The *Wall Street Journal* has the largest circulation of any daily print news source in America (circulation of two million). CBS "Evening News" has a "circulation" almost ten times as large, and CBS is one of three "equal" networks. Although there are revisionists who insist that networks do not dominate the national news audience,[48] nothing else approaches the size of the audience for television news, estimated at fifty-five million viewers per night.

Equally important is the composition of that audience. Network television has been able to produce a news viewership that is somewhat bottom heavy, with people at the lowest end of the social spectrum likely to consume the highest proportions of television news. No responsible news medium has ever done that. Radio, closest relative to television, never even came close.[49] Robert Bower's research from the 1970s shows that people with an eighth-grade education not only watch more television than the college-educated, they also watch news in higher proportions than any other group.[50] Taken together, the size and shape of the television news audience generates a viewership that is a breed apart from everything else.

In trying to understand how network news has influenced public opinion it might be just as important to appreciate the uniqueness of its audience as the singularity of its content. It is the size of audience, for example, which explains how millions of Americans came to recognize a physically nondescript John Anderson in just a matter of weeks in 1980. Because of the enormous audience of television, in a month's time almost an entire population could pronounce, if not spell, Bani Sadr's name. Sadegh Gotzbazadeh, Iranian foreign minister at the time of the original take-over of the American embassy in Tehran, became a household word through the wonders of network news and its vast audience. Even the growth in the importance of single-issue voting is partially explained by the size and shape of the network news audience.[51] With network content reaching a part of the audience rarely exposed to any sort of serious news medium, issues almost had to become more important. Before television brought news to this informationally disadvantaged class of viewers, party was reason enough to vote as they did.

We have ignored audience only because it is a given, something we have always appreciated as an extraordinary feature of television. Almost everybody knows about the unique television audience, but not too many consider the uniqueness of television content. Content has generally been the stepsister in theories about politics and television—a stepsister who needed to be appreciated for what she is, an essential component in any theory concerning the consequences of network news.

NETWORK NEWS OR "NEW JOURNALISM?"

Focusing specifically on campaign coverage, Martin Plissner at CBS accepted our notion that the early 1960s were the watershed in modern media, but not because of television. Plissner cited print reporting as the basis of the revolution—one print reporter, in fact. His name was Teddy White. According to Plissner, Teddy White was the watershed, almost on his own:

> Let me tell you what happened between 1960 and today. . . . In 1960, Teddy White wrote a book called *The Making of the President: 1960*, which suggested that the manner by which a man runs. . . and gets elected is extremely complicated. . . it involves much more than most people realized.

> Since 1960 you've had. . . political reporters who have become extremely sophisticated about the process—who have become specialists. . . . And it's these people and their talents which are (changing journalism), and not some kind of institutional decision to do it that way.

Plissner is not alone. In his *Pulse of Politics,* James Barber also singles out Teddy White's *The Making of the President* as the model that AP and the *New York Times* editors literally handed to their reporters in covering the campaigns after 1960.[52]

Of course, Teddy White is a symbol as well as model—a symbol of the "new journalism" as practiced in presidential campaigns. So the question becomes, was it network journalism or "new journalism" that helped produce a modest cultural transformation?

In one sense the question is moot. The public has fairly well stopped following national politics through print, traditional or otherwise. Television is the pre-eminent link between national affairs and the national public. But that point begs the original, more fundamental, question: is it network journalism or is it *all* journalism that has changed its approach to national politics? Our answer has two parts, but no simple solution. First, not all journalism has altered its approach.

As for the wires, they have changed, but not very much. We asked Helen Thomas to talk about the "new journalism," the wires, and her personal experience in the Washington press service since the early 1960s:

> I think basically I am as I was at the beginning. I still find myself curbing myself, and trying never to inject my own opinion.
>
> There is no question that there is more interpretation now and the whole aim is not just the straight "he said," "he added." But basically I think it is still the same format (as before). . . . I think we still try to toe the line.

UPI and AP still fill up traditional print with their own wire copy. And the wires still cover political leadership and politics in much the same tradition they have practiced for the last fifty years. So in that sense, when compared with the wires directly, it is television news that has made the difference.

But, in fact, daily print has changed. It has become less like the wires. By Campaign '80, the news syndicates and news services had made the *Columbus Dispatch* and *Seattle Times* read just a wee bit more like the eastern press than had ever been the case before. Young reporters working in the local press identify more with the lessons of *All the President's Men* than with the lessons in the AP handbook on style and protocol. In his study of American newspapers in the late 1970s, Stephen Hess had to admit that "increasingly, the content of the news from Washington in papers around the country looks more and more like the *New York Times.*"[53]

"New journalism," the avowedly unobjective news form of the 1960s, has seeped into the prestige press, and the prestige press has been seeping into traditional print. Traditional newspapers contain more criticism, more analysis, more skepticism than the wires, and more than they carried in the past. But if Rubin and Rivers are right, traditional newspapers still do not do nearly as much of that in their hard news coverage as network television and the eastern press. So in the last analysis, even if we concede that traditional print has shifted some, it has not shifted much, not enough to produce the changes in behavior and opinion that have characterized this last political generation.

One could argue that the difference really involves "old news" and "new media," not wires and television. But the wires were, and are, the old news; the networks are the new media, at least when we talk about mass communication from Washington to the rest of the nation. It is the network news people who bring the news, the stories, and the themes about national politics to the rest of the country. Network news people never really subscribed to the "new journalism." Basically, they subscribe to the *Washington Post* and the *New York Times*. But it was the networks who brought their own short form of new journalism, borrowed in part from the *Washington Post* and *New York Times*, to the American public. So it is the networks who have altered the basic line and style of communication between the capital and the public at large.

DEMOGRAPHICS

Virtually every major trend in mass politics since the 1950s can be pegged to shifts in American demography. The transition from print and radio toward television has coexisted with other, equally important social trends, the most important of which have been increasing wealth and rapidly rising levels of formal education.

Political scientists have offered demographic factors such as education and age to explain changes ranging from the decline in party to the growth in crime. More important, demographic changes also explain away some of our findings, such as increasing political interest, political activism, issue awareness, and so forth. Part of the reason that mail flow to Washington has jumped so dramatically is demographic. A richer, more literate society means more letters to Congress and to the president.

But demographics do not work nearly so well in explaining the marked increase in presidentialism. Nor do demographic changes explain growing public cynicism toward government and political leadership. And demographics fail miserably to explain the decreasing tendency to vote. In fact, given what *has* changed in American sociology in the last twenty years, with nineteenth-century history as our guide, we should be less cynical, less alienated, less likely to miss out on the vote.[54] Evidently, demographic theory has its limitations.

CAUSES OR CONSEQUENCES

It is, of course, possible that network news has not caused any of these changes, but that the news has merely reflected changes in the electorate. Specifically, network news might be a consequence of audience, not a cause. We know that on a day-to-day basis the networks are much more sensitive to audience than are wires or newspapers. So, it makes good sense to assume that network news has grown more presidential, more critical, and so forth, in order to keep pace with a public opinion which has been shifting in those same directions. Theoretically, then, networks, because of intense ratings competition, have been influenced more by viewers than vice versa.

To some degree the entire process must be circular, with the networks affecting the public and the public affecting the networks in return. Yet, sensitive as we are to this problem, we see media as the more important, more original force; not a first cause, to be sure, but a cause nonetheless. We cling to our view for three reasons. First, the overwhelming majority of the quantitative research that looks at this problem mathematically supports us. High-powered statistics indicate that the media influence the public more than vice versa.[55] Second, in several instances and issues the networks have been out ahead of the public, "leading" public opinion. Consider some classic examples: Howard K. Smith's attacks on white racism in America during the early 1960s; Morley Safer's coverage of U.S. marines burning villages in Vietnam before the war became unpopular; Dan Rather's legendary 1974 confrontation with President Nixon during a nationally televised press conference concerning Watergate.

The point is not that the networks have been courageous, let alone correct. The point is that the networks have been willing, on occasion, to step outside public opinion in areas as important as civil rights, Vietnam, and Watergate. Not as willing to push as the eastern dailies, perhaps, but not as unwilling as the wires or traditional print.*

Campaign '80 provided its own best evidence for rejecting the notion that network news simply reflects public opinion. The case involves the now historic Edward Kennedy interview which Roger Mudd conducted in November 1979, an interview in which Mudd implicitly labeled Kennedy's explanation of Chappaquiddick as bunk, and in which Mudd embarrassed Kennedy badly with questions about his wife and politics. When Mudd did that interview he knew that at that time Kennedy was by far the most popular figure in the Democratic party, perhaps the most popular figure in the nation. So, whatever else he was attempting to do, Mudd was not trying to pander to favorable public opinion concerning Kennedy. Mudd was very much "ahead" of public opinion at that point.

We have a third reason for rejecting the notion that the networks have only mirrored electoral change. To argue that networks mechanically reflect public tastes and opinions implies that networks consider audience their major reference point. But we have a hard time accepting that premise. Networks no doubt do consider audience in constructing news, but we find that networks defer to other journalists in deciding matters of focus and tone. Network journalism has taken its focus and tone neither from the public, nor from the wires, nor from traditional print. Instead, we would argue that the networks have taken as reference point prestige print. Public opinion very possibly influences network news less than the *Washington Post* and *New York Times* influence network news. Granted this pattern of influence is speculative, but it is speculation that will merit our further consideration.

MEDIA OR EVENTS?

Inevitably one has to ask if media systems explain much contemporary political change, or if all this has come as mere consequence of real world events. Consider the case of political cynicism. Although

*David Halberstam argues that the wires, by practicing safe journalism, virtually buried the more aggressive and critical reporting being practiced in Vietnam. Editors chose the safer wire copy whenever it was available.

we have said that moving from wires to networks has, since 1960, played a role in lessening public esteem for presidential candidates, the most obvious counterargument would be that recent candidates simply deserve less esteem. Most journalists believe that reality and events caused this change, not the media.

Had Lyndon Johnson not misrepresented his position about peace in Vietnam; had Barry Goldwater not suggested that the East Coast be allowed to float off into the Atlantic; had Richard Nixon not lied about Watergate; had George McGovern not sworn to back Tom Eagleton 1,000 percent; had Jimmy Carter rescued the hostages; had Reagan not blamed trees for air pollution: candidate images would not have fallen quite so fast or so consistently over the years. But had all those things happened in a wire-based news system and not in a world of network news, the erosion would have not, we suspect, come so quickly or so fully.

Events are not events until they get themselves communicated. Ron Nessen, former press secretary to Gerald Ford and former NBC news correspondent, is fond of saying that if it didn't happen on network television, then it didn't happen. Media do decide, to some limited degree, which of the events on a particular day will be represented and how those events will be played. But different types of media choose different events as newsworthy, and cover them in different ways.

CBS correspondent Robert Pierpoint tells a fascinating story in *At the White House.* In March 1962, Pierpoint was covering President Kennedy on one of his trips to California. Pierpoint was serving as a pool reporter, covering the events for his own network and for other networks as well. Traveling in the motorcade, Pierpoint followed Kennedy to an estate where he had been staying outside Palm Springs. Pierpoint continues:

> Douglas Cornell of Associated Press and I were sitting quietly in the desert darkness chatting when suddenly the front door of the house burst open and the light streaming out revealed JFK emerging with a woman on his arm.
>
> Kennedy pulled her along toward the limousine, and then, opening the door, laughingly shoved her in the back seat.
>
> After a few minutes of silence, the front door of the house opened again and another woman came out. It was one of President Kennedy's sisters.

"Come on, Mildred," she shouted, and as the light went on again in the car we could see 'Mildred' disentangling herself from the President of the United States.[56]

Pierpoint never reported the event. Nor did he mention it in his report for the pool, denying those reporters a chance to use what was very clearly the day's "top" story. Pierpoint says, reflecting the new morality of the newer journalism, "I might report a similar incident were I to witness it today."

We do not deny that he would go with that story today, nor would we discourage him. But Pierpoint's nonreporting of this nonevent makes several important points about reality and the news media. First, in a world in which the press decides what not to report, the press becomes almost as important as the events themselves in the formulation of perceived reality. Second, in a world in which the press changes its mind as to what it will not report, those changes in content become at least as much an effect of media as an effect of the events per se. Third, the obverse also applies: what press considers worthy of emphasizing becomes quite obviously a major part of "reality." Pierpoint's decision not to report on Kennedy's extracurricular life means that "reality" was not the only thing determining Kennedy's political image.

Finally, Pierpoint's current willingness to go with this sort of story tells us that almost all the media have changed. Conceivably, the wires might still not go with this sort of thing, unless, of course, the story had broken in some other medium. But, in general, the networks have, since 1963, altered the definition of "all the news that's fit to print." Had this particular Kennedy story been covered objectively and fully and visually, it is more than likely that Kennedy's image would not have been quite so charismatic. Compared with Jimmy Carter's remark about "lust in my heart," a major press gaffe in 1976, John Kennedy had committed something on the order of a morally impeachable offense.

Which brings us full circle and back to Jimmy Carter, back to Campaign '80, and back to Carter Day in Philadelphia (chapter 1). CBS covered the events of Carter's Day; UPI covered the "same" events. Reread those two stories and the conclusion is clear: events count, but media count too.

The Prestige Press, The Networks, and The Washington Community: The New Two-Step Flow of Media

Throughout this book we have made passing, almost cryptic references to the influence of something called "the prestige print press." Broadly defined, prestige print includes *Time* and *Newsweek,* the *Boston Globe,* the *Los Angeles Times,* the *Wall Street Journal,* and extends all the way to *U.S. News and World Report.* But no matter how narrowly defined, prestige print always includes the *Washington Post* and the *New York Times,* the two American dailies which stand in a class of their own.[57]

In chapter 5, we pointed out that one of the best interpretations for John Anderson's great success with CBS in the early campaign was that the *Washington Post* and *New York Times* had, as early as 1979, been treating Anderson to lots of very good press. In chapter 10, we pointed out that recent research suggests that people who work at CBS and the other networks have similar opinions, and even similar personalities, to those who work at the *Washington Post* and the *New York Times.* All of this at least implies that prestige print has played a very important role in the creation of the television news genre and that prestige print also plays an indirect role in the effects we have attributed to TV news. Although it is very late in the play to introduce another character, we do consider it essential to point out that what the networks have given us did not begin spontaneously or in a vacuum. Instead, network journalism, as a news form and as political factor, begins in part with prestige print.

For thirty years there has been considerable speculation about a two-step flow of mass communication. The original notion, offered by Elihu Katz and Paul Lazarsfeld, was that political content goes from a news source to a collectivity of "opinion leaders" and then to the public at large. In national politics there is a two-step flow but not as Katz and Lazarsfeld imagined it thirty years ago.[58] In the United States, political communication runs a different route—from the *Post* and *Times* through the networks and then on to the general public.

Under the wire system, the wire people produce their own national copy in keeping with the traditions of AP and UPI. But the network correspondents and editors identify more closely with the people who control the elite print press. The network reporters and editors see themselves as part of the prestige press, not part of traditional print. None of the network correspondents we interviewed bothered to read the wires or wire copy on the campaign trail, where wire copy was, admittedly, in relatively short supply. But reporters always seemed to find a way to spend time with the major dailies and to read them, especially the *Post* and *Times*. For the networks, the elite press counts for much; traditional press counts for little. One anonymous person at CBS made this point with a hammer:

> The wires don't count. Wires don't even belong in the discussion.
>
> In all fairness, for coverage of a political campaign, if you've got the CBS correspondents out in the field reporting, if you read the *Washington Post*, the *New York Times,* the *Wall Street Journal.* . . you're not likely to miss much by not reading the wires.

The network relationship to the prestige press extends beyond identity and includes personnel. James Wooten reported the 1976 campaign for the *New York Times,* the 1980 campaign for ABC. After Charles Krause finished reporting about Latin American politics for the *Washington Post,* he moved over to "Evening News." The networks and the prestige newspapers sometimes exchange staffs and editors as well as status.

Tied closely with elite print in status and in personnel, the networks have not had to invent their own news form *de nouveau.* They borrowed it in part from the prestige press. At least in its coverage of the presidency and presidential campaigns, network journalism has given America what it has never had before, an abbreviated national newspaper in the manner of the *Washington Post* and the *New York Times.* So, in covering Washington and the presidency, network news has brought the style and vocabulary of the prestige print press to places as far away from Washington as Pasadena and Pensacola, and Peoria too.

This premise does not hold so well for foreign news or local politics. The networks literally and figuratively do not have the time for those. But the premise holds particularly well in those areas where the networks have decided to compete. To be specific, it holds for the presidency and the presidential campaign. In those two topics, "the networks," according to one veteran correspondent at ABC, "have brought the *Washington Post* to the rest of America"—not necessarily in length, or in depth, but in approach and tenor.

Marshall McLuhan believed that network television had made the world a "global village." Our perspective is much narrower. As we understand it, covering national politics as it does, network television has extended somewhat the Washingtonian news approach to the rest of the population. And, by adopting a news format much more in keeping with prestige print (a format that is more analytical, more thematic, more critical than traditional print), the networks have shifted the electorate toward an image of national politics that comes close to the image held by the Washingtonians themselves. By borrowing their style of reporting from prestige print, the networks in the last two decades have changed somewhat the disposition and vocabulary of national news and the general public. Cynical but interested, savvy and involved, the electorate has come to view the presidency, the president, and the political leaders in Washington the way professional Washington has almost always viewed them.

In 1964, over three-quarters of the nation believed it "could trust the government in Washington to do what's right 'most of the time' or 'all of the time.' " By 1978, the figure was well below one-third![59] Although there are other explanations for this dramatic change, the shift from traditional print to network journalism is, in our opinion, as good as any. We suggest that the networks, by emulating the tone of the prestige press, have shifted public opinion so that it reflects the thinking of the Washington press and political community. What percentage of the Washington press, or even the Washington establishment, "would trust the government in Washington to do what's right all of the time?"

That declining trust in government is partially a media effect and reflects a new form of national journalism seems fairly clear. But, given that the news content of the networks is rarely dishonest or irresponsible, there seems only a little merit in blaming the networks for their role in this process. Rather than blaming the networks one might even prefer arguing that traditional print was insufficiently critical of national political leadership. One could even regard the new approach as "historic," a reflection of early American journalism when press hostility was very much in vogue[60] (when George Washington was described as an infidel, and worse).

Even the politicians were more hostile then, expressing in almost every way their doubts about centralized government. Assume for a moment that there had been a national government in Washington, D.C., in 1787. Assume that we might have asked the farmers the same "trust" question: how often can you trust the government in

Washington to do what's right? Which of the founders would have said "always" or "most of the time"? Hamilton? Maybe. Jefferson? Doubtful. Madison? Never.

If Madison were somehow able to watch the "Evening News" as it implied over and over again that the government was up to no good, Madison might well conclude with Cronkite that "that's the way it is." We doubt very seriously that Madison would have found network coverage adequate, but doubt too that he would have found it unduly hostile, given the press he faced.

Does one blame the networks for increasing cynicism, or does one credit them for fostering realism? Practically speaking, that surely depends on whether or not one is the target of the news coverage. But from the philosophical perspective, the answer tends to hinge on the motives of the newspeople. To the extent that all this "realism" is simply a function of competition for ratings, blame is in order. To the extent that the network approach is based in a pristine commitment to serving as watchdog, the emphasis on blame diminishes. But if we were to cover the networks the way they cover leadership, we would have to assume the darker motive, the influences of ratings instead of principles. Either way, the evidence is fairly convincing: wittingly or unwittingly, network journalism has been a factor, though clearly not the only factor, in reshaping our political culture.

Summary

A generation ago, Bernard Cohen made an observation which has become catechism for students of mass media and national press:

> The press is significantly more than a purveyor of information and opinion. It may not be successful much of the time in telling people what to think, but it is stunningly successful in telling its reader what to think about.[61]

Cohen drew his conclusion from the period just before television. We would add a corollary that takes network news into account. The media not only tell us what to think about, but also *how* to think about it. This has almost nothing to do with partisan thinking. It pertains almost wholly to the way we approach and respond to politics and politicians. Traditional print approached national politics and political candidates descriptively and officially and so did its readership. Network news approaches them more like the *Washington Post* and the *New York Times,* analytically and critically, and so, too, does its audience. There never were too many political roman- . tics reading the *New York Times* or *Washington Post.* There are increasingly fewer political romantics watching the "Evening News." As of now, only traditional print might possibly sustain that kind of romanticized political culture. But almost nobody reads, or writes, that kind of news anymore.

Chapter 13

Reprise: Reviewing the Day's Top Stories

Ours is an independent newspaper—as independent as circulation will allow.

—A TRADITIONAL AMERICAN NEWSPAPER

At its best, journalism is a kind of window on the world.. . . At something less than its best, journalism is a screen on which. . .images dance to today's seeming truths, tomorrow's undoubted foolishness.

—PAUL WEAVER, *FORTUNE* MAGAZINE

BOOKS ought not to follow the format of the inverted pyramid. Books merit a wrapup, a clean set of conclusions. We come at last to half a dozen such conclusions. As one might expect, there is good news and bad news about the news. First the bad news.

More Objectivity Than "Truth"

American media work hard at being honest, being factual, being objective. But we found that the press did a much better job of being objective than at reaching "truth," when "truth" is defined hypothetically as a valid representation of a larger reality. Different as they may be, both CBS and UPI came closer to objectivity than to "truth."

Commercial news media fail to convey "truth" for three reasons. First, "truth" is elusive, if not beyond discovery. Second, "truth" is rarely sensational enough to render it newsworthy. Finally, as watchdogs, the news media have a built-in bias against "truth" in favor of half-truth. We do not know which factor (illusiveness, sensationalism, or role as watchdog) counts the most in impeding "truth." But we saw all three factors operating in network and wire coverage of Campaign '80.

Consider first the extensive coverage of Billy Carter and his personal loans from the Libyans. Without transcripted conversations and without confessions, the press could not have known the truth concerning Billy's influence over American policy toward Libya. So with "truth" virtually unknowable, the press offered not "truth" but fact and Objective Reporting. One might even commend the press in this instance, both for its refusal to draw conclusions about Billy Carter and its scrupulous adherence to the rules of fairness in following the case. When the news media fail to give us "truth" due to limitations on evidence, the "failure" is not that of commercialism or sensationalism but of responsible journalism.

Much less commendable is the tendency to miss out on "truth" when the reasons do reflect sensationalism. Consider, for example, Jimmy Carter's public utterances during the general campaign. Given that the press had grumbled throughout 1980 about Carter's Rose Garden strategy and his refusal to campaign on the issues and his record, one might have expected great interest by the media in what Carter did say when he finally left the confines of the Rose Garden. It was not so.

In the opening week of the general campaign the only Carter "speech" to receive more than passing quotation, especially by the networks, was his harsh criticism of Ronald Reagan for slurring the South. What Carter said about affirmative action, the economy, or labor relations during that week received scant, though factual, attention. His comment: "I resent very deeply what Ronald Reagan said about. . . Tuscumbia, Alabama. . ."[1] made all three evening news shows and the wires. Factual, yes. Truthful, not necessarily.

On occasion, the need to be entertaining pushes the commercial media close to limits of untruthfulness. Perhaps the most famous example in campaign news came in 1976, when Jerry Ford personally bumped up against the difficult problem of factuality before "truth." On several occasions, as president or as candidate, Ford had slipped, tripped, fallen, or bumped his head—often while on camera. All the media picked up on Ford's supposed clumsiness, and, of course, the coverage was factual. Yet Ford was, in truth, perhaps the most physically adept president in history. To be "factual," he was our only president to have been a college football "All-Star" or to have been MVP with a major college football team.[2]

In Campaign 80 "truth" also lost out to factuality in instances much more serious than a candidate's physical coordination. And in these instances "truth" lost out principally for reasons having to do with the press's own watchdog bias. Reagan's campaign coverage proves the point.

The press dutifully, and factually, covered Reagan's communications gaffes: his public pronouncements that trees cause pollution, that evolution is just a theory, and so forth. What the media, especially the networks and eastern papers, did not cover nearly so fully were Reagan's persuasiveness and winning style. Reagan's remarkable personal charm went basically without remark. In their turn, Jimmy Carter, and then the nation were surprised by Reagan's communication skills, in part because the press had covered only half the truth—that Reagan was an imprecise communicator, but not that he was an effective communicator.

Reagan's press coverage after his election points up the same thing. Take, as example, the now legendary case of Reagan's first public and sustained fight with the Washington press corps concerning coverage of policy. In March of 1982, Reagan complained openly that the media were ignoring his successes in reducing inflation and emphasizing instead what he considered to be the sad legacy of the Carter administration: increasing unemployment. Reagan attacked the networks particularly harshly for traveling to "South Succotash" and overcovering individual cases of unemployment.

Whatever the merits of his case for claiming personal success with inflation, while at the same time blaming Carter for unemployment, Reagan was right about one thing: during his first year and a half in office, the media had completely deemphasized coverage of inflation and had shifted toward emphasizing unemployment.

This shift represents neither anti-Reaganomics by the press, nor a dearth of hard evidence about declining inflation. It suggests little more than a long-standing bias of the news media, particularly the networks and the eastern dailies, in favor of policy failure and against policy success. Coverage of increasing unemployment during the Reagan administration was factual and generally objective; at the very least, objectivistic. But moving toward coverage of unemployment has dramatic implications for "truth" about the state of the economy, not to mention the Reagan administration.

We do not suggest that the American media transform themselves from watchdog to lap dog by emphasizing success instead of failure. We suggest instead that practitioners and consumers of American journalism appreciate the problem: independent and commercial news sources have a much higher probability of being factual than of providing "truth."

The Myth of an Imperial Media

For the last dozen years, political analysts have seemed compelled to use the adjective "imperial" to describe any one of several national political institutions. Arthur Schlesinger, Jr. began it all in 1973 with *The Imperial Presidency*.[3] Once the word "imperial" was popularized, we all moved quickly to a theory of an imperial judiciary, toyed with the notion of an imperial Congress and skipped on to a consideration of the imperial bureaucracy. Now we have most recently been exposed on several occasions to the theory of the "imperial media."

The contemporary notion of an imperial media actually goes back a decade, starting with an essay in *Commentary* magazine by Daniel Patrick Moynihan.[4] More recently, *Commentary* has gone a step further, publishing a piece by *Los Angeles Times* correspondent Joseph Kraft—an essay specifically titled "The Imperial Media."[5] In fact, Kraft is only one of many contemporary press critics to label the media imperial.[6]

We can accept many of Kraft's premises and complaints: that news people have become celebrities; that fame has gone to the collective head of the Washington press; that the media have grown more openly hostile toward government; that the press has become compulsive about the First Amendment; that network correspondents hypocritically complain about the star system while milking the networks for multimillion dollar contracts. But our own content research shows that Kraft has overstated the case and that his point that the networks and the eastern press have "traded objectivity for bias" goes much too far. Media may be much less obsequious than in the past but they did not, during Campaign '80, trade in objectivity for bias, nor did they behave very imperially.

We began this research believing that CBS would behave more imperially than it did. Compared with the wire, all the evening news shows were less objective, less descriptive, and less respectful of the people and events they covered in 1980. But the networks were much more obstreperous than imperial.

It is true that CBS was more critical of every single candidate than was UPI, and that virtually no one on CBS conducted his campaign in the glow of good press. But in the end, about 75 percent of the news time on "Evening News" was either nonevaluative, or ambiguous in its messages about the candidates. CBS also was more than twice as negative in its overall coverage as UPI. But that particular fact ought not to conceal another, that the majority of the stories were balanced, were tied closely to sources, and were fair.

Virtually every reporter we asked was convinced that Jimmy Carter had exploited the media on the morning of the Wisconsin primary, and that he knew precisely what he was doing when he shepherded the wires and networks into the Oval Office at 7:00 A.M. to make his announcement about the possible breakthrough in Iran. The networks never quite got over the April Fool's Day press conference, and CBS News had that press conference in mind when it put together its feature-length exposé on the Carter Rose-Garden campaign. But nobody at UPI or CBS ever explicitly said what he or she thought about that April 1 press conference, and never reported that Carter had probably used them and the voters in the state of Wisconsin.

And so it went. Practically every reporter felt Carter was hiding behind the hostages, yet few said so, at least not directly. Almost every reporter we asked felt that Reagan's supply-side economics was absurd, yet none said so, ever. Most reporters felt that there was nothing to the Billy Carter affair, yet, even there, none said so.

Our point is not that CBS, or even UPI, played patsy in Campaign '80; clearly they did not. Our point is that they did not play emperor either. The campaign reporting we watched and read stayed inside the laws of truth and fairly well inside the rules of responsible reporting. There are, to be sure, stars at CBS News and in all the prestige media, stars who are exorbitantly paid and overly pampered. But celebrity status is not necessarily imperialism. In their behavior and their copy, American media may at times, be impish, impertinent, even impudent, but they are very rarely imperial.

Network correspondents and members of the prestige press frequently underplay their own importance. But modern press critics generally err in the other direction, attributing too much to the legal license of the press and, above all, failing to appreciate the self-imposed limitations under which the press still operates.

The Hyperbole of Hegemony

At the other end of the spectrum are those who believe that the media have been, and remain, handmaidens of the establishment. These critics argue hegemony theory, that the media are not imperial but are instead effete—water carriers for a system based in bourgeois capitalism. In chapter 3, we reviewed Todd Gitlin's research concerning the status quo orientation of American news content.[7] Herbert Gans has made similar points in his research with CBS, NBC, Time, and Newsweek. For Gans, and for the "hegemonists" he cites, American news media "help maintain order, warn against disorder, and act as moral guardians, [and] function as agents of social control."[8]

We found evidence that corroborates some of what Gans says. First, in their reporting and in their private interviews, none of our reporters expressed anything approaching antisystem opinion. Most spoke as if they were moderates, or "not very political." Second, fewer than 1 percent of the news stories explicitly criticized our less than perfect mechanisms for electing presidents. In fact, CBS and UPI pretty much ignored electoral institutions, covering candidates and issues instead. But just as the "imperialist school" overstates the arrogance of the modern news media, the "hegemonist school" exaggerates their level of diffidence.

The hegemonists make two important miscalculations. To begin, they tend to dismiss media criticism of elected leadership as irrelevant to basic public opinion. Yet, while it may be true that our newspeople never overtly denigrated the constitutional presidency, let alone the constitution, on several occasions they did show disdain for the person holding the title. And while one might see this as simply "bad press" for Carter, or whomever, the public may, having watched the criticism of the officeholders themselves, come to be less enthusiastic about the offices involved. In fact, the public has, to say the least, grown less enthusiastic. Even economic institutions, the very essence of capitalism, have, during the age of modern media, suffered major losses in public approval.[9] Increasingly critical coverage of politics means less legitimacy for almost all facets of society, not, as the hegemonists assert, more social control.

The second hegemonist miscalculation involves perspective. It is true that the Earth represents far less than a speck of dust in a limitless universe. Even within its own limited galaxy, our planet is at best miniscule. But, it remains the only earth we've got. And to us it looms very large. The hegemonists dismiss too forcefully the fact that some criticism not only exists in modern political journalism, but that it has expanded generously since 1960.[10] Since then all our major news sources have become more critical, even the wires. And with network news virtually replacing traditional print as the main source of political information, the new media have become something approaching a delegitimizing force in our politics.[11] In short, even if the new messages are defined as objective, the networks have, by practicing a new form of news, probably played a real part in the growing disenchantment with American politics.[12] So, even though the press itself believes in the American system, media content has not really served as blanket reinforcement for the status quo.

More Consequential Than Powerful

Press critics frequently confuse political power with political consequences. Power should be defined as capacity plus *intent;* consequences entails something much less premeditated. Television cameras, as an example, have great consequences for politics simply because they exist. But cameras, on their own, have by our definition no political power, because they "behave" without intent. Obviously news people perform their tasks less mechanically than cameras. Nonetheless, if political intent is part of the definition of power, it makes real sense, given what we have now learned about content, to regard the national media as more consequential than powerful.

Remarkable as it may seem, the premeditated power of the news media has probably been on the wane during the last fifty years. As consequential as radio and television have been in our political system, they have failed to reach the level of raw political power that some elements of the press enjoyed during the nineteenth and early twentieth centuries. James David Barber, in his historical review of American press, shows how George Harvey and his *Harper's Weekly* quite literally set out as early as 1908 to nominate Woodrow Wilson for president, and by 1912 had accomplished their task.[13] Under Harvey's direction, *Harper's* not only ran articles on "the Predestination of Woodrow Wilson," it also ran for an extended period, a banner on the editorial page of every issue proclaiming, "For President, Woodrow Wilson."[14]

According to David Halberstam, Henry Luce essentially devoted his *Life* and his *Time* magazines to the nomination and election of Wendell Willkie. In Halberstam's history of the American press, Luce "invented" Willkie, and, says Halberstam, "invent is precisely the right word."[15]

This is not the way the networks, let alone the wires, behave. Not once in his history of CBS does Halberstam claim that Chairman William Paley tried to get somebody nominated or elected president. The idea that Chairman Paley would suggest to Lesley Stahl or Bill Plante how to slant the story in favor of somebody's nomination or election not only flies in the face of what we saw on camera, it contradicts almost everything we have read about the day-to-day realities of network news. If anything, the Paleys of network television intervened only to keep the reporters from being too tough on incumbents, regardless of their party or political philosophy. Naked interventionism by owners and publishers in presidential campaign reporting or the nominations process is a thing of a simpler past, and most assuredly not part of the network news system.

But what about the power at the reportorial level? Has the power to make or break candidates or philosophies merely devolved to the people who produce and edit the news? If one looks at the past thirty years of American political history, then the logical answer is no. It makes little sense to assume that network news has been pro-conservative or Republican. Almost all media critics see the political coloration of network news people and network news to be moderately liberal or Democratic. Yet since the age of television and big national media, the liberal candidate for president has lost in three out of four chances; the conservatives have done better in Congressional elections; the Great Society has become a political label that practically every politician shuns. Ironically, with the coming of the network news system, Republicanism and conservativism have made something of a comeback. If the modern national media intended to help the left, they have, as of the 1980s, apparently failed. If the national media really intended to help out the conservatives, then that hidden agenda would have to be considered one of history's most remarkable conspiracies.

One might say that we have defined power too narrowly and that if one looks beyond partisanship, the modern press has been very powerful. For example, the media did not like Carter and, we might assume, wanted him to lose in 1980, and lose he did. One might call that a case of media power. But our first response is that we suspect that the national press did in 1980 what it did in 1976, gave most of its vote to Jimmy Carter, despite having given him so much bad press. Our second response is that Carter's case proves that media are more consequential than powerful. Consider the press coverage of the hostages.

Whatever their reasons for hyping the hostage story as much as they did, we do not think that the media were trying to aid and comfort Jimmy Carter and his campaign, not by late 1979 at any rate. Yet by covering the story as they did, the news media not only "helped" Carter, they "saved" him, at least until the primaries had been won. Nothing in the history of television was so great a media event as the hostage crisis. Never had so much coverage been given to so few, and never had any president risen so quickly on so little.[16] The media frenzy, which Carter had in fact helped to create, was unprecedented and, given the stakes, so too was the public response.

But at the beginning of the crisis there was little media power involved. Mostly there were media consequences. If anything, the first two months of the hostage crisis showed the networks to be somewhat powerless, not only as a premeditated shaper of public opinion, but as an institution as well.[17] Networks dutifully reported most of the official news coming out of the State Department and the White House, even though the reporters sensed that the entire affair was a public relations bonanza for the Carter campaign. By February, the media had staged a minor comeback of sorts, implying that Carter was hiding in the Rose Garden and merely trying to manipulate the press. But Carter's amazing success in the primaries was a tribute not so much to press power but to media consequences.

Later on, of course, the media fell over themselves to cover every aspect of the last minute negotiations and the anniversary of the crisis. And again, as far as the candidates and the election were concerned, that last minute coverage was objective. But it too had its consequence, dramatizing as it did Carter's record in office. This is not to say that the networks and press distinguished themselves in their coverage of the hostages. The level of coverage and the intensity went wildly beyond any objective standard of importance. But the hostage crisis epitomizes the difference between intended effects and "unintended" consequences of the modern American media.

The hostage crisis implies that the national media can, in the short run, play a major role in producing effects that nobody in the press ever intended. But the crisis in American political parties suggests that modern media also produce long-term, and unintended, consequences. And again the emphasis belongs on consequence, not power.

Practically nobody denies that American political parties have grown weaker during the age of electronic journalism. David Broder, perhaps the single most noted chronicler of American party politics, has not only pointed out the rapid decline of party in the age of television, he lists television as the first of four causes of that decline.[18]

Broder argues that television, by focusing on personalities, not parties, has made the institutional party less salient and less relevant to voters, to candidates, and to rank-and-file. But, in fact, we found CBS only slightly less interested in parties than UPI. Both devoted less than 1 percent of their campaign coverage to parties, as parties. There was little difference between media in their indifference to party per se.

But Broder was on a right track. All national media tend to ignore institutional parties in covering politics and campaigns. The fact is when CBS and UPI bothered to cover parties, the story often dealt with party decline. Media either ignore party or concentrate on its flaws and diseases.

We found no major differences between print and network coverage of party, which is why we have not considered party until now. But we are convinced that by virtually ignoring the institutional party, the media have been consequential, have worked to diminish the meaning and power of political party. But again the effect was unintended.

Back in Campaign '60 and Campaign '40, there was much less campaign news (half as much), and the percentage of copy about parties was slightly higher. That being the case, the modern media have watered down even more completely the relative attention to the institutional parties. What's more, television has jumped into campaign coverage somewhat more enthusiastically than traditional print. Given those facts, network news has, perhaps, made party less salient at a more rapid rate than print. But we can only conclude that all our news media, not just television, played a part in decreasing the relevance of party. In short, the relationship between the national news media and party system suggests that the press is more consequential than powerful.

Networks also tend to be more consequential than powerful when it comes to non-news programming. One of the most important social consequences of network television has been a reduction in regional dialect, as networks consistently provide audiences with reporters and entertainers who have no clear regional accent. This is not cultural imperialism: networks sought to hire the least common denominator, not to change national speech patterns. And so too in political affairs.

National media are not powerless, obviously. First, media do help to define an agenda; second, media influence voter perceptions as to winners and losers, especially in primaries; third, media can, and sometimes do, run with a story and virtually destroy a political leader, as was the case with vice-presidential nominee Thomas Eagleton in 1972; fourth, under special circumstances, the national press corps not only takes a position, it lets that position show, as it did with the civil war in Nicaragua. Yet behind each of these powers is another reality. Governments play a major role in defining the news agenda which the media then disseminate; media tend to undercut the bandwagons they create by criticizing most the people who win; media almost always impair reputations on the basis of documents or leaks from political leaders; and rarely do the media see issues as open and shut as the Nicaraguan revolution.

Perhaps the press comes closest to raw political power when it criticizes to an ever increasing degree the incumbent president. But seemingly, it does that with little regard for the philosophy or politics of the incumbent. Even here the power is less than raw: the press tends to unmake incumbents, not make successful candidacies.

It goes too far to say that the media have done more to our politics by accident than on purpose. But most critics of modern media fail to recognize that the press does not construct daily news reports to achieve a partisan or political end. The ends are usually unrelated to partisan political goals.

Probably the one "political" dimension in which networks have sought to achieve a purpose has been the area of public cynicism. Network reporters do seem to want to make the public more aware of the frailties and inadequacies of their elective leadership. The networks have succeeded. If there is one clear-cut example of media power in the age of television news it must be the networks' contribution to our increasing political malaise. But consider other consequences that probably were less intended: an ever-increasing presidential orientation; a heightened sensitivity toward personality; a more "political" public; a nation that, despite Reagan's new federalism, thinks more and more about Washington, and less and less about state capitals.

For twenty years or so, most critics have complained about the overt power of television news and have consistently overlooked the relatively inadvertent consequences of that news form. Given what we saw, given the attitudes of the news people we interviewed, given the relationship between the national press and the people it covers, we think the conventional interpretations of media power are somewhat misdirected. America has not adopted the politics in which Dan Rather believes, but American politics have, for good or ill, taken on much of the coloration of the news form Rather presents.

Medium Is Part of the Message

We have resisted from the outset the theory that, in and of themselves, sound and video represent the essence of network journalism: the McLuhanite notion that "medium *is* message." We have suggested instead that network journalism differs from other news forms not so much as a matter of technology but as a function of intense competition and craft attitudes of network reporters and editors. But regardless of the real reasons, we know that even when reduced to words and sentences, network journalism presents a measurably different world of politics and campaigns—different from the world of old-line print. Traditional wire-based print and network journalism share enough that replacing the former with the latter has not transformed our news system radically. But networks have changed the tone and tenor of American political communication. Even without consideration for audio-visuals, medium can be part of the message. Network news has influenced the message.

More Good News Than Bad News About News

In September 1981, CBS media critic Jeff Greenfield asked CBS News producer Don Hewitt if "60 Minutes" had ever exonerated anybody; had ever investigated a charge, found the focus of the investigation innocent and then told the audience that the case was closed. Hewitt stammered badly, said he couldn't remember and that he'd have to check. Apparently the answer was "no"; "60 Minutes" had never broadcast an investigation that turned up anything favorable. We refuse to fall into the same mold—saying something bad or saying nothing at all.

CBS and UPI were often superficial, were sometimes petty, and were generally geared to covering events and people instead of institutions, formal process, or public policy. And, of course, both sources virtually ignored candidates outside the mainstream and offices other than presidential. But then there is the good news. Jody

Powell, Carter's press secretary, and Lyn Nofziger, the man who handled press for much of the Reagan campaign, acknowledged to us that the coverage in 1980 was honest and practically void of partisan bias. Honesty and political neutrality are no mean achievements for a free and commercial press. If Powell and Nofziger can both look back on press coverage in 1980 and consider it to have been reasonably acceptable, so can we. At the risk of adding disincentives for improvement in 1984, we admit that we found as much to like as to dislike in the media coverage of the Carter-Reagan campaign.

Watching the nightly news will not produce a populace in keeping with the Athenian ideal of democracy. Neither will reading the wire. Nor will reading the *New York Times* or the *Washington Post.* All mass media have massive limitations. And mass democracy has massive limitations as well. Citizens, after all, fail to reach the Athenian ideal at least as often as their leaders or their news media.

In the last analysis, the commercial media did a better job in 1980 than most critics allowed, albeit a worse job than the media themselves pretended. Such is the nature of institutions—better than their critics challenge, worse than their own public relations departments claim. The press is a highly visible political institution and is growing more visible year by year. In a free society, visible political institutions inevitably attract criticism and generally behave defensively in the face of that criticism. The press is no exception on either count. Still, if history is the bench mark, the news media have improved.

Consider one last historical case, the Lincoln-Douglas debates. We have criticized the networks for the size and shape of their coverage of the 1980 debates and the debate about the debates. It may well be that the coverage of the Carter-Reagan debate was the low point in Campaign '80, overdone and, in some ways, irresponsible. Jimmy Carter had good reason to complain about press coverage of his one-time-only debate. But consider how Abraham Lincoln must have felt on the morning of August 22, 1858, when he saw the news coverage of his first debate with Stephen Douglas in Ottawa, Illinois. The *Chicago Times,* a pro-Douglas daily, played it this way.

THE CAMPAIGN

Douglas Among the People
Lincoln Breaks Down.
Lincoln's Heart Fails Him!
Lincoln's Legs Fail Him!

Lincoln's Tongue Fails Him!
Lincoln's Arms Fail Him!
Lincoln Fails All Over!
The People Refuse to Support Him!
The People Laugh at Him!
Douglas the Champion of the People![19]

Quite obviously the nineteenth-century American press failed to cope with problems of fairness as well as problems of the market place. At the very least, our national media, networks included, have learned how to handle the rudiments of fairness, if not the pressures of commercialism. Modern media may not be great, but they seem to be gaining on their own history.

Most of our political institutions in the last hundred years have managed to improve, and the press is no exception. A good part of that improvement on all sides has probably come through criticism —criticism by the press and criticism of the press. As the press knows, criticism can be constructive, and we found several places in Campaign '80 where constructive criticism could be applied. And in the end, when we consider how much better journalism might have been in that election, we do come away feeling more than a little dissatisfied. But when we consider how much worse the media might have been, we also come away feeling ever so slightly relieved.

Notes

Chapter 2

1. Dennis T. Lowry, "An Evaluation of Empirical Studies Reported in Seven Journals in the '70s," *Journalism Quarterly* 56 (2) (Summer 1979): 262–268, 282.

2. In 1972, for example, there were five book-length studies of the media coverage of the campaign: C. Richard Hofstetter, *Bias in the News: Network Television Coverage of the 1972 Election Campaign* (Columbus, Ohio: Ohio State Press, 1976); Robert S. Frank, *Message Dimensions of Television News* (Lexington, MA: Lexington Books, 1973); Thomas E. Patterson and Robert McClure, *The Unseeing Eye: The Myth of Television Power in National Elections* (New York: Putnam, 1976); American Institute for Political Communication, *The 1972 Presidential Campaign,* (Washington, D.C., 1974); Alternative Education Foundation, *Report on Network Treatment of the 1972 Democratic Presidential Candidates.* In 1976, the number had been diminished to three, and only one of those offered a systematic investigation of content, per se. And that one book was considerably more interested in effects than content. See Thomas E. Patterson, *The Mass Media Election: How Americans Choose Their President* (New York: Praeger, 1980); James D. Barber, ed., *Race for the Presidency: The Media and the Nominating Process* (Englewood Cliffs, N.J.: Prentice Hall, 1978); Edwin Diamond, *Good News, Bad News* (Cambridge, MA: MIT Press, 1978). In 1980, ours appears to be one of only two full-scale analyses of media behavior in the campaign. The other is Jeff Greenfield's *The Real Campaign: How the Media Missed the Story of the 1980 Campaign* (New York: Summit, 1982).

3. Walter Cronkite, "What It's Like to Broadcast News," *Saturday Review* 53 (December 12, 1971): 53–55.

4. Dennis T. Lowry, "Agnew and the Network TV News: A Before/After Content Analysis," *Journalism Quarterly* 48 (Summer 1971): 205–210.

5. Interview with Arnold Sawislak, May 27, 1981. Hereafter, unless indicated otherwise, comments from journalists and editors which were received during interviews with the authors will not be referenced.

6. Arthur Miller, Edie Goldenberg, and Lutz Erbring, "Type-Set Politics: Impact of Newspapers on Public Confidence," *American Political Science Review* 73 (1979): 67–84.

7. In modern times, the most widely read example of the noneffects of campaign media is Patterson and McClure's *The Unseeing Eye.* But in 1980, Patterson changes his position slightly and finds more media effects in the 1976 campaign; see Patterson, *The Mass Media Election.* A major investigation of the 1972 campaign found media

to have been practically inconsequential in moving voters or opinion. See C. Richard Hofstetter, Cliff Zukin, and Terry Buss, "Political Imagery and Information in an Age of Television," *Journalism Quarterly* 55 (3) (Autumn 1978): 562–570. The most acerbic denials of media effects come in *Good News, Bad News* and *The Tin Kazoo,* both by Edwin Diamond.

8. Michael J. Robinson, "Political Legitimacy in an Era of Electronic Journalism," *Television as a Social Force: New Approaches to TV Criticism,* ed. Richard Adler (New York: Praeger, 1975) pp. 97–139; David H. Weaver, Doris A. Graber, Maxwell E. McCombs, and Chaim H. Eyal, *Media Agenda-Setting in a Presidential Election* (New York: Praeger, 1981).

9. Michael Grossman and Martha Kumar, *Portraying the President: The White House and the News Media* (Baltimore: Johns Hopkins University Press, 1981), pp. 53–61. Also see Leon Sigal, *Reporters and Officials: The Organization and Politics of Newsmaking* (Lexington, MA: D.C. Heath, 1973), p. 5.

10. Patterson, *The Mass Media Election,* pp. 11–14.

11. Miller, et al., "Type-Set Politics," pp. 68–69.

12. Stephen Hess, *The Washington Reporters* (Washington, D.C.: Brookings Institution, 1981), p. 93.

13. A. Kent MacDougall, "Grinding It Out: AP, UPI Fight Fiercely for Front-Page Space as They Cover the World," *Wall Street Journal,* 18 January 1968, p. 1; cited in Bernard Roshco's *Newsmaking* (Chicago: University of Chicago Press, 1975), p. 68.

14. Lutz Erbring, "News Media Monitoring and Modeling Public Opinion Dynamics," xeroxed, (Chicago: University of Chicago, June 1980), p. 6.

15. Donald Shaw, "Surveillance vs. Constraint: Press Coverage of a Social Issue," *Journalism Quarterly* 56 (Winter 1969): 707–712.

16. Hess, *The Washington Reporters,* p. 93.

17. Edward J. Epstein, *News From Nowhere: Television and the News* (New York: Random House, 1973), p. 42.

18. Maxwell McCombs and Donald Shaw, "Structuring the Unseen Environment," *Journal of Communication* 26 (Spring 1976): 21.

19. John W. C. Johnstone, Edward J. Slawski, and William W. Bowman, *The News People: A Sociological Portrait of American Journalists* (Urbana, Ill.: University of Illinois Press, 1976), p. 224. According to their respondents, the top twenty-six news organizations in "overall prominence," along with their total rating points were:

ORGANIZATION	TOTAL POINTS
1. *New York Times*	1008
2. Associated Press	698
3. United Press International	456
4. *Washington Post*	372
5. *Wall Street Journal*	333
6. *Los Angeles Times*	190
7. *Newsweek*	165
8. *Christian Science Monitor*	148
9. *Time*	145
10. CBS News	121
11. *Chicago Tribune*	61
12. NBC News	56
13. *U.S. News and World Report*	56
14. ABC News	54
15. *St. Louis Post-Dispatch*	53
16. *Washington Star*	52
17. *Chicago Daily News*	45

18. *National Observer*	44
19. *New York Daily News*	41
20. *Minneapolis Tribune*	38
21. *Milwaukee Journal*	37
22. *San Francisco Chronicle*	35
23. *Boston Globe*	34
24. *Chicago Sun-Times*	32
25. *Philadelphia Inquirer*	29
26. *Houston Post*	29

20. Ibid.

21. Ours is not the first book-length study to choose CBS as best case. Using a similar rationale, Ernest Lefever also picked CBS "Evening News" in his *TV and National Defense* (Boston: Va. Institute for American Strategy Press, 1974), pp. 15–16. And more recently, Todd Gitlin also chose CBS over the other networks in his *The Whole World is Watching: Mass Media in the Making and Unmaking of the New Left* (Berkeley: University of California Press, 1980). In their monumental study of White House press relations, Michael Grossman and Martha Kumar also used CBS, *Portraying the President*. Finally, Richard Rubin and his associates chose CBS, too, in their comparison of print and television coverage of American politics between 1960 and 1975 in *Press, Party and Presidency* (New York: W.W. Norton, 1981).

22. See rankings in footnote 19.

23. The "Canons" are reprinted in Wilbur Schramm, ed., *Mass Communications* (Champaign, Ill.: University of Illinois Press, 1949), pp. 236–238.

24. *A Free and Responsible Press* (Chicago: University of Chicago Press, 1947).

25. John Hulteng, *Playing It Straight: A Practical Discussion of the Ethical Principles of the American Society of Newspaper Editors* (Chester, Conn.: ASNE, 1981).

26. Using a more stringent definition of campaign news, Doris Graber found 13 percent of all newspaper news to be presidential campaign news, and 15 percent of the television news to be about the campaign. Her study included presidential election years 1968, 1972, and 1976. Doris A. Graber, *Mass Media and American Politics* (Washington, D.C.: Congressional Quarterly Press, 1980), p. 165.

27. Closest perhaps to our own research is C. Richard Hofstetter's analysis of the 1972 campaign. Hofstetter's analysts reached agreement 87 percent of the time, not surprising given his interest in visuals. C. Richard Hofstetter, *Bias in the News* (Columbus: Ohio State University Press, 1976), p. 26.

28. For a discussion concerning the importance of nonliteral content research see Robert S. Frank, *Message Dimensions of Television News*, and Frank's "The Grammar of Film in Television News," *Journalism Quarterly* 51 (Summer 1974): 245–250.

29. We found a diversity of opinion, but generally found that the networks do tend to behave as a class. See, for example, James B. Lemert, "Content Duplication by the Networks in Competing Evening Newscasts," *Journalism Quarterly* 51 (Summer 1974): 238–234. Hofstetter's massive study found negligible differences among the networks; see Hofstetter, *Bias in the News*. For a different opinion about network differences, see George Comstock and Robin E. Cobbey, "Watching the Watchdogs: Trends and Problems in Monitoring Network News," *Television Network News: Issues in Content Research*, eds. William C. Adams and Fay Schreibman (Washington, D.C.: George Washington University, 1978), pp. 47–63.

30. See Gary D. Malaney and Terry F. Buss, "AP Wire Reports vs. CBS TV News Coverage of Presidential Campaigns," *Journalism Quarterly* 56 (3) (Autumn 1979): 602–610.

31. William C. Adams, "Visual Analysis of Newscasts: Issues in Social Science Research," *Television Network News: Issues in Content Research*, ed. William C. Adams and Fay Schreibman (Washington, D.C.: George Washington University, 1978), pp. 155–178.

32. Richard Pride and Gary Wamsley, "Symbol Analysis of Network Coverage of the Laos Incursion," *Journalism Quarterly* 49 (Winter 1972): 635–640, 647.

33. Adams, "Visual Analysis of Newscasts," pp. 155–178.

34. Elihu Katz, Hanna Adona, and Pnina Parness, "Remembering the News: What the Picture Adds to Recall," *Journalism Quarterly* 54 (2) (Summer 1977): 231–239. Also Alan Booth, "The Recall of News Items," *Public Opinion Quarterly* 34 (1970–71): 604–610.

Chapter 3

1. Conrad's remarks are transcribed in *The Wilson Quarterly* 1 (3) (Spring 1977): 84.

2. Walter Lippmann, *Public Opinion* (New York: Macmillan Co., 1922), p. 223.

3. Barbara Walters interview, ABC "World News Tonight," 8 October 1980.

4. Edith Efron, "Do the Networks Know What They're Doing?" *The News Twisters* (Los Angeles: Nash Publishing, 1971), pp. 173–207.

5. See, for example, most recently, Stephen Hess, *The Washington Reporters*, (Washington: Brookings, 1981); Herbert J. Gans, *Deciding What's News: A Study of CBS Evening News, NBC Nightly News, Newsweek and Time* (New York: Pantheon Publishers, 1979); Elie Abel, ed., *What's News* (San Francisco: Institute for Contemporary Studies, 1981); David Paletz and Robert Entman, *Media Power Politics* (New York: Free Press, 1981).

6. Bill Green, "Janet's World," *Washington Post*, 19 April 1981, p. A13.

7. *In the Public Interest–II* (New York: National News Council, 1979).

8. *Newsweek*, 4 May 1981, p. 51.

9. *A Free and Responsible Press* (Chicago: University of Chicago Press, 1947).

10. *Nieman Reports*, 4 April 1950, p. 30.

11. For a discussion of the problems of objectivity in covering McCarthyism, see Edwin Bayley, *Joe McCarthy and the Press* (Madison, Wisc.: University of Wisconsin Press, 1982).

12. George E. Lardner, Jr., "Two Views of Objective Reporting: An Analysis" (M.A. thesis, Marquette University, May 1962), pp. 9–10, in Lou Cannon, *Reporting: An Inside View* (Sacramento, Calif.: California Journal Press, 1977), p. 44.

13. Doris Graber, *Mass Media and American Politics* (Washington, D.C.: Congressional Quarterly, 1980), p. 168.

14. Donald Matthews, " 'Winnowing:' The News Media and the 1976 Presidential Nominations," in *Race for the Presidency*, ed. James D. Barber (Englewood Cliffs, N. J.: Prentice Hall, 1978), p. 67.

15. Quotation cited in Oliver Gramling, *AP: The Story of News* (New York: Farrar and Rinehard, Inc. 1940), p. 39.

16. Todd Gitlin, *The Whole World is Watching* (Berkeley, Calif.: University of California Press, 1980).

17. Ibid., p. 17.

18. Ibid., pp. 27–28.

19. Ibid., pp. 270–271.

20. George Gerbner, "Ideological Perspectives and Political Tendencies in News Reporting," *Journalism Quarterly* 41 (3) (1964): 495–508.

21. CBS/*New York Times* poll, August 1980.

22. CBS/*New York Times* poll press release, 22 October 1980, p. 11.

23. *Weekly Compilation of Presidential Documents* 16 (36–40) (September 1980).

24. Colin Seymour-Ure, *The Political Impact of Media* (Beverly Hills, Calif.: Sage, 1974), p. 223.

25. James D. Barber, "Characters in the Campaign," *Race for the Presidency*, ed. James D. Barber, p. 114–115.

26. Leo C. Rosten, *The Washington Correspondents* (New York: Harcourt, Brace, 1937), p. 220.

27. Edward J. Epstein, *News from Nowhere* (New York: Random House, 1973), chapter 2; also see Herbert Gans, *Deciding What's News* (New York: Pantheon Books, 1979), chapters 6 and 10.

28. Gans, *Deciding What's News*, p. 186.

29. Barber, *Race for the Presidency*, chapters 5, 6, and 7.

30. Montague Kern, "The Invasion of Afghanistan: Domestic vs. Foreign News," *Television Coverage in the Middle East*, ed. William C. Adams (Norwood, N.J.: Ablex Publishing, 1981), pp. 106–127.

31. For a scholarly review of subjectivity in hostage news, see David Altheide, "Iran vs. U.S. TV News: The Hostage Story Out of Context," *Television Coverage*, ed. Adams pp. 128–157.

32. The classic attack is Ernest W. Lefever's *TV and National Defense: An Analysis of CBS News, 1972–73* (Boston, Va.: Institute for American Strategy, 1974). Lefever argues that the liberal press produced liberal news bias.

33. Peter Braestrup argues that the press coverage of Vietnam was subjective and biased, but not because of ideology so much as organizational factors. *Big Story: How the American Press and Television Reported and Interpreted the Crisis of Tet 1968 in Vietnam and Washington* (Boulder, Co.: Westview Press, 1977).

34. For a discussion of "60 Minutes" subjectivity concerning the Saudis, see Jack Shaheen, "Images of Saudis and Palestinians: A Review of Major Documentaries," ed. William C. Adams, 89–105.

Chapter 4

1. Miami Herald v. Tornillo, 418 U.S. 241 (1974).

2. *In the Matter of the Handling of Public Issues Under the Fairness Doctrine and the Public Interest Standards of the Communications Act* (Fairness Report) Federal Communications Commission, 48 F.C.C. 2d, 1 (1974).

3. The single greatest liberalization occurred in 1975. The Federal Communications Commission ruled that debate between candidates did *not* fall within the limitations of the equal time rule. Networks and stations were then free to televise debates and refuse time to those not included, so long as the debate was sponsored by someone other than the candidates. The Commission also ruled that year that press conferences could, if bona fide news events, be considered as outside the limitations prescribed under Section 315(a)(4) (the equal time provision). Petitions of Aspen Institute and CBS, Inc. 55 F.C.C. 2d, 697 (1975).

4. Speech to the National Association of Broadcasters, Dallas, Texas, 7 April 1982, cited in the *Washington Post*, 8 April 1982, p. D 14.

5. In their classic study, *Television in Politics: Its Uses and Influences* (Chicago: University of Chicago Press, 1969), Jay G. Blumler and Dennis McQuail argue that the liberal party in Britain profited directly from greater access to television, but their case involved nonnews coverage and did not lead to liberal party victory, just increase in attitudinal support, pp. 206–207.

6. The Hutchins Commission Report lists among its five major press values a commitment to "full access" for the day's intelligence and news.

7. See Robert Batlin, "San Francisco's Newspapers' Campaign Coverage: 1896, 1952," *Journalism Quarterly* 31 (Summer 1954): 297–303; Malcolm Maccoby, "Newspaper Objectivity in the 1952 Campaign," *Journalism Quarterly* 31 (2) (Summer 1954):

285–296; Jae-Won Lee, "Editorial Support in Campaign News: Content Analysis by Q Method," *Journalism Quarterly* 49 (4) (Winter 1972): 710–716.

8. David Halberstam, *The Powers That Be* (New York: Dell Press, 1980), p. 167.

9. Ibid., p. 168.

10. Peter Clarke and Susan Evans, *The Broken Quill: Journalism in Congressional Campaigns.* Forthcoming 1983, chapter 4.

11. Bill Peterson, "Flying High, From 'Sustained Whimsy' To Fatigued Frustration," *Washington Post,* 31 October 1980, p. A3.

12. Thomas E. Patterson, *The Mass Media Election: How Americans Choose Their President* (New York: Praeger, 1980), pp. 43–48.

13. Ibid., p. 45.

14. Jeff Greenfield, *The Real Campaign: How the Media Missed the Story of the 1980 Campaign* (New York: Summit, 1982), chapter 3.

15. Patterson, p. 46.

Chapter 5

1. *Playing It Straight: A Practical Discussion of the Ethical Principles of the American Society of Newspaper Editors,* John Hulteng, (Chester, CT: Globe Pequot Press, 1981).

2. Current policy requires that broadcasters "must devote a reasonable percentage of . . . broadcast time to public issues," but neither the Fairness Doctrine nor law requires that broadcasters grant access to candidates for office at the state or local level. On the other hand, both public law as outlined in the Federal Communications Act and the Fairness Doctrine do require that once time is given to one candidate or to one viewpoint, reasonable opportunity must be given to the other side for response. For a full discussion see Steven J. Simmons, *The Fairness Doctrine and the Media,* (Berkeley, CA: University of California Press, 1978).

3. See Simmons, *The Fairness Doctrine and the Media,* especially chapter 4.

4. Under the terms of the "equal opportunities" law, Section 315a of the Federal Communications Act, candidates are entitled to something approaching strict equality in access to time for advertising. The Fairness Doctrine is more "liberal," requiring only "reasonable standards of fairness for political points of view and response to personal attack." FCC, *Fairness Doctrine and Public Interest Standards, Fairness Report Regarding Handling of Public Issues,* 39 Fed. Reg. 1974.

5. Committee for Fair Broadcasting of Controversial Issues, 35 FCC 2d 283, 292 (1970).

6. The largest study ever conducted of network coverage of a campaign includes information about successfulness and failure in the campaign as *a* if not *the* major component in its measure of good press/bad press. See C. Richard Hofstetter, *Bias in the News: Network Television Coverage of the 1972 Election Campaign* (Columbus, Ohio: Ohio State University Press, 1976). The only direct comparison between wire news and network news campaign coverage relied almost totally on references to success or failure as a measure of good press or bad, a methodology which, we believe, was the principal reason CBS seemed in that study to be no less critical than Associated Press. See Gary D. Malaney and Terry F. Buss, "AP Wire Reports Vs. CBS TV News Coverage of a Presidential Campaign," *Journalism Quarterly* 56 (3) (Autumn 1979): 602–610. Apparently, Michael Grossman and Martha Kumar also used success as a measure of good press in their content analysis of CBS, the *New York Times* and *Time* Magazine, which would explain why Kumar and Grossman found press coverage more favorable than we did. See *Portraying the President* (Baltimore: Johns Hopkins University Press, 1981).

7. Hofstetter, *Bias in the News,* p. 50.

8. Doris Graber, *Mass Media and Politics* (Washington, D.C.: Congressional Quarterly, 1980), pp. 167–168.

9. Edith Efron, *The News Twisters* (Los Angeles: Nash Publishing, 1971).

10. For a refutation that shows how much neutral or ambiguous press really did exist in Efron's collection of network news stories, see Robert L. Stevenson, Richard A. Eisinger, Barry M. Feinberg, and Alan B. Kotok, "Untwisting *The News Twisters:* A Replication of Efron's Study," *Journalism Quarterly* 50 (Summer 1973): 211–219.

11. Robert Lichter and Stanley Rothman, "Media and Business Elites," *Public Opinion* 4 (5) (November 1981): 43.

12. Ibid., p. 43.

13. Efron, *The News Twisters,* p. 47.

14. Ibid., p. 47.

15. Charles Peters, "Tilting at Windmills," *Washington Post,* 24 February 1980, p. B2.

16. Jeff Greenfield, *The Real Campaign: How the Media Missed the Story of the 1980 Campaign* (New York: Summit Books, 1982), p. 43.

17. For a more comprehensive discussion of Reagan's honeymoon press in November, see Michael Robinson and Margaret Sheehan, "Brief Encounters with the Fourth Kind: Reagan's Press Honeymoon," *Public Opinion* 3 (December/January 1981): 56–59.

18. Charles Seib, "Enough of Chappaquiddick," *Washington Post,* 16 November 1979, p. A21.

19. Tom Shales, "Teddy's Torment: A TV Soap Opera," *Washington Post,* 22 November 1979, p. C1.

20. "The Senator and the Shah," *Washington Post,* 4 December 1979, p. A20.

21. Greenfield, *The Real Campaign,* chapter 4.

22. Tom Shales, "Petty for Teddy," *Washington Post,* 30 January 1980, p. B1.

23. For a historical account comparing media events in 1976 and 1980 see Michael J. Robinson, "The Media in 1980: Was the Message the Message?" in *The American Elections of 1980,* ed. Austin Ranney (Washington, D.C.: American Enterprise Institute, 1981), pp. 177–216.

24. "Reagan Sags, Carter Soars in Iowa Poll," *Des Moines Register,* 11 January 1980, p. 1.

25. Data provided by S. Robert Lichter and Stanley Rothman.

26. "Campaign Notes," *Washington Post,* 11 April 1980, p. A3.

27. Hofstetter, *Bias in the News,* pp. 32–36, 197–207.

28. Dan Balz, "Anderson Climbs Uphill Toting Heavyweight Issues," *Washington Post,* 17 November 1979, p. A2.

29. Greenfield, *The Real Campaign,* chapters 6 and 11.

30. Michael Robinson and Karen A. McPherson, "The Early Presidential Campaign on Network Television: Accuracy and Imbalance in the Evening News," *Social Responsibilities of the Mass Media,* ed. Allan Casebier and Janet Casebier (Washington, D.C.: University Press of America, 1978): 5–41.

31. Remarks recorded at Aspen Institute Seminar on Media, Easton, Maryland, 11 July 1981.

32. Betty Cuniberti, "End of Ear Era at *Washington Post?" Los Angeles Times, View,* 19 November 1981, p. 9.

33. Grossman and Kumar, *Portraying the President,* chapter 11.

34. Ibid., p. 279.

35. David Broder, "Outlook," *Washington Post,* 23 October 1977, p. C7.

36. David Morgan, "The Fall, Rise and Fall of Jimmy Carter: Journalists and Presidential Reputations," mimeographed (University of Liverpool, undated), p. 26.

37. Jonathan Alter, "Rooting for Reagan," *Washington Monthly,* 12 (11) (January 1981):12.

38. Ibid., p. 12.

39. Tom Shales, "The Harassment of Ronald Reagan: TV's Assault on a Candidate, 1980," *Washington Post,* 31 October 1980, p. C1, 4.

40. Alter, "Rooting for Reagan," p. 13.

Chapter 6

1. Paul Weaver, "Newspaper News and Television News," *Television as a Social Force: New Approaches to TV Criticism*, ed. Richard Adler (New York: Praeger, 1975), p. 91.

2. Thomas Patterson and Robert McClure, *The Unseeing Eye: The Myth of Television Power in National Elections* (New York: G.P. Putnam, 1976), p. 36.

3. Thomas Patterson, *The Mass Media Election: How Americans Choose Their President* (New York: Praeger, 1980), p. 40.

4. Ibid., pp. 34–35.

5. Jefferson letter to John Norvell, cited in Dan Schiller, *Objectivity and the News: The Public and the Rise of Commercial Journalism* (Philadelphia: University of Pennsylvania Press, 1981), p. vi.

6. Alexis de Tocqueville, *Democracy in America* (New York: Alfred A. Knopf, 1945), p. 185.

7. Paul Lazarsfeld, *Radio and the Printed Page: An Introduction to the Study of Radio and Its Role in the Communication of Ideas* (New York: Duell, Sloan and Pearce, 1940), p. 213.

8. Ibid., p. 211.

9. Cited in William E. Bicker, "Network Television News and the 1976 Primaries," *Race for the Presidency: Media and the Nominating Process*, ed. James D. Barber, (Englewood Cliffs, N.J.: Prentice-Hall, 1978), p. 104. This entire collection contains an interesting description and analysis of the problems involving issue coverage in a presidential campaign.

10. Patterson, *Mass Media Election*. Estimates appear on p. 28, with references to the work of Lazarsfeld and Berelson from the 1940s campaigns. Those early studies presented figures only for the general election. See Paul Lazarsfeld, Bernard Berelson, and Hazel Gaudet, *The People's Choice* 3rd ed. (New York: Columbia University Press, 1968), pp. 115–119; also Bernard Berelson, Paul Lazarsfeld, and William McPhee, *Voting* (Chicago: University of Chicago Press, 1954) p. 240.

11. Taken from John Russonello, "Newspaper Coverage of the 1976 and 1968 Presidential Campaigns," (B.A. thesis, Drew University, May 1977). This is just one of several quotations reported to Russonello by prominent journalists such as David Broder of the *Washington Post*, James Naughton of the *New York Times*, Jim Wiehart of the *New York Daily News*. Because Russonello promised anonymity to all of these reporters as to specific quotations, we have used those quotations to build this argument, but cannot identify the particular reporter, instance by instance.

12. Robert Kaiser, "TV on the Trail: A 3-Course Menu for Fluff," *Washington Post*, 10 October 1980, pp. A1, A7.

13. Doris Graber, *Mass Media and American Politics* (Washington, D.C.: Congressional Quarterly, 1980), pp. 178–180.

14. Patterson, *Mass Media Election*, p. 35.

15. Stephen Hess, *The Washington Reporters* (Washington, D.C.: Brookings, 1981), table 22, p. 166.

16. Patterson, *Mass Media Election*, pp. 34–36.

17. Chris Arterton, "The Media Politics of Presidential Campaigns," *Race for the Presidency*, ed. James D. Barber (Englewood Cliffs, N.J.: Prentice-Hall, 1978), pp. 48–51.

18. R. Emmett Tyrrell, Jr., "The Wise and the Wisenheimers," *Washington Post*, 3 November 1980, p. A21.

19. See "Battle for the Morning: Today, Good Morning, America and Morning Fight to Be First," *Time*, 1 December 1980, pp. 62–66.

20. Dan Rather with Mickey Herskowitz, *The Camera Never Blinks: Adventures of a TV Journalist* (New York: William Morrow and Co., 1977), p. 270.

21. Thomas Griffith, "The Age of Cronkite Passes," *Time*, 9 March 1981, p. 42.

22. Osborn Elliott, "And That's The Way It Is," *Columbia Journalism Review* (May/June 1980): 51.

23. Frank Greve, "GOP's Switch Trips Media," *San Jose Mercury*, 18 July 1980, p. 1.

24. Ibid.

25. Jeff Greenfield, *The Real Campaign: How The Media Missed the Story of the 1980 Campaign* (New York: Summit Books, 1982), p. 169.

26. John Sears, "How Presumptuous Can the Press Get," *Washington Post*, 30 October 1980, p. A23.

Chapter 7

1. Doris Graber, "Press and TV as Opinion Resources in Presidential Campaigns," *Public Opinion Quarterly* 40 (3) (Fall 1976): 285–303.

2. David Broder, "The Nos. 2 on the Campaign Trail," *Washington Post*, 22 October 1980, p. A23.

3. Jack Germond and Jules Witcover, "Governors Get Short Shrift in Media Attention," *Washington Star*, 19 October 1980, p. A3.

4. For a statement of the problem and a review of the relevant literature, see Michael J. Robinson and Karen A. McPherson, "The Early Presidential Campaign on Network Television: Accuracy and Imbalance in the Evening News," *Social Responsibilities of the Mass Media,* ed. Allan Casebier and Janet Jenks Casebier (Washington, D.C.: University Press of America, 1978); also, *Race for the Presidency: The Media and the Nominating Process,* ed. James D. Barber (Englewood Cliffs, N.J.: Prentice-Hall, 1978).

5. Michael J. Robinson, "TV's Newest Program, the Presidential Nominating Game," *Public Opinion* 1 (May/June 1978): 41–46; Michael J. Robinson and Karen A. McPherson, "Television News Coverage Before the 1976 New Hampshire Primary: The Focus of Network Journalism," *Journal of Broadcasting* 21 (2) (Spring 1977): 177–186.

6. Michael J. Robinson, "News and Reality in the Early Presidential Campaign: The Case of Spring 1976," *The Party Symbol,* ed. William Crotty (New York: W.H. Freeman, 1980).

7. Michael J. Robinson, "The Media in 1980: Was the Message the Message?" *The American Elections of 1980,* ed. Austin Ranney (Washington, D.C.: American Enterprise Institute, 1981), pp. 177–211.

8. For a dialogue as to blame in the problems in covering primaries, see "TV News and Politics," in the *Wilson Quarterly* 1 (3) (Spring 1977): 73–90.

Chapter 8

1. Newton Minow, John B. Martin, and Lee M. Mitchell, *Presidential Television* (New York: Basic Books, 1973), p. 166.

2. "Inside Story, with Hodding Carter," "Mr. President . . . Mr. President?" Public Broadcasting Service, 18 November 1981.

3. A. J. Liebling, *The Press* (New York: Ballantine Books, 1964), p. 139.

4. Edward Epstein, *Between Fact and Fiction: The Problems of Journalism* (New York: Random House, 1975), chapter 1.

5. Leon V. Sigal, *Reporters and Officials: The Organization and Politics of Newsmaking* (Lexington, Mass.: Heath, 1973), p. 124.

6. William Adams and Phillip Heyl, "From Cairo to Kabul with the Networks, 1972–1980," *Television Coverage of the Middle East,* ed. William Adams (Norwood, N.J.: Ablex Publishing, 1981), pp. 1–39.

7. Don Oberdorfer, "Hostage Seizure: Enormous Consequences," *Washington Post,* 23 January 1981, p. A10.

8. Adams and Heyl, "From Cairo to Kabul," p. 28.

9. Ibid., p. 30.

10. Edward Epstein, *News From Nowhere* (New York: Random House, 1973).

11. Quoted in Fran Lukas, *New York Times Magazine,* 15 May 1977, p. 22ff.

12. "Mr. President. . . Mr. President?" Public Broadcasting Service.

13. Quoted in Michael Grossman and Joyce Kumar, *Portraying the President: The White House and the News Media* (Baltimore: Johns Hopkins University Press, 1981), p. 43.

14. Grossman and Kumar, *Portraying the President,* pp. 40–45.

15. Ibid., p. 259.

16. Daniel Patrick Moynihan, "The Presidency and the Press," *Commentary* 51 (3) (March 1971): 41–52.

17. David Paletz and Robert Entman, *Media Power Politics* (New York: The Free Press, 1981), chapter 4.

18. Kathy Sawyer, "The White House Has Become 'Nation's Fire Hydrant,' Mondale Says," *Washington Post,* 10 October 1980, p. A3.

19. Grossman and Kumar, *Portraying the President,* especially chapter 12.

20. Jeff Greenfield, *The Real Campaign: How the Media Missed the Story of the 1980 Campaign* (New York: Summit Books, 1982), p. 128.

21. Grossman and Kumar, *Portraying the President,* p. 316.

22. Paletz and Entman, *Media Power Politics,* pp. 64–65.

23. Ibid., pp. 65–78.

24. Grossman and Kumar, *Portraying the President,* p. 305.

25. "Mr. President. . . Mr. President?" Public Broadcasting Service.

26. Robert Pierpoint, *At the White House: Assignment to Six Presidents* (New York: G. P. Putnam's Sons, 1981), p. 71.

27. Grossman and Kumar, *Portraying the President,* p. 301.

Chapter 9

1. Lou Cannon, *Reporting: An Inside View* (Sacramento, Calif.: California Journal Press, 1977), pp. 64–65.

2. Thomas E. Patterson, *The Mass Media Election: How Americans Choose Their President* (New York: Praeger, 1980), p. 26.

3. Doris Graber, "Press and TV as Opinion Resources in Presidential Campaigns," *Public Opinion Quarterly* 40 (3) (Fall 1976): 289.

4. C. Richard Hofstetter, *Bias in the News: Network Television Coverage of the 1972 Election Campaign* (Columbus, Ohio: Ohio State University Press, 1976), p. 54.

5. Patrick Caddell, Carter's pollster, is convinced that voters did shift their allegiance from Carter to Kennedy during the primaries because voters wanted to send the electorally successful Carter a message. Whatever their motives, primary voters shifted dramatically toward Kennedy as Carter's nomination became certain.

6. Paul Weaver, "Newspaper News and Television News," *Television As A Social*

Force: New Approaches to TV Criticism, ed. Richard Adler (New York: Praeger, 1975), pp. 81–94.

7. Ibid., p. 92.

Chapter 10

1. Erik Barnouw, *Tube of Plenty: The Evolution of American Television* (London: Oxford University Press, 1975), pp. 168–169.

2. Ibid., pp. 169–170.

3. Ralph de Toledano, *One Man Alone: Richard Nixon* (New York: Funk and Wagnalls, 1969), p. 319.

4. There is an enormous literature, popular and critical, that sees only ratings when explaining the content and composition of network television. For an unsympathetic treatment, see Rose K. Goldsen, *The Show and Tell Machine: How Television Works and Works You Over,* (New York: Dial Press, 1977), especially chapter 13; see also A. Frank Reel, *The Networks: How They Stole the Show* (New York: Charles Scribners Sons, 1979), especially pp. 98–104. For a somewhat more sympathetic treatment, see Robert MacNeil, *The People Machine: The Influence of Television on American Politics* (New York: Harper and Row, 1968), p. 27.

5. Dan Rather, with Mickey Herskowitz, *The Camera Never Blinks: Adventures of a TV Journalist* (New York: William Morrow and Co., 1977), p. 271.

6. Ibid.

7. Ron Powers, *The Newscasters: The News Business As Show Business* (New York: St. Martins Press, 1978), p. 201.

8. Jane O'Reilly, "I'm Down On the Floor, Can You Hear Me?" *New York Magazine,* 31 July 1972, p. 29.

9. Gary Gates, *Air Time: The Inside Story of CBS News* (New York: Harper and Row, 1978); Gates opens his book with the following quote: "The name of this business is time on the air," p. vii.

10. Fred Friendly, *Due to Circumstances Beyond Our Control* (New York: Random House, 1967), p. 257.

11. Edward J. Epstein, *News From Nowhere: Television and the News,* (New York: Random House, 1973), pp. 91–100.

12. Ibid., pp. 4–5.

13. Alexis de Tocqueville, *Democracy in America* (New York: Alfred A. Knopf, 1945), vol. 1, p. 194.

14. H. L. Mencken, *Prejudices: Sixth Series* (New York: Alfred A. Knopf, 1927), p. 15.

15. The first study was John Johnstone, Edward Slawski, and William Bowman, *The News People: A Sociological Portrait of American Journalists and Their Work* (Urbana: University of Illinois Press, 1976); then comes Stephen Hess, *The Washington Reporters* (Washington, D.C.: Brookings, 1981). Still unpublished are the findings from Stanley Rothman and Robert Lichter, although preliminary findings about political attitudes appear in "Media and Business Elites," *Public Opinion* 4 (October/November, 1981).

16. Johnstone, et al., *The News People,* p. 114.

17. Ibid., p. 115.

18. Ibid., pp. 123–131.

19. Stephen Hess, *The Washington Reporters,* appendix, table 11.

20. Ibid.

21. Johnstone, et al., *The News People,* p. 224.

22. Hess, *The Washington Reporters,* appendix, table 12.

23. Ibid., appendix, table 11.

24. Ibid., p. 124.

25. Ibid.

26. William A. Henry, III, "News As Entertainment: The Search for Dramatic Unity," *What's News: The Media in American Society,* ed. Elie Abel (San Francisco: Institute for Contemporary Studies, 1981), p. 134.

27. Timothy Crouse, *The Boys on the Bus* (New York: Random House, 1972), p. 141.

28. Jane O'Reilly, "I'm Down on the Floor," p. 30.

29. Stanley Rothman and Robert Lichter, unpublished research made available through the authors.

30. William Safire, "Stand-Up Savants," *New York Times,* 9 October 1980, p. A35.

31. Barbara Walters, "The Tomorrow Show," NBC, 14 October 1981.

32. Bernard Cohen, *The Press and Foreign Policy* (Princeton: Princeton University Press, 1963).

33. Epstein, *News From Nowhere.*

34. Leon Sigal, *Reporters and Officials: The Organization and Politics of Newsmaking* (Lexington, MA: Heath, 1973).

35. David Altheide, *Creating Reality: How TV News Distorts Events,* (Beverly Hills: Sage, 1976); more recently, with Robert Snow, *Media Logic,* (Beverly Hills: Sage, 1979).

36. Epstein, *News From Nowhere,* p. 258.

37. For a good discussion of the politics and reality of the Fairness Doctrine, see Fred Friendly, *The Good Guys, The Bad Guys and the First Amendment: Free Speech vs. Fairness in Broadcasting* (New York: Random House, 1976).

38. Henry, "News As Entertainment," p. 133.

39. Tom Shales, "Losing the Picture for 1000 Words," *Washington Post,* 21 February 1980, p. D1.

40. Ibid., p. D8.

41. Herbert Gans, *Deciding What's News: A Study of CBS Evening News, NBC Nightly News, Newsweek and Time* (New York: Pantheon Books, 1979), p. 93.

42. Sam Donaldson, remarks to the National Construction Industry Legislative Conference, Hyatt Regency Hotel, Washington, D.C., 1 March 1982.

Chapter 11

1. Richard Neustadt, *Presidential Power,* rev. ed. (New York: John Wiley, 1976).

2. Jeff Greenfield argues that Bush's "politics of momentum," a campaign based on coverage of early primary successes, was dangerous, misdirected and bound to produce added suspicion within the press corps toward George Bush. Greenfield devotes an entire chapter to what he considers Bush's ill-conceived media strategy. In *The Real Campaign* (New York: Summit Books, 1982), chapter 2.

3. "Reagan Sags, Carter Soars in Iowa Polls," *Des Moines Register,* 11 January 1980, p. 1.

4. CBS/*New York Times* poll, 27 September 1980, p. 1.

5. Cited in Michael Grossman and Martha Kumar, *Portraying the President: The White House and the News Media* (Baltimore: Johns Hopkins University Press, 1981), p. 48.

6. James J. Kilpatrick, "Of Presidents and Press: What will Reagan Do?" *Washington Star,* 27 December 1980, p. A9.

7. Judy Woodruff, "Diary of a TV Reporter," *Washington Post Magazine,* 16 April 1981, p. 11.

8. Grossman and Kumar, *Portraying the President,* p. 259.

Chapter 12

1. Historians of journalism have yet to agree on the point at which the press became objective. Dan Schiller traces the birth of objectivity all the way back to the 1830s. See *Objectivity and the News: The Public and the Rise of Commercial Journalism* (Philadelphia: University of Pennsylvania Press, 1981). Donald Shaw considers 1880 the turning point. See "News Bias and the Telegraph: A Study of Historical Change," *Journalism Quarterly* 44 (Spring 1967): 3–12,31. Ben Bagdikian implies that the age of objectivity really began during the time of the first World War in *The Information Machines: Their Impact on Men and the Media* (New York: Harper & Row, 1971), p. 272.

2. Shaw, "News Bias and the Telegraph", p. 6.

3. Ibid., p. 31.

4. Peter Sandman, David Rubin, and David Sachsman, *Media: An Introductory Analysis of American Mass Communications*, 2nd ed. (Englewood Cliffs, N.J.: Prentice-Hall, 1976), p. 55.

5. Schiller, *Objectivity and the News*, chapter 7.

6. See Gaye Tuchman, "Objectivity as Strategic Ritual: An Examination of Newsmen's Notions of Objectivity," *American Journal of Sociology* 77 (1977): 660–679.

7. Christopher Sterling and Timothy Haight, *The Mass Media: Aspen Institute Guide to Communication Industry Trends* (New York: Praeger, 1978), p. 278.

8. Stephen Hess, *The Presidential Campaign: As Essay*, revised edition, (Washington, D.C.: Brookings, 1978), chapter 7.

9. Kevin Phillips, *Mediacracy: American Parties and Politics in the Communications Age* (New York: Garden City, Doubleday and Co., 1975), p. 132.

10. Hess, *The Presidential Campaign*, pp. 84–85.

11. George Watson, cited in Michael Grossman and Martha Kumar, *Portraying the President: The White House and the News Media* (Baltimore: Johns Hopkins University Press, 1981), p. 48.

12. David Halberstam, *The Powers That Be* (New York: Dell, 1979), pp. 15–16.

13. See, for example, Harold Mendelsohn and Irving Crespi, *Polls, Television and the New Politics*, (Scranton, PA: Chandler, 1972). See also Gene Wyckoff, *The Image Candidiates: American Politics in the Age of Television*, (New York: Macmillan, 1968).

14. Walter Lippmann, *Public Opinion* (New York: Macmillan, 1922), chapter 1.

15. Theodore H. White, *The Making of the President, 1972* (New York: Bantam, 1973), p. 327.

16. The literature on agenda-setting has burgeoned in the last ten years, beginning with Maxwell McCombs and Donald Shaw, "The Agenda-Setting Function of the Mass Media," *Public Opinion Quarterly* 36 (1972): 176–187. More recent studies include Donald Shaw and Maxwell McCoombs, *The Emergence of American Political Issues: The Agenda-Setting Function of the Press* (St. Paul: West Publishing, 1977), and David Weaver, Doris Graber, Maxwell McCombs, and Chaim Eyal, *Media Agenda-Setting in a Presidential Election: Issues, Images and Interest* (New York: Praeger, 1981). Most recently, Shanto Iyengar and Mark Peters, "Experimental Demonstrations of the 'Not-So-Minimal' Political Consequences of Mass Media," American Political Science Association Convention, New York, 1981.

17. Shaw and McCombs, *The Emergence of American Political Issues*, p. 105.

18. Iyengar and Peters, "Experimental Demonstration," pp. 10–12.

19. Weaver et al., *Media Agenda-Setting*, chapter 10.

20. Arthur Miller, Edie Goldenberg, and Lutz Erbring, "Type-Set Politics: Impact of Newspapers on Public Confidence," *American Political Science Review* 73 (1979): 80.

21. Ibid., p. 79.

22. Statistics on assassination taken from William J. Crotty, ed., *Assassinations and the Political Order* (New York: Harper & Row, 1971).

23. Walter Dean Burnham, "Shifting Patterns of Congressional Voting Participation in the United States," American Political Science Association paper, New York, 1981. For a general discussion, see Richard Brody, "The Puzzle of Political Participation in America," in *The New American Political System*, ed. Anthony King (Washington, D.C.: American Enterprise Institute, 1978), pp. 287–324.

24. Figures provided by Arthur H. Miller through the Center for Political Studies, Ann Arbor, Michigan.

25. Weaver, et al., *Media Agenda-Setting*, p. 203.

26. Samuel Kirkpatrick, William Lyons, and Michael Fitzgerald, "Candidates, Parties and Issues in the American Electorate: Two Decades of Change," *American Politics Quarterly* 3 (July 1975): 262.

27. Scott Keeter, "Television and the Role of Candidate Personality in Voter Decisions" (Paper presented to the Northeast Political Science Association, Tarrytown, New York, November 1978).

28. Gerald Pomper, *Voter's Choice: Varieties of American Electoral Behavior* (New York: Dodd-Mead, 1975), p. 199.

29. Ibid., pp. 199–201.

30. Dick Dabney, among many, has made a very similar argument. "When," wrote Dabney, "a certain kind of candiate begins to run for high office, the networks immediately ask 'will he stumble.' Before long we are told he has stumbled. . . and it is suggested that 'his campaign may be in trouble'. . . and from there it's only a short step to 'he's slipping in the polls'. . . to a solemn proclamation that 'he hasn't got a chance.' " "Little is said," concluded Dabney, "about the networks' own role in getting him to a spot where he hasn't got a chance." "Stumbling on the Stump," *Washington Post*, 2 September 1980, p. A21.

31. Cited in Dan Nimmo and Robert L. Savage, *Candidates and Their Images: Concepts, Methods and Findings* (Pacific Palisades, CA: Goodyear, 1976), p. 131.

32. Ibid.

33. See, for example, Shaw and McCombs, "The Agenda-Setting Function," pp. 155–156.

34. Weaver et al., *Media Agenda-Setting*.

35. Alan Booth, "The Recall of News Items," *Public Opinion Quarterly* 34 (1970–71): 604–610.

36. Richard Rubin and Douglas Rivers, "The Mass Media and Critical Elections: A First Report" (Paper presented to the Northeast Political Science Association, Tarrytown, New York, November 1978). That research has been recently expanded in Richard Rubin's *Press, Party and Presidency* (New York: W.W. Norton & Company, 1981), especially chapter 7.

37. Rubin and Rivers, "The Mass Media and Critical Elections," p. 21.

38. Ibid., p. 26.

39. Paul F. Lazarsfeld, *Radio and the Printed Page: An Introduction to the Study of Radio and Its Role in the Communication of Ideas* (New York: Duell, Sloan and Pearce, 1940), p. 219.

40. Norman Nie, Sidney Verba, and John Petrocik, *The Changing American Voter*, enlarged edition (Cambridge, Mass.: Harvard University Press, 1979), p. 274.

41. Halberstam, *The Powers That Be*, p. 30.

42. Lazarsfeld, *Radio and the Printed Page*, p. 211.

43. *In re The Yankee Network*, Inc., 8FCC333 at 340, 1941, cited in Sydney Head, *Broadcasting in America: A Survey of Television and Radio* (Boston: Houghton Mifflin, 1972), p. 436.

44. David G. Clark, "H.V. Kaltenborn's First Year on the Air," *Journalism Quarterly* 42 (1965): 373–381.

45. Head, *Broadcasting in America*, p. 170.

46. Halberstam, *The Powers That Be*, p. 72.

47. Thomas Patterson, *The Mass Media Election: How Americans Choose Their President* (New York: Praeger, 1980), p. 26.

48. John P. Robinson, "The Audience for National TV News Programs," *Public*

Opinion Quarterly 35 (1971): 403–405. See also George Comstock et al., *Television and Human Behavior* (New York: Columbia Press, 1978), chapter 3; and Patterson, *The Mass Media Election*, pp. 59–61.

49. According to Lazarfeld's research, people in the highest social strata were at least three times as likely to listen to serious programming on radio as were those in the lowest stratum. Lazarsfeld, *Radio and the Printed Page*, p. 44.

50. Robert Bower, *Television and the Public* (New York: Holt, Rinehart and Winston, 1973), p. 132.

51. Michael Robinson, "Television and American Politics: 1956–1976," *Public Interest* 48 (Summer 1977): 23.

52. Barber, *The Pulse of Politics*, pp. 82–85.

53. Hess, *The Washington Reporters*, p. 112.

54. Brody, "The Puzzle of Political Participation in America," in the *New American Political System*, ed. Anthony King (Washington, D.C.: American Enterprise Institute, 1978), pp. 287–324.

55. See, for example, Shaw and McCombs, *The Emergence of American Political Issues*, chapter 6; also Weaver, Graber, McCombs, and Eyal, *Media Agenda-Setting in a Presidential Election*, chapter 9.

56. Pierpoint, *At the White House*, pp. 193–194.

57. Grossman and Kumar, *Portraying the President*, pp. 52–69.

58. Elihu Katz and Paul Lazarsfeld, *Personal Influence: The Part Played by People in the Flow of Mass Communication* (Glencoe, Ill.: The Free Press, 1955).

59. Data for 1964 appear in Arthur Miller's "Political Issues and Trust in Government: 1964–1970," *American Political Science Review* 68 (3) (September 1974): 953. 1978 data provided by Arthur Miller.

60. For a classic statement on wide open press criticism before the age of objectivity, see Frank Luther Mott, *American Journalism: A History, 1690–1960*, 3rd ed. (New York: Macmillan, 1962).

61. Bernard Cohen, *The Press and Foreign Policy* (Princeton: Princeton University Press, 1963), p. 13.

Chapter 13

1. *Weekly Compilation of Presidential Documents*, 2 September 1980, vol. 16, no. 37, p. 1610.

2. Ron Nessen devotes a full chapter to the cause and consequences of this media-based and inaccurate portrayal of President Ford. See *It Sure Looks Different From the Inside* (Chicago, Ill.: Playboy Press, 1978), pp. 163–178.

3. Arthur Schlesinger, Jr., *The Imperial Presidency* (Boston: Houghton Mifflin, 1973).

4. Daniel P. Moynihan, "The Presidency and the Press," *Commentary*, March 1971, pp. 41–52.

5. Joseph Kraft, "The Imperial Media," *Commentary*, May 1981, pp. 36–47.

6. See, for example, William P. Cheshire, "The Imperial Press," *National Review*, 17 August 1979, pp. 1020–1023.

7. Todd Gitlin, *The Whole World is Watching: Mass Media in the Making and Un-Making of the New Left* (Berkeley, Calif.: University of California Press, 1980).

8. Herbert Gans, *Deciding What's News: A Study of CBS Evening News, NBC Nightly News, Newsweek and Time* (New York: Pantheon Books, 1979).

9. According to the Harris poll, between 1966 and 1979, the percentage of people expressing "a great deal of confidence" in nine major institutions fell from 43 percent to 23 percent. Confidence in major companies fell dramatically from 55 per-

cent to 18 percent. Statistics cited in *Public Opinion* (October/November 1979), pp. 30–31.

10. Michael Grossman and Martha Kumar, *Portraying the President: The White House and the News Media* (Baltimore: Johns Hopkins University Press, 1981), chapter 10.

11. Michael J. Robinson, "American Political Legitimacy in an Era of Electronic Journalism: Reflections on the Evening News," in *Television As a Social Force: New Approaches to TV Criticism,* ed. Richard Adler, (New York: Praeger, 1975).

12. ———, "Public Affairs Television and the Growth of Political Malaise: The Case of the Selling of the Pentagon," in the *American Political Science Review* 70 (2) (June 1976): 409–432.

13. James David Barber, *The Pulse of Politics: Electing Presidents in the Media Age* (New York: Norton, 1980), chapter 7.

14. Ibid., p. 124.

15. David Halberstam, *The Powers That Be* (New York: Dell, 1979), p. 101.

16. No incident ever received as much play. Only the Watergate scandals and the War in Vietnam were able to attract as much television news coverage, but both of these stories went on much longer in time. See William Adams and Phillip Heyl, "From Cairo to Kabul With the Networks, 1972–1980," in William C. Adams, *Television Coverage of The Middle East* (Norwood, N.J.: Ablex, 1982), p. 29.

17. Jeff Greenfield, *The Real Campaign: How the Media Missed the Story of the 1980 Campaign* (New York: Summit, 1982), p. 117.

18. David Broder, "Of Presidents and Parties," *The Wilson Quarterly* 2 (1) (Winter 1978): 105–114.

19. Cited in Lee Mitchell, *With the Nation Watching: Report of the Twentieth Century Fund Task Force on Televised Presidential Debates* (Lexington, Mass.: Lexington Books, 1979), p. 24.

Index